WORK-LIFE BALANCE IN ARCHITECTURE

This book seeks to improve the work lives of architects of diverse demographics who do not fit, or want to replicate, the traditional '24/7' white, male architect lifestyle. Aimed at a workforce whose life and career expectations have changed drastically in recent years, it helps readers of different generations to make informed choices about their careers – enabling students, educators, and professionals to prioritise wellbeing and offer their design and practice voice to enhance a built environment for all.

Work-Life Balance in Architecture examines what it means to play the 'game of architecture' – to choose to study and pursue a career in architecture rather than another profession. The book shows the economic, social, and professional structures within which architectural education and practice operate and reveals the impact of a corporate, neoliberal 'big business' mentality on wellbeing.

After setting out the context exacerbating work-life imbalance, the book discusses the paths an architect may take – whether this leads to a career in practice or not in architecture at all – and how alternative gameplay moves can advantage or disadvantage those of different gender, class, ethnicity, race, or age at different career stages. It concludes by examining how the places in which an architect works, the time available to work, and critiques of perpetual neoliberal economic growth can enhance the lives of all architects today.

Australian born, **Igea Troiani** (PhD) is a Professor of Architecture and Head of Division of Architecture at London South Bank University. She has taught or practiced architecture in Australia, Germany, China and the United Kingdom. As a practice-centred academic, her research over the last 26 years has focused on the production of the architect. She has authored five books, 50 articles and book chapters, and was editor-in-chief of *Architecture and Culture* from 2012–2022. She is Chair of Women in Architecture (WIA UK) and a mother of two.

WORK-LIFE BALANCE IN ARCHITECTURE

Playing the Game

Igea Troiani

Routledge
Taylor & Francis Group

LONDON AND NEW YORK

Cover design by Né Santelmo, Porto, 6 November 2023
Designed cover image: Taal Safdie and Moshe Safdie in front of Habitat 67.
© Safdie Rabines Architects

First published 2024
by Routledge
4 Park Square, Milton Park, Abingdon, Oxon OX14 4RN

and by Routledge
605 Third Avenue, New York, NY 10158

Routledge is an imprint of the Taylor & Francis Group, an informa business

British Library Cataloguing-in-Publication Data
A catalogue record for this book is available from the British Library

Library of Congress Cataloging-in-Publication Data
Names: Troiani, Igea, author.
Title: Work-life balance in architecture : playing the game / Igea Troiani.
Description: Abingdon, Oxon : Routledge, 2024. | Includes bibliographical references and index.
Identifiers: LCCN 2023044008 (print) | LCCN 2023044009 (ebook) | ISBN 9780815392187 (hardback) | ISBN 9780815392194 (paperback) | ISBN 9781351199834 (ebook)
Subjects: LCSH: Architecture—Vocational guidance. | Work-life balance.
Classification: LCC NA1995 .T76 2024 (print) | LCC NA1995 (ebook) | DDC 720.23—dc23/eng/20240202
LC record available at https://lccn.loc.gov/2023044008
LC ebook record available at https://lccn.loc.gov/2023044009

ISBN: 9780815392187 (hbk)
ISBN: 9780815392194 (pbk)
ISBN: 9781351199834 (ebk)

DOI: 10.4324/9781351199834

Typeset in Times New Roman
by codeMantra

To Andrew, Lola, and Valentino Dawson,
my mother and father, and Jennifer Taylor.

CONTENTS

PART I

Life in Architecture under Neoliberalism

1

WORK-LIFE IMBALANCE IN ARCHITECTURE

An Introduction

FIGURE 1.1   Architect, Moshe Safdie, and his daughter, Taal, observe the construction of Habitat 67 in Montreal. Taal, now an architect, lived in the apartment complex. Photograph courtesy of Taal Safdie. Photographer and date unknown.

DOI: 10.4324/9781351199834-2

Work-Life Imbalance in Architecture

Work-life imbalance in architecture has become an increasingly important issue for women and men architects to address since the feminisation and diversification of the profession, even more so post-pandemic. Many, but not all, architects with family and children – architect-mothers and architect-fathers (Figure 1.1) – juggle balancing work and home responsibilities (Fleetwood 2006, p. 1) including family, sometimes having a detrimental effect on their health, wellbeing, job-satisfaction, work, and home life. Architecture, however, which has always been and remains a long and arduous course of study, roughly equivalent to studying medicine, is increasing in its excessive toll on many of its workers with or without having demands outside work. There are a rising number of studies commissioned by institutes of architects, architecture journals, and independent researchers recognising that aspects of architectural education can be harmful to wellbeing and solutions need to be sought. (Troiani 2021; McLean, Holgate, and Bloice 2020; Waite and Braidwood 2016) Notoriously recognised for being poorly remunerated, life in professional architectural practice can continue to be taxing particularly, but not exclusively, in the early career years. Working as a practitioner in the architectural marketplace is highly competitive and as the media image of the architect becomes more important for brand identity, the profession itself has lost, and continues to lose, efficacy and relevance in building. There has been a parallel decline in wellbeing and job satisfaction pre- and post-graduation for many architects.

The primary aim of this book is to study work-life balance in architecture to enhance the lives and wellbeing of architects. It seeks to improve the work lives of architects of diverse demographics who do not fit, or want to replicate, the traditional white-male architect lifestyle of working a 24/7 work life. It is written to support changing work life for an assorted range of architectural students, educators, and practitioners of different gender, race/ethnicity, class, and age to enable them to sustain and flourish so as to contribute positively to the profession by offering their design and practice voice to enhance a built environment for all.

Work-life balance,[1] is broadly defined as the balance of "work, family and lifestyle" including leisure activities. (Francis, Fulu, and Lingard in Lingard and Francis 2009, p. 2) Alternative meanings of balance define it as "a situation in which different elements are equal or in the correct proportions" or as "mental or emotional stability." (Oxford Dictionary online 2018) In metaphysics, balance is understood as a point between two opposite forces that is desirable over purely one state or the other; and an imbalance means stronger forces of power dominate weaker forces. In architecture, work-life balance can be understood as the harmony and equilibrium between work – which was traditionally enacted in the distinct spatial domains of the university or office – and home, but which now happens in a multitude of places everywhere and anywhere, including the construction site and at times inside and outside normal 9 to 5 work hours. In this fluid space of post-industrialised and digitised work, many modern workers, of which architects are only one part, struggle to find personal and professional equilibrium. This has led to a rise in the generic research on wellness, wellbeing, and work-life balance.

Wellness first appeared in the English language in 1654, and "like adding 'ness' to 'ill' to make 'illness' it was a way to designate the state of being well (i.e. absence of disease)". (Zimmer 2010) While it in fact has deeper origins in Antiquity, appearing in the writings of Plato, Socrates, Epicurus, and Aristotle, the word fell out of favour in the 1800s to the mid-1960s, resurfacing in 1961 in the writings of the American doctor, Halbert L. Dunn who is recognised as the 'father of the wellness movement'. Dunn sought "new terminology to convey the positive aspects of health that people could achieve beyond simply avoiding sickness." (Zimmer 2010 quoted in Scaria et al. in Kim and Lindeman ed. 2020, pp. 3–4) The common everyday term, wellbeing, as the state of being well, conveys the positive attributes of both physical health and mental health experienced by avoiding sickness, exhaustion, or burnout. While the wellbeing of workers is "a key determinant of the productivity of an economy" (Huber, Lechner, and Wunsch, 2015, p. 170) and is a primary concern of employers because it has the capacity to reduce sickness absenteeism, this book focuses on the benefits to an individual's physical, spiritual, or phenomenological wellbeing and in relation to their life experiences and career trajectory in architecture. This book examines how to improve the wellbeing of architects for greater job-satisfaction and retention for longer, happier careers at work, and if not always possible, to understand some of the primary reasons behind their lack of being able to do so in order to explore ways to make systemic changes that would improve the situation in the future.

Like wellness studies, work-life balance emerged as a topic of serious research in the 20th century in the fields of public health and wellbeing. Initial research sprang up around 'work/family border theory' (Clark 2000), which adopts an outlook centred on the conflict between divided types of mutually-exclusive domains of daily life activities. Subsequent research has examined imbalanced or unequal levels of engagement and satisfaction in work life and home life and adopted "a conflict-based outlook." (Ong and Jeyaraj 2014, p. 2) Management researchers, Jeffrey H. Greenhaus, Karen M. Collins, and Jason D. Shaw (2003) argue that in order to achieve work-life balance, real and psychological time must be committed to roles in both domains. Balancing commitments at home and work "is a zero-sum game where[by] committing resources to one domain is seen as taking away resources from the other." (Ong and Jeyaraj 2014, p. 2)

Work-life balance has become a catchphrase of the millennial generation, many of whom do not want to replicate the lives of the generation of their parents or grandparents, and are seeking out healthy, rather than unhealthy, work environments that are more about 'work-leisure' or 'play-care.' (Kane 2004, p. 179) A growing sentiment is that having a life outside of work is not unreasonable; in fact it should be a priority, but achieving this differs depending on the understanding of gendered labour divisions. Whereas initially women, more so than men, struggled to achieve work-life balance because they had care commitments to juggle with work demands, nowadays architects of different genders, particularly those in the younger generations, are becoming growingly concerned about what a satisfying inside–outside architecture work life might be. Key ingredients that enhance job satisfaction and wellbeing include acquiring and sustaining enough wealth to live the life one wants and aspires to live through strong networks of wealthy clients and a healthy and productive office workforce. While books like *Design your Life* (Nash 2022) offer a guide to how an architect can achieve a work-life balance through their *own* design, this book goes one step further to analyse how the possibility of doing so is premised on the limits prescribed by governmental, societal, and architectural institutional structures in which architectural work is enacted, but which are out of an architect's control.

In the U.K., where this book is written, and in many other countries, neoliberal entrepreneurism is the most common mechanism through which to increase social and professional mobility and acquire wealth, success, and esteem. Neoliberalism is generally understood to be a *laissez-faire* economic system in which business transactions are free from economic regulatory restriction. It is driven by the desire for individual economic independence and continuous growth although it is defined both positively or negatively, depending on what aspect of the neoliberal system is focused upon. Social scientist, Janet Newman (2012, p. 157) writes that unlike other scholars such as the British sociologist, Bob Jessop (2002) and Canadian geographer, Jamie Peck (2004) who emphasise "the role of the state in securing political and ideological reform in order to enable the expansion … of corporate capital," British social geographer, David Harvey "views neoliberalism as a class-based political project of creating new means of capital accumulation." According to Harvey (2007, p. 2), "Neoliberalism is in the first instance a theory of political economic practices that proposes that human well-being [sic] can best be advanced by liberating individual entrepreneurial freedoms and skills within an institutional framework characterized [sic] by strong private property rights, free markets, and free trade." In order to do this, Harvey (2005, p. 23) maintains that neoliberalism "has entailed much 'creative destruction'" of institutions and institutional powers and "also of divisions of labor [sic], social relations, welfare provisions, technological mixes, ways of life, attachments to the land, habits of the heart, ways of thought, and the like." Winning in a neoliberal work environment has health and wellbeing benefits for those who are or can transition to the 'haves' of society. It can, however, be detrimental to the health and wellbeing of those in society who are the 'have-nots.'

Due to the now inextricable relationship between money and lifestyle wellbeing, most research on work-life balance is driven by promotion of what is termed here, 'the neoliberal imperative' to make workers happier, more productive, and efficient. Unhealthy workplaces tend to nurture unhealthy workers, which then affects the health of a business. As writer, musician, consultant, activist, curator, and facilitator of the 'play ethic', Pat Kane (2004, p. 179) points out, "Employers and politicians [are] both worried about skyrocketing degrees of sick leave in general and the competition for talent at higher levels." Business has responded accordingly, and as such there are a multitude of self-help books in virtually every field in the popular press, mainly from a business-oriented perspective in order to increase productivity through flexi-time or other work-time models that allow more time for leisure and rest inside and outside work. In the main, these books avoid discussing how neoliberalism's essential requirement of depleting resources, both human and geographical, to create profits, are counter-productive to a sustainable world and a sustainable balanced model of work for a diverse group of workers in the construction industry.

In *Managing Work-Life Balance in Construction*, Helen Lingard and Valerie Francis (2009) uncover many of the already well-known reasons why women and men working in the construction industry suffer differing levels of 'career strain' and build upon earlier arguments, such as the one presented by Phyllis Moen (2003) that argues that imbalances are due to a lag in governmental policy changes to support work-life balance in the industry. While the research by Lingard and Francis (2009), done in Australia, is extensive and revealing, it does not focus entirely on architecture, nor does it critique the institutional frameworks that create the challenges that face working women and men in architecture who also have demanding commitments outside work. While the book, *Design your Life* (Nash 2022) addresses the topic, there is no book in architecture that examines work-life balance through the economic lens of neoliberalism, where one is constantly playing the money game, as this book does. Conflicts inside and between professional and personal life can have an unprecedented effect on an architect's ability to play the game and can, as a consequence, be life changing.

For aspiring, emerging, and practising architects, architectural education and architectural practice exist as particular kinds of games that are played. The rules of architectural play, like any business, are premised on surviving in an aggressive and competitive gamespace. While playing the game of an architect's life is like no other profession's game, the way in which an architect's life path has been affected by capitalism and heightened by neoliberalism has parallels with tactical, competitive gameplay that has evolved in the development of the game industries in the U.K. and U.S.A. The study of the motives of neoliberal gameplay and gamespace allows a later reading of balancing life inside and outside work as an architect.

Philosophers and political scientists, but not architects, have critically analysed the social impact of the dramatic change that neoliberal 'governmentality' directed purely towards an economic imperative has had on knowledge, labour, productivity, education, democracy, freedom, and equality of the body polis. An early critic of neoliberalism, French philosopher Michel Foucault addressed in his writings the key relationship between 'governmentality' and power exertion on the body polis. According to Foucault (2008, pp. 259–260), neoliberal power provides an "image, idea, or theme-program [sic] of a society in which there is an optimization [sic] of systems of difference, in which the field is left open to fluctuating processes, in which minority individuals and practices are tolerated, in which action is brought to bear on the rules of the game rather than on the players."

From 1978 to 1979 – the eve of the elections of both British Prime Minister, Dame Margaret Thatcher and American President, Roland Reagan – Foucault examined neoliberalism through a series of lectures he delivered in Paris that considered the relationship between 'governmentality' (or "the art of government") and the exertion of power on the body politic. In the book of his collated lectures entitled *The Birth of Biopolitics*, Foucault (2008) notes the changing association between biology and politics ("biopolitics") and the powerful role that *homo oeconomicus* – discussed in detail in the next chapter – plays in neoliberalism. 'Biopolitics' is a form of rationality applied to political governance that is used to administer everyday life and people. Foucault's theory of governmentality is deeply intertwined with a theory of surveillance and monitoring through technologies of governing. For Foucault, neoliberal governments have enforced a belief in "installing 'economic' logics of calculation (constituted through discourses of markers, efficiency, managerialism, consumer choice and individual autonomy) and strategies for promoting 'self-governing' subjects.'" (Newman 2012, p. 157) In *Discipline & Punish: The Birth of the Prison*, Foucault (1995, p. 221) explains how, under our current economic system, "the two processes–the accumulation of men and the accumulation of capital–cannot be separated and are co-existent." Consumption of human labour (capitalist polity) and resources allow neoliberalism to operate as a system of a growing accumulation of wealth (capitalist economy). This constructs a specific model of success where social, cultural, and economic capital defines an individual's identity and worth through accruing more and more by exploiting lower-cost resources and/or human labour.

Since the late 1970s, some 40 years on, Britain, its English-speaking colonies (former and current overseas territories), and other Western countries have dramatically altered the rituals of daily life because of neoliberalism. As the American political theorist Wendy Brown (2015, p. 31) notes, "neoliberalism literally *marketizes* all spheres" and "configures human beings exhaustively as market actors" in a world where everything is for sale, and everything can be bought. Every aspect of life is nowadays quantified, monetised, and commoditised around playing the game of an economically-motivated lifestyle. Neoliberalism prioritises economisation, financialisation, careerism, creativity, entrepreneurship, corporatisation, globalisation, internationalisation, competition, etc., and has normalised them all in our everyday life. Its demands on the body of the worker, and here, the body of the architect, result in the challenge to attain work-life balance. It also affects the relationship an architect has with the architecture they produce.

Architecture and Neoliberalism

The neoliberal drive for increased production and consumption through economic rationalism after the 1970s is arguably the most significant factor affecting our everyday life, environment, climate, and wellbeing. Today, in many modern developed countries in the West and the East, dominant neoliberal agendas have altered the way we work and the products of our work. Here architecture is foregrounded as a professional example within a complex social, economic, and political system.

For many architects, work has changed dramatically in the neoliberal age, such that the very core of how an architect works has only scant resemblance to its former modes of privileged, leisurely, autonomous, artistic, socially-oriented, and site responsive practice. The work of the architect is commonly understood to be the design of buildings and the spaces that surround them. In architecture, however, under neoliberalism, the products of architecture (buildings and the spaces in-between and around them), the nature of the production process, and quality of architectural work, and body of the architect have all been radically transformed without the architect having any control.

The privatisation of the architecture profession has accentuated economic optimisation and productivity through a long work hours culture, enacted across a non-stop 24/7 global marketplace. Most architects have shifted from working in the home-artist studio to both the global corporate office and something in-between, post-pandemic, this means that the architectural office is everywhere, including the home. From being able to work everywhere an architect can work anywhere in the world without having to be there. No longer is architecture the stable, lifelong profession it once was where work was local or only in an architect's home country. Emerging and established architects are freer than ever before to move to work anywhere in the world from their office or own home.

Architects working under neoliberalism have exploited and benefited from its promotion of globalisation, rapid urbanisation, and development. To meet targets set by governments in many countries, the architectural workforce in Higher Education (H.E.) and practice has increased, and the demands for global growth and productivity within architecture schools are being felt professionally, environmentally, and corporeally.

However, the maximum productivity treadmill that has driven many architecture schools and practices since the increased privatisation of architectural education and practice is suffering from strain. Due to the fact that architectural workers have been encouraged for decades to work across, consume, and develop local and international projects in the West and the East "with vigor [sic] and skill" – to quote Dutch architect Rem Koolhaas (in Owen 2009, p. 1) – some are or are beginning to suffer because of performance time pressures and overwork. A growing number are questioning their career path. It is because the image and reality of a professional life in architecture is not what people think it will be, and is also changing so rapidly and unpredictably, that want-to-be and practicing architects of all generational levels need to better understand how they can enact their professional life for better work-life, social, and environmental balance.

Capital accumulation flourishes in what Polish philosopher Zygmunt Bauman (2000) calls 'liquid modernity.' Predating postmodernity and predicated on the neoliberal drive for freedom of choice, 'liquid modernity' is the current modern era in which we live that has shifted focus from citizen to individual, from state institution to corporation, from quite simply, living a life grounded in solidity to living in continual fluidity. No longer do we live in 'heavy modernity' (Bauman 2000, p. 47) where our life paths and behaviours are mostly circumscribed, we have (in theory) all the freedoms in the world to create new ways of living and working. These freedoms, however, bring with them additional complications and pressures that differ to those experienced by earlier generations working in architecture and, more broadly, in early forms of industrial capitalism.

Marxist economists, Ben Fine and Alfredo Saad-Filho (2019, p. 2) see that neoliberalism "represents a new stage in the development of capitalism emerging in the wake of the post-war boom." Neoliberalism draws upon the post-WW2 theory of Austrian economist, Ludwig von Mises and American economist, Milton Friedman:

> albeit in sharply dissimilar and logically incompatible ways, that differently endowed property-owning individuals exchanging goods, services and information in minimally regulated markets constitute the most desirable form for allocating resources and should prevail over an interventionist role of the state.
>
> *(Fine and Saad-Filho 2019, p. 7)*

By prioritising individual freedom, neoliberalism promotes an individually-centred rather than 'egalitarian concept of self and society.' (Fine and Saad-Filho 2019, p. 7) In the pursuit for advancement, a neoliberal mindset seeks out individual advancement through financialisaton that sells and exploits. Many architects who are willing servants to neoliberalism are happy to play along in the game of greedy capital accumulation for the individual gain of mostly their clients, and sometimes themselves, because they see no other choice for survival, because it suits them, or because they are uncritical of the system of property development in which they work. It is the contradiction that for an architect to strive for self-worthiness, they are encouraged by neoliberalism to exploit others.

The current literature on architecture and neoliberalism focuses mostly on the products of architecture not the product of the architect. *The Architecture of Neoliberalism* (Spencer 2016) shows "how contemporary architecture became an instrument of control and compliance." Other writers examine architecture's relation to money and capital flows (Deamer ed. 2014; Andrachuk et al. eds. 2014; Gabrielsson and Mattsson eds. 2017) by focusing mostly on the commonly-produced objects and typologies of neoliberal architecture that directly result from increased financialisaton for private investment and capital accumulation. The non-exhaustive list includes "shopping malls, corporate headquarters, museums, performance spaces, sports stadia, transportation hubs, and gleaming megatowers" (Sklair 2017, p. 5), and now semi-private or private university campuses, hospitals, and schools, etc., in which mostly high profile or corporate architects are working with wealthy clients. The converse end of the economic spectrum are social architectures including self-build and affordable housing, civic and religious centres, public universities, hospitals, schools, etc., which are for community groups or funded by the state. (Awan, N. et al. eds. 2011; Fishman and Kubey 2018) It seems that architects, to varying degrees in different countries, are dividing into different architectural social classes: those that 'work for the [corporate] man' and those that want to 'give it to the [corporate] man.'

Theorisation of architectural labour in relation to architecture serving capitalism is a growing field of scholarship of which American architect, Peggy Deamer (ed. 2015) is a leading scholar. Others examine how computational, including parametric or digitally-generated, architectural design enhances neoliberal production. (Poole and Shvartzberg eds. 2015) The former divide between, and production requirements of, academia and practice is shifting because of rising consumerism, globalisation, corporatisation, and the emergence of digital-based design in the 1990s. (Hight 2012, p. 414 in Sklair 2017, p. 30) The effects of neoliberalism on the producers of architecture, architects, has not been foregrounded in architectural literature and this book's aim is to remedy that gap in literature.

Working in architecture is unlike working in any other, even related, profession or design field and it is the understanding of architecture's *internal* institutional and cultural limitations in relation to a neoliberal, liquidly modern lifestyle that is under analysis here. So, if the neoliberal working environment does not slow down or get replaced by another political drive, how can architects better navigate their professional and personal lives at the various life stages of their careers? The purpose of the book is not to provide quantitative research that work-life balance in architecture is becoming more difficult to achieve (as this is common knowledge) or to provide definitive remedial solutions. Instead, the book aims to provide a reflective qualitative guide for prospective or current architectural students, academics, and practitioners at all life stages to better understand the systems and pathways possible in architectural labour in order to best help navigate through them. It focuses on what it means to play the game of architecture today, i.e., to choose to study architecture over another profession or design career in an international, global market; and to undertake meaningful work in architectural life – both at university and professional practice – beyond neoliberalism. This book argues that the ability for an architect to achieve work-life balance or harmony, and to successfully play the game of life in architecture, is dependent on a range of personal factors and on the political (neoliberal in the case of the U.K.), social, and economic environments in which they can operate at various stages of their work life.

While this book is based on secondary literature, including found conversations recording the academic and practice experiences of women and men architects of all socio-economic classes working and living in various countries including the United Kingdom, Europe, and U.S.A., it goes beyond only architectural literature. It builds upon and is framed around theoretical research in philosophy, sociology, economics, business, gender studies, and visual culture to offer readers an understanding of the social, economic, and professional structures in which architectural education and practice operate. Illustrations in the book have been chosen carefully and are purposely few. Limited to two figures per chapter, they resist the neoliberal tendency for flooding spectators with images that lose impact, lingering longer than a fleeting moment. Taken from visual culture and mass media, they have been selected because they depict images powerfully of a life in architecture. In this sense, they resist the game of producing a happy flow of architectural images, as is discussed in the next chapter.

Playing the game of life in architecture in a liquidus, neoliberal world can mean choosing to study or work locally or internationally (either in-person or remotely); an urban or rural life; more or less work or home life; or between a career or family or both. While there is an apparent freedom to make life choices at each life stage, neoliberal governance, and a history of social stratification and modern professionalisation, means that participation in a professional architectural life can have, or has, limits for different types of architectural workers. This book endeavours to increase criticality about what it means to live and work as an architect by examining how working in a neoliberal age is affected by the state and how governance affects the city, nature, society, and the potential for genuine individual freedom. For almost 50 years, Harvey has researched the relationship between capitalism and society and his writings on the stealth rise in neoliberalism are expanded here to understand the British context of architectural labour post 1970s, which in turn will provide a context for architectural life after this period.

A History of Neoliberalism

In 1973, after moving from Britain to Baltimore, Harvey, born in the former dockyard town of Gillingham in Kent, first published *Social Justice and the City*.[2] In it, Harvey employs a Marxist framework to analyse the relationship between the economic processes of capitalism and its impact on the 'polis' – the city and its citizens. Most significantly, Harvey expands upon the theory of economic 'reproduction' presented by Karl Marx (1970–1972/1867) in *Capital: A Critique of Political Economy* to show the means by which society re-creates itself, both materially and socially, and then how the means of capital circulation dictates the socio-spatial form and evolution of the polis.

Building upon his research on ghetto formation, Harvey (1972) calls for revolutionary change in order to tackle economic, social, gender, and class inequality. At the basis of Harvey's (1972, pp. 261–274) proposal is the need to understand the connection between the process of global market exchange and urban development. Globalisation, marketisation, corporatisation, and monopolisation, to name but a few features of neoliberalism, are fundamental factors at play in regard to *what* land is attributed higher or lower value, *how* that land is capitalised upon – if it can be capitalised upon – by *who* had the finances to do so. Expanding upon the study by German art historians, Reinhold Bentmann and Michael Müller (1992)

FIGURE 1.2 Conservative leader Margaret Thatcher (bottom right) visiting the Parker Family, of Ascot Close, Northolt, in London, who were among the first to buy their terrace council house from Ealing Borough Council after the Conservatives took control of the council in May 1978. Harry Greenway (left), Tory candidate for Ealing North, looks on. Photograph by PA/PA Archive/PA Images. Date taken: 20 April, 1979.

of the villas and connection to wealthy clients of the 16th century Italian architect, Andrea Palladio, Scottish sociologist Leslie Sklair (2017, p. 11) contends in *The Icon Project: Architecture, Cities and Capitalist Globalization* that "certain buildings and spaces can serve specific class interests expressed in their aesthetic and symbolic qualities." The market is controlled by the affluent classes who have wealth to play it. Their participation in urban development drives the market and creates a surplus economy through new building development and redevelopment that, in the process, depletes and exploits resources – both material and human. This is a fundamental feature of the economic system of capitalism and is heightened under neoliberalism, which presents itself as the system through which to allow everyone the opportunity to become a player in the global marketplace. Most architects enact their everyday life within this space of economic transaction and so it is essential that aspiring or established architects understand the socio-political history of neoliberal *laissez-faire* economics because it has a direct impact on their daily work.

In *A Brief History of Neoliberalism*, Harvey (2005) explains the emergence of *laissez-faire* economics and how it has come to proliferate in the contemporary world. He traces its origins in the U.S.A. to Lewis Powell's 1971 confidential memorandum to the U.S. Chamber of Commerce and its steady evolution under the Jimmy Carter administration in the 1970s through to the Reagan administration of the 1980s. In the U.K., Thatcher's government, inspired by Reaganomics, sought early neoliberal reforms such as the privatisation of state-owned assets, deregulation and reduction in taxes, and social welfare. Neoliberal economic policy that diminished welfare support for the 'have nots' has continued ever since. While it is unremarkable that Sir John Major's Conservative government picked up where Thatcher left off, the British author and journalist, Sir Simon Jenkins (2007) claims in *Thatcher and Sons: A Revolution in Three Acts* that Thatcher's legacy continued throughout Sir Anthony (Tony) Blair's years of Labour government, manifesting itself in his economic, domestic, and foreign policies that were later collectively called 'Blairism.' In 2013, when Blair (quoted in BBC News 2013) was asked about Thatcher and her administration, he stated, "I always thought my job was to build on some of the things she had done rather than reverse them." In "Thatcher's Children, Blair's Babies, Political Socialization and Trickle-down Value Change," Grasso et al. (2019) conclude that "Thatcher's Babies" are in fact less Thatcherite (neoliberal-authoritarian) by nature than "Blair's Babies," inferring there is an evolutionary process to the rise of neoliberal thinking in subsequent generations of Britons.

Thatcherism, and its spin-off governments, have had an insurmountable impact on the current labour market in architecture in the U.K. and the neoliberal modes of production and market exchange architecture is now subject to. What Thatcherism did was pose welfare politics as 'a threat of sorts to capitalist market exchange.' (Harvey 1972, p. 277) Thatcherism incited a shift in focus from the communal to the self, from social architecture to private architecture, and to the desire for increased production and consumption of everything in architecture understood to be a commodity. It is contended here that the foundation of Thatcher's economic policy in fact came from her experience of growing up and seeing the running of her father's business and revolves around the value of a Protestant work ethic.

Thatcher was one of two daughters of Beatrice Ethel Stephenson and the English grocer, Methodist preacher, and politician, Alfred Roberts. She grew up in provincial Grantham and was inspired by her father's advocacy of freedom through hard work and entrepreneurism. According to Thatcher (1995, p. 21), her father was an 'old-fashioned liberal'; Roberts was motivated by *On Liberty* by the English philosopher and political economist, John Stuart Mill (Mill, Philp, and Rosen 2015 [1859]). In the book, Mill argues for individual responsibility and financial soundness. Having lived through the Great Depression of the 1930s and coming from a frugal but reasonably well-off middle-class family, Thatcher worked her way up the socio-economic ladder, studying chemistry on a scholarship at the University of Oxford from 1943–1947, then becoming a barrister and a politician; initially Secretary of State for the Department of Education and Science (DES) from 1970–1974. At the DES Thatcher worked to challenge student unions in response to what she termed 'student princes.' (Thatcher 1995, pp. 185–187) In 1974, Thatcher founded the Centre for Policy Studies (CPS) for which she became the first deputy chairman. Co-founded with British politician, Sir Keith Joseph, the CPS is a non-profit making organisation funded by donations from companies and individuals that develop policies on privatisation, low-tax, and family support independent of all political parties and interest groups. It seeks to create a free society through a belief in free market economics. The British think tank "promotes policies to limit the role of the state, to encourage enterprise and to enable the institutions of society – such as families and voluntary organisations – to flourish." (www.cps.org.uk)

Only three years after forming the CPS, in May 1979, Thatcher was elected the first female Prime Minister of the U.K. As Prime Minister, Thatcher and her policies encouraged women and men in Britain to work hard for personal gain in order to move from depending on state welfare to becoming self-sufficient and prosperous within free, neoliberal markets. In her memoirs, *The Path to Power* she admits that her "upbringing and early experience" also allowed her to gain "a sympathetic insight into... 'capitalism' or the 'free-enterprise system.'" (Thatcher 1995, p. 566) Thatcher (1995, p. 566) claims she saw "... it was satisfying customers that allowed... [her] father to increase the number of people he employed.... [She] knew that it was international trade which brought tea, coffee, sugar and spices to those who frequented... [the] shop. And, more than that,... [she] experienced that business, as can be seen in any marketplace anywhere, was a lively, human, social and sociable reality: in fact, though serious it was fun." According to Thatcher (1996, p. 566), "There is no better course for understanding free-market economics than life in a corner shop."

Thatcher expanded the economic model she witnessed in her father's family business as the economic model for her government. Britain began to be run like a shop, engaging in buying and selling for growth. In 1979 Thatcher appointed Milton Friedman, from the Chicago school, as her economic advisor. "He and his colleagues had been making waves by promoting 'economic liberalism'... Within a few years of meeting Thatcher, Friedman was advising the US treasury, and most world bodies were beginning to adopt what became known as 'neoliberal' ideas." (Vidal, Ncube, Bromund, and Ghosh 2013) With Friedman and another of her economic advisors, Alan Walters, Thatcher embarked on a campaign to encourage privatisation of property, deregulate industry, lower taxes, withdraw funding to the public sector, and debilitate trade unions to facilitate global free trade and free markets that promoted global competition, all in order to restore economic power and superiority to Britain.

According to the traditional Conservative, Roger Scruton (1979 in Scruton 1981, p. 200) in "The Ideology of the Market," Thatcher and Joseph's CPS sought three goals for British people: to improve "the standard of living, the quality of life and... freedom of choice." Scruton, however, sees that because the three goals "may not be compatible," Thatcher and Joseph ironically deprioritised 'quality of life' through policy making. Joseph "impress[ed] on the British public that the freedom of the market is no more than a consequence of that higher and more generalized [sic] freedom which is the Englishman's birthright. He... spoke of the merchant and the industrialist as 'wealth creators', who must be given again their freedom to invest, to speculate, to engage in enterprises, the rewards or losses of which will be automatically confiscated or sustained by a vigilant sovereign state." (Scruton 1979 in Scruton 1981, pp. 200–201) According to Scruton (1979 in Scruton 1981: 201), under Thatcherism, "the invisible hand of self-interest" was used as "a constitutional device."

As part of Thatcher's push to make Britons independent from the state, in August 1980, only one year after being elected as PM, she passed a Housing Act to allow tenants the 'Right to Buy' their homes from their local authority. As the British writer, journalist, and academic, Anna Minton (2017, pp. 27–28) notes in *Big Capital: Who is London For?*: "During the 1980s, council estates began to change. The impact of ...Thatcher's flagship Right to Buy policy that saw the sell-off of millions of council homes at very large discounts, which began in the 1980s and continues to this day, is well known and cannot be underestimated." Thatcher saw the 'Right to Buy' (RTB) scheme as a way to empower less well-off Britons to gain independence from the state by owning their own property. She embarked on a media publicity campaign being photographed with families such as the Parker Family, of Ascot Close, Northolt, in London, who were among the first to buy their terrace council house from Ealing Borough Council (Figure 1.2).

Importantly, Minton notes that the RTB scheme allowed the British government the opportunity to withdraw funding for social housing so that far less housing for low-income people is available in the U.K. today. It remains a paramount problem in contemporary Britain. While Minton's statistics are from 2017, the picture has not changed. Minton (2017, p. 27) explains that "In 1978, the last year before ... Thatcher came to power, the government built 100,000 council homes and the private sector built 150,000. There was no shortage of housing. Since 1979, while private sector house building figures have remained about the same, the government builds hardly any." Clearly only one of many factors, Thatcher's RTB scheme forced a shift in the kind of labour enacted by architects working in the U.K. from producing more public national projects to private and commercial national and international projects.

The legacy of Thatcher's neoliberalism has deeply affected the types of labour enacted in architectural education and practice in the U.K. This is because later Labour governments did not resist the neoliberal drive to increase the need to 'pay for what you get' including H.E. tuition fees were first introduced in the U.K. in 1998 by the Blair Labour government. Students studying architecture in the U.K. at state universities were initially required to pay £1,000 a year for tuition. This has steadily risen, with variations, in universities in Scotland, Wales, and Northern Island, whose fees differ to the roughly £9,000 a year tuition implemented following the Browne Review published in 2010. Chaired by the former chief executive of British Petroleum (BP), Lord Browne of Madingley, the Review led to the removal of a price cap on university fees they can charge. This weaned universities off government funds and forced them to become more independent self-governing subjects. In 2022, Domestic or Home students who study architecture in U.K. architecture schools are means tested and take out student loans for tuition costs, and possibly for living costs depending on the capital available to them through their individual or family wealth. In a spiral of rising debt before graduation from a long five-year (three-year undergraduate degree and two-year postgraduate degree) architectural education, British graduates are increasingly matching the once shocking post-graduation debts of their American private architecture school contempories. Draft proposals have been produced to reduce the number of years of study for an architectural education and some are gaining traction. What the increase in student fees and loans has done is force universities to become entrepreneurial.

The entrepreneurial university, and architecture schools within them, have had to revamp and restructure their 'businesses' to expand university campuses and markets by recruiting larger numbers of national and international students, or in some instances, through forming international academic partnerships. There are large waves of international students from countries around the world who have the personal wealth and opportunity to study as international students in the West; the case of China's opening up is discussed here as but one example, to showcase how it offers the potential of architectural market expansion for both architecture schools and architects.[3]

The opening up of China as a new international market and as a country able to expand into new international markets has had a startling effect on the world economy – and within it the architectural economy – particularly in the U.K. Architectural labour, when enacted as a global practice, has been affected by the shift in the West–East economic power relation. In Great Britain and China, architectural education and practice have been altered in the name of 'global citizenship' and in the name of internationalisation. Architects in Europe and other western countries who were unable to find work due to unemployment post-2008 fiscal crisis, or simply saw market opportunities and experience elsewhere, were drawn to China during its frenzied phase of construction. Whether unemployed or no longer wanting to be limited by small scale projects with small budgets in their home country, China offered many young or established architects grander work opportunities not available at home. The ability for Chinese students to study architecture overseas informs their practice on their return and has expanded their network of opportunities for commissions.

Architectural education, which has transformed due to neoliberalism in the U.K., U.S.A., and Australia to name but a few, has affected the study of architecture in China too. Some of these universities have entrepreneurially created academic alliances with Chinese universities, in an increased market of privatised architectural education, so that Chinese and other international students can experience a U.K. or U.S. accredited architectural education *in* China. Students from China and other wealthy Eastern countries have also become at times a high proportion of commodity stock of many British universities, providing essential money to subsidise, maintain and sometimes increase the profitability of U.K. universities. What is clear is that from the U.K. to the U.S.A. and Australia to the PRC, architectural practice and education is at the mercy of government policy changes enacted within competitive world markets and the volatility of crises outside industry which have economic impact. Neoliberal *laissez-faire* economics has a knock-on effect on consumption and production of architectural labour and on the body of the architect entering or operating within the architectural workforce. Making the choice and having the opportunity to decide where to study and work in architecture relates to how to play the game in the profession. As it has marked parallels with the evolution of competitive board games that build skills in making life choices that improve one's economic positioning, *The Game of Life*, as a game that teaches skills in accumulation of capital will now be discussed.

Playing *The Game of Life*

The Georgian era (1714 to c. 1830–1837) in Britain was a period that saw large social change due to the Industrial Revolution. It was a time in which class divisions and divisions of labour were intensified due to new modes of industrial production and consumption. It was also the period in which boxed games, a product of industrialised processes of printing production, emerged as a form of leisure and moral teaching about decision making in the modern world. During the Enlightenment Age, the notion of game playing was a means of self-improvement. Games like chess were as much about learning morals as partaking in 'idle amusement' because playing chess developed "several very valuable qualities of the mind, useful in the course of human life,... for life is a kind of Chess, in which we have often points to gain, and competitors or adversaries to contend with, and in which there is a vast variety of good and ill events, that are, in some degree, the effect of prudence, or the want of it." (Franklin 1750)

Continuing in this vein of learning life skills through play, in 1800, the English children's author and game designer, George Fox, designed the children's game, *The Mansion of Happiness: An Instructive Moral and Entertaining Amusement.* The game encourages players to choose between virtues and vices, the former allowing players to advance in contrast to the latter, which resulted in retreat from the goal. Fox's *The Mansion of Happiness* showed gamers in the U.K. and beyond, to America, how life choices needed to be made carefully to succeed.

Responding to the aftermath of an America that was reeling from major recession (1837 to the mid-1840s) the American boxed games industry began in 1843 with William and Stephen B. Ives's path game, *The Mansion of Happiness*, a version of Fox's game. In keeping with the desire to teach the player about morality at the time, it rewarded virtue and punished vice (Whitehill 2004, p. 28) and became an instant success with the public of all ages, leading to the growth of other board games concerned with wealth acquisition. Like *The Mansion of Happiness*, *The Landlord's Game*, patented by Elizabeth Magie in 1904, sought to teach its players about the moral relationship between wealth and society through acquiring property. Magie designed *The Landlord's Game* (which later became *Monopoly*)[4] to teach players the theories of political economist Henry George (1879), specifically his 'Single Tax Principles' and other philosophies set out in *Progress and Property: An Inquiry into the Cause of Industrial Depressions and of Increase of Want with Increase of Wealth: The Remedy.* (Whitehill 2004, p. 72) *Progress and Poverty* studies the paradox of rising inequality that accompanies economic and technological progress and particularly how anti-monopoly reforms can remedy social injustice.

Following on from the popularity of these games, in 1860, the American business magnate, game pioneer, and publisher Milton Bradley, also inspired by *The Mansion of Happiness*, created his first morality board game, *The Checkered Game of Life*, using the pattern of a standard checkerboard. Based on a snakes and ladders approach to winning or losing by climbing the ladder, the object was to be the first player to reach "'Happy Old Age' while trying to avoid 'Ruin'." (Miller 2005, p. 24) The modern version of *The Checkered Game of Life*, co-designed by game designer Reuben Klamer in 1959, is *The Game of Life* (or *Life*). Still popular today, it is a simulated search for the "meaning of life" (Lou 2003: 10) that follows the traditional path developed in 1950s America centred on the 'American dream.' In *The Game of Life* players replicate a person's travels from university to retirement, with jobs, marriage, and having children as options to choose from on the way. They can choose a College Path, a Career Path, Get Married, Start a New Career, etc.

From 1959 the rules changed to suit the times, swinging between societal and moral responsibility and personal gain and ambition. The 1960s version of *The Game of Life* allowed a player who had reached the "Day of Reckoning" "to choose between moving on to "Millionaire Acres" (if they had a lot of money), or trying to become a "Millionaire Tycoon" (if they had little or no money) with the risk of being sent to the 'Poor Farm'" (https://en.wikipedia.org/wiki/The_Game_of_ Life). In 2007, *The Game of Life: Twists and Turns* was released as a way to learn to better negotiate life's challenges. Moving with the zeitgeist, *The Game of Life Fame Edition* (2013) allows players to be a music artist, supermodel, or other type of celebrity to build instant fame and wealth. Responding to the digital generation of gamers, the video game, *The Game of Life: 2016* for iOS and Android made by Marmalade Game Studio allows children to play online with their friends, teaching players how to compete early on in real-life fantasy game space.

No matter what version, like *Monopoly*, each path in *The Game of Life* aims for the gradual accumulation or growth of property, which in turn presents more options from which to potentially accrue more capital. In Harry Lou's (2003) book, *The Game of Life: How to Succeed in Real Life No Matter Where You Land*, he argues that the game was invented and is played because it allows the gamer or player to have "one foot in fantasy and one in reality." (Lou 2003: 10) Lou claims the game isn't about acquiring wealth, but instead is about living life. Nor is it about finding happiness because the game is paved with setbacks and obstacles, [5] much like everyday life. (Lou 2003, p. 11) What is key to playing in *The Game of Life* is the importance of making the 'right' choice at a given moment on an individual's journey for optimal end of life rewards. While there is no version of *The Game of Life* for architects, it presents a useful aperture through which to analyse career ambition and the potential for success through beating the competition. Competitive gaming, whether friendly or not, moral or not, can be seen as a seminal aspect of learning life skills for navigating everyday life.

According to the Australian new media theorist, McKenzie Wark (2007, p. [001]) in the contemporary world the 'gamespace' of a board game or a video game or indeed everyday life is "everywhere" and is a "speculation sport" enacted in an "atopian arena." To explore the philosophical limits of "gamespace," Wark creates a fictitious computer game called 'The Cave™,' which is based on Plato's Allegory of the Cave. As a site of contest and struggle, gamers focus in 'The Cave™' on "the act of targeting" which assigns "a unique value" to the target. (Walk 2007, p. [149]) 'The Cave™' has an interior world in which we choose to participate (or not) that legitimates targeting carefully and being victorious over rivals. 'Gamespace' also has an external world of spectatorship. "OUTSIDE each cave is another cave; beyond the game is another game. Each has its particular rules; each has its ranks of high scores." (Wark 2007, p. [014])

Wark (2007, p. [011]) contends that gamespace, like neoliberalism, while seeming to be devoid of the old class divisions, in fact conceals them "beneath levels of rank, where each agonizes [sic] over their worth against others as measured by the size of their house and the price of their vehicle and where, perversely, working longer and longer hours is a sign of victory. Work becomes play." Players are required to become a team player where "your work has to be creative, inventive, playful— ludic." (Wark 2007, p. [011]) When you are in creative control of the gamespace you are no longer the worker who engages in 'dull, repetitive work,' instead it is lively, as Thatcher wished it to be, because the "the commerce of play—making it into the major leagues" insists that "play becomes everything to which it was once opposed. It is work, it is serious; it is morality, it is necessity." (Wark 2007, p. [011])

Replicating the neoliberal disbelief in the welfare system, Wark (2007, p. [012]) notes that no longer is the gamer "interested in playing the citizen." Gamespace in fantasy or real life is premised on the competitive self, but unlike reality, the gamespace of the board or virtual game requires successfully completing levels, in adherence to rules. Anthropological research reiterates the value of competitive playing-to-win in all facets of life and in the formation of socio-cultural value-creation.

According to the Franco-American literary critic, philosopher, and essayist, (Francis) George Steiner (in Huizinga 1970/1949, p. 10), "Play, as [the Dutch cultural historian, Johan] Huizinga defines it, is an activity which proceeds within certain limits of time and space, in a visible order, according to rules freely accepted, and outside the sphere of necessity and material utility." Huizinga agrees, as does Wark, that play is enacted with utmost seriousness, which opposes the very concept of what it means to play. "Thus the cheat is far less hated or chastised than the spoil-sport, the man who somehow subverts and shatters the validity, the importance of the game." (Steiner in Huizinga 1970/1949, p. 10)

In *Homo Ludens* (which roughly translates as Playing Man), Huizinga (1970/1949, p. 48) states that the 'play-instinct' underpins almost every aspect of civilized [sic] social behaviour. Culture arises from and evolves through play "between two parties or teams." (Huizinga 1970/1949, p. 67) "When two people are pitted against each other – whether they are philosophers or warriors, artists among their peers or jurists in a court of law – their intention is to win or succeed. And their weapons are the techniques of play: imagination, simulation, the chance moment...." (Kane 2004, p. 54)

However, play against an opponent involves uncertainty that puts success at stake. "Success gives a player a satisfaction that lasts a shorter or longer while as the case may be." (Huizinga 1970/1949, p. 70) Winning in any gamespace is a sign of superiority that conjures up more than simply the winning of the game played, but also "honour and esteem" which "accrue to the benefit of the group to which the victor belongs." (Huizinga 1970/1949, p. 70) The essence of gaming is a spirit of competition and a drive to win and succeed. For Huizinga, it manifests most strongly as 'sportive competition' as a cultural phenomenon played by *Homo Ludens*.

Broadly parallel to Harvey's definition of neoliberalism, these board games are "a ...political project of creating new means of capital accumulation" through 'sportive competition.' The board game and life motives and choices analogy, enacted in the spirit of play in gamespace, provide an aperture through which to contemplate the game of life to accrue personal and professional capital – social, economic, and cultural (Bourdieu 1986/1983 in Richardson 1986, pp. 241–258) – when architecture is chosen as a career path. The professional gamespace in which architects operate today occurs mostly through neoliberal rules of competitive play. It follows Thatcher's (1995, p. 566) argument that the game of business "though serious [... is] fun" and offers everyone new freedoms and liberties that have not been imaginable under any previous form of governance. However, the paradox of neoliberalism enacted in architectural life is that it offers the promise of individual freedom, sometimes at the architect's own risk and through taking freedoms from others. Consumption of human labour (capitalist polity) and resources allows neoliberalism to operate as a system of growing accumulation of 'self' wealth (capitalist economy). This constructs a specific model of success where social, cultural, and economic capital defines an individual's identity and worth through knowing how to play the game, accruing more and more on the way by exploiting lower-cost labour or resources. The ability and need to progress is uneven for women and men (at the time of writing this book), for example because an individual can start at a different point of advantage or disadvantage, so the playing field in which they have come differs. This is discussed in more detail in the next chapter.

For an architect to participate, win or lose, in the game of an architectural life it is important to understand: 1) image/identity formation under neoliberalism; 2) work-life choices identified at different life stages of professional progression in academia or professional practice; and 3) the effect of neoliberal demands on where, how and when architects work and live life in relation to their wellbeing and the future of work-life balance beyond neoliberalism. The three-part structure of the book examines these three themes.

Part 1 discusses "Life in Architecture under Neoliberalism" and consists of this chapter, "Work-Life Imbalance in Architecture: An Introduction"; Chapter 2, "Celebrity Architect as *Homo Oeconomicus*"; and Chapter 3, "Starting from a Different Position: Architect as *Femina Domestica*." Chapter 2 examines the space of an architect's labour and identity positioned as Foucault's *homo oeconomicus* – economic wo/man – and discusses the architect without any family care responsibilities who is committed entirely to work in an effort to achieve global brand status through 24/7 global practice. Chapter 3 examines the female and male forms of Brown's *femina domestica* – domestic wo/man – who divides their labour between work and non-work/home. It sets out the traditional white male model of *homo oeconomicus* architect, which many female and male architects replicate, and examines how gender, race/ethnicity, class, and age have been historical factors of discrimination that create intersectional inequalities in architectural career progress for those who do not fit the traditional white male model. The dreams that all diverse groups have about their personal and professional identity brand formation are discussed in relation to the neoliberal enterprising self.

Part 2 is entitled "Gameplay Moves: Become an Architect (or Not)." It consists of three chapters which follow the progression of choosing (or not) to enter or progress into a later stage in a life in architecture. Chapter 4, entitled "The Choice to Study Architecture or Not" discusses some reasons girls or boys choose from a young age to study architecture rather than another creative industry. Chapter 5, "Academic Capitalism and Architectural Education" sets out the working life of students of architecture and architectural educators within the context of "academic capitalism" (Slaughter and Leslie 1997) and reveals how it can positively or negatively affect the minds and bodies of architecture workers in H.E. Chapter 6, "A Neoliberal Life in Architectural Practice" discusses the intrinsic relationship architecture has with capital (its production of buildings, land value, and development practices) and capital consumption (of the environment, resources and human labour, and its own workforce) within a neoliberal society that encourages a profit-oriented entrepreneurial, corporate 'big business' philosophy at the higher echelon. It outlines some of the effects on the professional, personal, and societal life and wellbeing of women and men 'starchitects.'

Part 3, "Work-Life Balance in Architecture Beyond Neoliberalism" consists of three chapters. Chapter 7, "The Sites of Neoliberal Architectural Labour: Work, Home, Everywhere" discusses where architectural labour has taken and takes place in the university, office, and remotely. A balance of onsite and remote work can also offer positive areas for future change in the life work patterns of architectural workers at all career stages. Chapter 8, "24/7 Architectural Capitalism, No Time and No Sleep" centres on how the time and modes of production to produce and administer architectural students and architecture for a global market operating 24/7 (Crary 2014) can affect the architectural worker's wellbeing. Many architectural workers have suffered mental and physical health problems or death from overwork and so the culture of architecture work must change. The book concludes with Chapter 9 entitled "Playing the Game of Life in Architecture Beyond Neoliberalism." It summarises the current game of playing out a life in architecture as discussed in previous chapters and reflects on Aristotle's notion of 'eudaimonia' in relation to long-term rather than short-term job and life satisfaction. In *The Nicomachean Ethics*, Aristotle (1947) argues that 'eudaimonia' is not about short-term pleasurable sensations, as 'liquid modernity' encourages contemporary society to believe, but is the possible outcome of the totality of one's life, how we participate in life-in-full, across the private and public domains. This final chapter argues that if architects are to regain balance in their work life, the rules of the game in which they operate need revising in terms of architecture's relationship to neoliberalism.

The main purpose of the book is to encourage architects to make careful life choices for personal, societal, and environmental balance. It aims to challenge the dominant image of a 'successful' architectural life in the public domain as that of the architectural worker devoted entirely to work, consuming themselves and all around them. It asks deeper philosophical questions about what neoliberalism demands of the architectural 'self as enterprise' (Kelly 2006) versus the enterprise of the architect self. In order to do this, the next chapter will examine the relationship between identity formations in architecture to establish the current dominant models and patterns of architectural work-life to later consider them in relation to more diverse groups of people entering the profession. Those identity formations rely arguably, as Sara James (2017, p. 296.9) notes in *Making a Living, Making a Life*, on the choice to balance or not "fulfilment in work and love." The next chapter looks at the architect's dream to be deeply in love with and driven by their work.

Notes

1 While the phrase work-life balance continues to be used and is adopted here, it has arguably been debunked by "work-family balance" (Frone 2003), "work-life harmony" (Ong and Jeyaraj 2014), or "work-life integration." While many writers on the subject abbreviate it to WLB, this research refrains from doing so because it is important to keep the word meanings present for the reader.
2 Inspired by East Coast American student activist movements with which he became affiliated, the book was a departure from Harvey's earlier scholarship undertaken at the University of Cambridge that used traditional quantitative research methods in geography.
3 This is because of the author's personal experience of having worked in a satellite campus of a U.K.-based university between 2018 and 2020.
4 Ironically, as the game became popular across college campuses, it lost its Georgian ambitions and turned into a game that improved the skills for profit making.
5 Setbacks in the game include being robbed, losing money after a slump in the stock market, having to pay taxes, etc.

References

Andrachuk, J., Forman, A., Bolos, C., and Hooks, M. eds. 2014. Issue title 'Money.' *Perspecta: The Yale Architecture Journal*, 47.

Aristotle; Rackham, H. 1947. *The Nicomachean Ethics*. Cambridge, Mass: Harvard University Press; London: W. Heinemann.

Attai, P. 2016. *The Full History of Board Games*. January 21, 2016. https://medium.com/swlh/the-full-history-of-board-games-5e622811ce89 Accessed May 06, 2021.

Awan, N., Schneider, T., and Till, J., 2011. *Spatial Agency: Other Ways of Doing Architecture*. London: Routledge.

Bauman, Z. 2000. *Liquid Modernity*. Cambridge: Polity Press.

Bentmann, R. and Müller, M. 1992. *The Villa as Hegemonic Architecture*. Atlantic Highlands, NJ: Humanities Press.

BBC News. 2013. Tony Blair: 'My job was to build on some Thatcher policies.' April 08, 2013. https://www.bbc.co.uk/news/av/uk-politics-22073434 Accessed November 06, 2023.

Bourdieu, P., 1986. The Forms of Capital. In Richardson, J. G. ed. *Handbook of Theory and Research for the Sociology of Education*. New York; Westport, Conn; London: Greenwood Press, pp. 241–258.

Brown, W. 2015. *Undoing the Demos: Neoliberalism's Stealth Revolution*. New York: Zone books.

Carducci, V. 2007. *Gamer Theory by McKenzie Wark*. June 05, 2007. https://www.popmatters.com/gamer-theory-by-mckenzie-wark-2496238666.html Accessed November 06, 2023.

Chamorro-Premuzic, T. 2013. Embrace Work-Life Imbalance. In *Harvard Business Review*, February 12, 2013. https://hbr.org/2013/02/embrace-work-life-imbalan Accessed November 06, 2023.

Clark, S. C. 2000. Work/family Border Theory: A New Theory of Work/family Balance, *Human Relations*, 53: 747–770.

Consolación, A., Caplliure, E.-M., Miquel, M.-J. 2016. Work-Life Balance in Firms: A Matter of Women? *Journal of Business Research*, 69 (4): 1379–1383.

Crary, J. 2014. *24/7: Late Capitalism and the Ends of Sleep*. London: Verso Books.

Deamer, P. ed., 2015. *The Architect as Worker: Immaterial Labor, the Creative Class, and the Politics of Design*. London: Bloomsbury Academic.

Deamer, P. ed., 2014. *Architecture and Capitalism: 1845 to the Present*. London: Routledge.

Dunham-Jones, E. 2014. Irrational Exuberance: Rem Koolhaas and the 1990s. In Deamer, P. ed. *Architecture and Capitalism: 1845 to the Present*. London: Routledge, pp. 150–171.

Fine, B. and Saad-Filho, A. 2019 August 09. Thirteen Things You Need to Know About Neoliberalism, *Critical Sociology*, 43 (4–5): 685–706.

Fishman, R. and Kubey, K. 2018. The Global Crisis of Affordable Housing: Architecture versus Neoliberalism, *Architectural Design*, 88 (4): 22–29.

Fleetwood, S. 2006. Why Work-life Balance Now? *The Lancaster University Management School (LUMS) Papers Series*, Lancaster, U.K.

Francis, V., Fulu, E., and Lingard, H. 2009. Is it a Problem? In Lingard, H. and Francis, V. *Managing Work-life Balance in Construction*. Abingdon: Spon Press, pp. 1–37.

Frone, M. R. 2003. Work-Family Balance. In Quick, J. C. and Tetrick L. E. eds., *Handbook of Occupational Health Psychology*. Washington, DC: American Psychological Association, pp. 143–162.

Foucault, M., Davidson, A. I. ed., and Burchell, G. (Trans). 2008. *The Birth of Biopolitics: Lectures of the Collège de France, 1978–1979*. Houndmills, Basingstoke, Hampshire [England]; New York: Palgrave Macmillan.

Foucault, M. and Sheridan, A. (Trans). 1995. *Discipline and Punish: The Birth of the Prison*. 2nd ed. New York: Vintage Books.

Franklin, B. 1750. The Morals of Chess. *American Philosophical Society*, 6: 159–161. Reprinted from *The Columbian Magazine*, 01 December 1786.

Gabrielsson, C. and Mattsson, H. eds. 2017. Issue title 'Solids and Flows: Architecture and Capitalism', *Architecture and Culture*, 5 (2).

George, H., 2012 [1879]. *Progress and Property: An Inquiry into the Cause of Industrial Depressions and of Increase of Want with Increase of Wealth: The Remedy*. London: Forgotten Books.

Gould, B. 2013. Margaret Thatcher's Contribution to Neoliberalism, *London Progressive Journal*. (April 12, 2013) http://londonprogressivejournal.com/article/view/1463/margaret-thatchers-contribution-to-neoliberalism Accessed November 06, 2023.

Grasso, M., Farrall, S., Gray, E., Hay, C., and Jennings, W. 2019. Thatcher's Children, Blair's Babies, Political Socialization and Trickle-down Value Change: An Age, Period and Cohort Analysis. *British Journal of Political Science*, 49 (1): 17–36. doi:10.1017/S0007123416000375

Greenhaus, J. H., Collins, K. M., and Shaw, J. D. 2003. The Relation between Work–Family Balance and Quality of Life, *Journal of Vocational Behavior*, 63: 510–531.

Harvey, D. 2010. *A Companion to Marx's Capital*. London: Verso.

Harvey, D., 2007. *A Brief History of Neoliberalism*. Oxford: Oxford University Press.

Harvey, D., 2006. *Social Justice and the City*. London: Wiley-Blackwell.

Harvey, D. 2005. Neoliberalism as Creative Destruction. *The Annals of the American Academy of Political and Social Science*, NAFTA and Beyond: Alternative Perspectives in the Study of Global Trade and Development, 610: 22–44.

Harvey, D. 2003 December. The Right to the City, *International Journal of Urban and Regional Research*, 27(4): 939–941.

Harvey, D. 2000. *Spaces of Hope*. Edinburgh: Edinburgh University Press.

Harvey, D. 1972 July. Evolutionary and Counter Revolutionary Theory in Geography and the Problem of Ghetto Formation, *Antipode*, 4 (2): 1–13.

Hight, C. 2012. Manners of Working: Fabricating Representation in Digital Based Design. In Crysler, C. G., Cairns, S., and Heynen, H., eds. *The Sage Handbook of Architectural Theory*. Los Angeles: Sage, pp. 410–429.

Huber, M., Lechner, M., and Wunsch, C. 2015. Workplace Health Promotion and Labour Market Performance of Employees, *Journal of Health Economics*, 2015–09, 43: 170–189.

Huizinga, J. 1970 [1938]. *Homo Ludens: A Study of the Play Element in Culture*. London: Temple Smith.

James, S. 2017. *Making a Living, Making a Life: Work, Meaning and Self-Identity*. London; New York: Routledge.

Jenkins, S. 2007. *Thatcher and Sons: A Revolution in Three Acts*. London: Penguin.

Jessop, B., 2002. Liberalism, Neoliberalism and Urban Governance: A State-Theoretical Perspective. In Brenner, N. and Theodore, N. eds. *Spaces of Neoliberalism: Urban Restructuring in North America and Western Europe*. Oxford: Blackwell, pp. 105–125.

Kane, P., 2004. *The Play Ethic: A Manifesto for a Different Way of Living*. Macmillan: Oxford.

Kelly, P. 2016. *The Self as Enterprise: Foucault and the Spirit of the 21st Century Capitalism*. London: Routledge.

Lilley, S. ed. 2011. *Capital and its Discontents: Conversations with Radical Thinkers in a Time of Tumult*. Oakland: PM Press.

Lingard, H., and Francis V. 2009. *Managing Work-life Balance in Construction*. Abingdon: Spon Press.

Lou, H. 2003. *The Game of Life: How to Succeed in Real Life no Matter Where you Land*. Philadelphia; London: Running.

Marx, K., and Engels, F. eds. 1970–1972 [1867]. *Capital: A Critique of Political Economy* or *Capital: A Critical Analysis of Capitalist Production*. London: Lawrence & Wishart. Vol. 2.

McClean, D., Holgate, P., and Bloice, L. 2020. *Mental Health in UK Architecture Education*. RIBA Research Grant.

Mill, J. S. 2015 [1859]. *On Liberty, Utilitarianism and Other Essays*, 2nd edition. Edited by Philp, M. and Rosen, F. Oxford: Oxford University Press.

Moen, P. 2003. Introduction. In Moen, P. ed., *It's about Time: Career Strains, Strategies and Successes*. Ithaca, NY: Cornell University Press, pp. 1–16.

Miller, R. H. 2005. *Inventors and Creators: Milton Bradley*. Detroit; New York: Thomas Gale.

Minton, A. 2017. *Big Capital: Who is London For?* London: Penguin Books.

Nash, C. 2022. *Design your Life: An Architect's Guide to Achieving a Work/Life Balance*. London: RIBA Publishing.

Newman, J. 2012. *Working the Spaces of Power: Activism, Neoliberalism and Gendered Labour*. London: Bloomsbury Academic.

Ong, H. L. C and Jeyaraj, S. 2014. Work–life Interventions: Differences Between Work–life Balance and Work–life Harmony and Its Impact on Creativity at Work, *Sage Open*, (July–September 2014), 1–11. https://doi.org/10.1177/2158244014544289

Owen, G. ed. 2009. *Architecture, Ethics and Globalization*. London; New York: Routledge.

Peck, J. 2004. Geography and Public Policy: Constructions of Neoliberalism, *Progress in Human Geography*, 28 (3): 392–405.

Poole, M. and Shvartzberg, M. eds., 2015. *The Politics of Parametricism: Digital Technologies in Architecture.* London: Bloomsbury Academic.

Scaria, D., Brandt, M. L., Kim, E., and Lindeman, B. 2019. What Is Wellbeing? In Kim, E. and Lindeman, B. eds. *Wellbeing,* Switzerland: Springer Nature Switzerland AG, pp. 3–10.

Sklair, L. 2017. *The Icon Project: Architecture, Cities, and Capitalist Globalization.* New York; Oxford: Oxford University Press.

Slaughter, S. and Leslie, L. L. 1997. *Academic Capitalism: Politics, Policies and the Entrepreneurial University*. Baltimore; London: John Hopkins University Press.

Scruton, R. 1979. The Ideology of the Market, *Cambridge Review*. (June 29, 1979). Republished in Scruton, R., 1981. *The Politics of Culture and Other Essays*. Manchester: Carcanet Press.

Spencer, D. 2016. *The Architecture of Neoliberalism: How Contemporary Architecture Became an Instrument of Control and Compliance.* London: Bloomsbury Academic.

Thatcher, M. 1995. *The Path to Power*. London: Harper Press.

Troiani, I. 2021. The Elephant in the Room: How Neoliberal Architecture Education Undermines Wellbeing, *Charrette*, 7(2), (December 2021): 9–33.

Vidal, J., Ncube, M., Bromund, T. R., and Ghosh, J. 2013. Margaret Thatcher: Her Impact and Legacy in Global Development. *The Guardian*, April 16, 2013. https://www.theguardian.com/global-development/poverty-matters/2013/apr/16/margaret-thatcher-impact-legacy-development Accessed November 06, 2023.

Waite, R., and Braidwood, E. 2016. Mental Health Problems Exposed by AJ Student Survey 2016, *Architects' Journal*, 243(16): 8–12.

Wark, M. 2007. *Gamer Theory*. Cambridge, Massachusetts; London: Harvard University Press. [This book is not paginated. Sections are numbered as [001] etc.]

Zimmer, B. 2010. Wellness. *The New York Times*, April 16, 2010. https://www.nytimes.com/2010/04/18/magazine/18FOB-onlanguage-t.html, Accessed May 06, 2022.

2

CELEBRITY ARCHITECT AS *HOMO OECONOMICUS*

FIGURE 2.1   Screen grab from *The Fountainhead* (Dir. King Vidor 1949) starring Gary Cooper (left) as Howard Roark and Henry Hull as Henry Cameron. Credit: Warner Brothers/Album. Copyright: Image ID: P0RF34, Alamy Stock Photo.

DOI: 10.4324/9781351199834-3

The Global American Dream, Neoliberalism, and the Image of the Architect

> The American Dream has served as a road map for the way we often envision the course of our lives. The rules of the game are well-known, as is the bargain that is struck. For those willing to work hard and take advantage of their opportunities, there is the expectation of a prosperous and fulfilling life.
>
> *(Rank et al. 2014, p. 1)*

Nowadays, the game of life for most in the developing world follows the road map of the American Dream, which Professor of Gender, Sexuality and Feminist Studies, Kathi Weeks (2011, p. 12) notes centres on a Protestant work 'ethic's productivist values,' and the notion that work is energising. Even if we work in a pure or partial form of a neoliberal-oriented society whether in the United Kingdom (U.K.), Europe, United States (U.S.A.), or Asia, etc., the construction of our identity is linked to *The American Dream*, even if it is a British Dream, or European Dream as others note for instance. For this reason, it is important to examine the link between the American Dream and identity formation of the architect.

As the American economic and social theorist Jeremy Rifkin (2004) points out in *The European Dream*, while other countries, politicians, and states have their own dreams for their national identity – which ironically are sometimes ideologically and politically polarised to the American Dream – it is the optimism, excitement, and hopefulness for the future and its connection with personal freedoms and rights that the American Dream exemplifies that enthrals people worldwide. Neoliberal conditions enabled by 'liquid modernity' (Bauman 2000) including advancement in technology, easier access to capital, and opportunities to work across the globe are greater than ever before. Consequently, it is arguably universally agreed, in theory, that it is more possible than ever before to achieve the American Dream anywhere in the world, not just in America. However, while the American Dream has global allure, as political scientist Jennifer Hochschild (1995, p. 25) points out it has also "kept … [people] striving in horrible conditions against impossible odds." Rank et al. (2014, p. 53) note that this "is the paradox and genius of America. It allows for hopes and dreams within the context of hardship and strife." As was the case for immigrants making their home in America and American nationals, "America has always been about the hope and promise of a good life." (Rank et al. 2014, p. 3) So, regardless of the fact that the American Dream can show signs of serious flaw, such as at times of economic and pandemic crises, society continues to play the game to achieve the American Dream rather than give it up because, according to Rifkin (2005, p. 2), it remains "the glue … [that] keeps us together." That, and the fact that capitalism and neoliberalism are so societally, environmentally, and culturally embedded in our lives, means that it is virtually impossible not to become a want-to-be, moving from a 'have-not' to a 'have' and participate in the life plight of the American Dream in some form.

The American Dream encompasses the post-war American image of a person having the ability to obtain "a well-paying and stable job, a house in the suburbs, a family with two or three children, a new car in the garage, and a two-week summer vacation" to someone who quickly-makes money such as the Sir Alan Sugar *Apprentice*-style rags to riches story. In its ideal form it links economic security with wellbeing (Cullen 2003, p. 29), with security deeply connected to private property ownership of the detached house and more. From the post-WW2 period, people dream (or have been encouraged by capitalism to dream) of owning their own home, ideally purpose-designed as a one-off by an architect. Set with this game goal, many people work all their lives to have access or gain enough wealth in order to acquire one or a vast number of private properties for personal security, but also to increase social status.

The American Dream and its osmosis throughout society occurs, in part, because of the creation and dissemination worldwide of media (movies) and the online platform (the internet) that has bound us into a global digital community. American movies setting out a protagonist's journey (typically an underdog) to get that girl or boy, to beat the corporation when it is has done us wrong, to stand up for what is true to our values, etc., i.e., through perseverance and tenacity, to win a life challenge or battle against all odds, have been the DNA stalemates of ambitions. They, along with other types of media, typify and promote global images of successful winners and contribute to how society constructs identity formations. Working tirelessly to win and be a winner, done through individual, less so collective, hard work, creative thinking, and entrepreneurism (which will be discussed more fully later) are also the hallmark of the contemporary neoliberal life. The heroic toil of the individual for freedom and independence from the state were essential human characteristics that British Prime Minster, Dame Margaret Thatcher and (former Hollywood actor), American President Ronald Reagan's administrations made valuable under neoliberal policy changes. That image of the heroic winner with an unrelenting work-ethic has also had a parallel lively history in architecture in print and digital media, particularly in film.

The construction of the image of the heroic architect had its heyday with the publication in 1943 of *The Fountainhead*, a non-fiction novel by the Russian American author, Ayn Rand. It was made into a black-and-white drama film of the same name three years later (Dir. Vidor 1949). *The Fountainhead* (Rand 2007 [1943]) is the story of the young, visionary modern architect, Howard Roark (played by Gary Cooper) (Figure 2.1) who maintains his integrity and resists conforming to popular design standards to battle the establishment against all odds for the fountainhead of achievement – success in building his avant-garde modern designs. Roark's rugged individualism is contrasted to architect and social climber, Peter Keating, who is a conformist that follows popular styles, gives clients what they want without question, and fails to pursue his own personal architectural agendas. The book uses Roark as the uncompromising creative who, in building the image of the modern American city, simultaneously builds his own heroic architectural persona. The story comes from Rand's affection for the image of the

American skyscraper. She saw it as the physical manifestation of individualism, which she considered superior to collectivism. All of this tied into her newfound political ideology, shifting from Soviet Communism to being "a part of the extreme right wing of American politics" and "an ardent supporter of the Republican Party." (Schleier 2009, p. 119)

After migrating from the Soviet Union to New York in 1926, Rand set out to write about the modern American city because she was instantly impressed with how the skyscrapers of Manhattan symbolised freedom and opportunity. (Schleier 2009; Ralston in Mayhew 2006, p. 70) Rand seized the opportunity to align the symbol of metropolitan architecture with the free spirit of its creative architect and of a new life for immigrants. As a then-assistant to the movie producer, Cecil B. DeMille, Rand wrote a script for the 1928 film, *Skyscraper* (Dir. Higgin). Although it was rejected, Rand developed the story into *The Fountainhead*. Fascinated by the skyscraper but knowing little about architecture or architects, Rand researched the stories of real-life architects and their struggles to build modern American cities. (Schleier 2009, p. 121) She read the biographies of the modern masters, Le Corbusier, Frank Lloyd Wright, and Louis Sullivan and used the personas of Wright and Sullivan as the basis for the characters of Roark and Henry Cameron respectively. Just like Wright, who had formerly worked for Sullivan, Roark was a former employee of Cameron. Just like Wright who was an artistically uncompromising architect visionary, so was Roark. Just like Wright, who worked on commissions for private clients, so did Roark. Just like Wright, who fell in love with the wife of someone in his professional circle,[1] Roark falls in love with the wife of someone in his professional circle.[2] Love and work are intertwined.

While doing her research on the persona of the heroic architect, Rand also undertook research on "public housing, which she employed for her critique of government-subsidized housing, the architectural nemesis of the novel that is destroyed by Roark." (Schleier 2009, p. 122) Rand was critical of public housing, which she aligned to Socialist ideology. From her reading of the *Architectural Forum* of 1938, Rand reiterated the journal's condemnatory claims that low-income Americans were being given housing at the expense of middle-income Americans. Identity constructions in *The Fountainhead* are not only of the 'ideal' architect but also privately-owned architecture that will come to symbolise the success of the architect as an individual, their posterity in architectural history, the city in which their project is built, and the power of that urban image to build a strong national image. While this is *the* dominant image of the architect in the popular press that can attract students to enter architecture, architects and architectural practices are becoming more varied. (Zaera-Polo and Abascal 2016)

First, images of the architect stretch across the spectrum of practitioners who refrain from engaging entirely, partially, or not at all with capitalist, neoliberal production. They range from architects designing and building collectively-motivated public projects to those who focus on producing private projects for individual patrons. Second, the gender, race, and class backgrounds of people choosing to study, teach, and practice architecture worldwide are more diverse than the 1920s of Rand's *The Fountainhead*. As such, understanding how to play the game of life in architecture requires understanding the multifarious types of architectural images that have existed and can exist other than the singular architectural genius. This broader understanding of a not-one-size-fits all architect when presented publicly could give emerging architects alternative role-models to aspire to. Only in the last 50 years has the profession examined the gamut of possibilities that are available for architect image formations.

Provoked in part by Roark's fictional character and the real-life Wright, in 1983, Andrew Saint published *The Image of Architect* to argue that there exist a multitude of images of architects of which individualist Roark is but one type, although all the types of architect Saint resents are male. There is no image of any type of woman architect recognised, but efforts have been made since to understand what a woman architect looks like. (Troiani 2012) In his book, Saint studies and distinguishes architects and architectural practices that range within the spectrum of those based on artisanship, sacrificing money for artistic freedom and integrity, to big business-oriented architects who are more focused on profit-making, with variations in-between.

Saint opens the book with the study of the category of the creative genius who has a singular artisan-driven practice, as exemplified by Wright. Saint then discusses the large American corporate practice of Sullivan and Adler who are a mixed model of creative genius (Louis Sullivan) who collaborates with his salesmen business partner, Dankmar Adler.[3] Saint then discusses the entrepreneur architect, British-born John Poulsen, who worked hard to win projects nationally and internationally at any cost and who was eventually convicted of fraud. Another chapter discusses the American real estate architect-developer, John C. Portman Jr., who made popular grand, private hotels with multi-storied interior atria such as the Westin Bonaventure Hotel in Los Angeles, 1974–1976, the subject of Fredric Jameson's (1992) *Postmodernism, or, the Cultural Logic of Late Capitalism*. At one end of the spectrum, creative or designer architects are presumed to spend substantial amounts of time designing and are committed to design excellence whilst also not being at the service of capital. At the other end of the spectrum, good commercial, corporate practices working in the spirit of enterprise act as client, architect, and developer. Business-oriented offices which only offer traditional architectural services fine-tune their production timelines through delegation of labour and efficient use of partners or employee skills. The business savvy architect is seen to be hard-headed and ruthless in their attitude to staff productivity, setting tight deadlines, and supporting a long-work hours culture while being friendly to clients to win jobs.

However, architects of both types, and everything in-between, have gradually changed their approach to business, no longer seeing it as something sullied that will damage their design integrity. Following the neoliberal logic that everything and anything including design ethics or integrity can be commodified, Saint (1983, p. 95) writes; "Though the managerial and artistic approaches to architecture continue generally to appear mutually opposed, in many of the biggest and most profitable practices they have happily co-existed." As most architects have come around to the need to be business-savvy rather than choosy as to who they work for or see that they can dictate to a client what architecture they will be given, as Sullivan did[4] (Lloyd Wright 1931, pp. 40–41 in Saint 1983, p. 16), creativity has become increasingly commodified for its capacity to define unique building designs to generate capital.[5]

The Creative Class, *Homo Oeconomicus*, and Entrepreneurship

As already outlined, the persona of the architect as creative is complex, being conditioned by historic constructions of the architect in the conflicting roles of 'artist' and 'professional.' While it is acknowledged that architects acquire reputational capital through the growth of their business, creativity has undoubtedly become an invaluable and powerful commodity in architectural production today. As architectural journalist and editor, Nancy Levinson (in Lamster ed. 2000, p. 27) writes; "Central to the mystique of architecture – in life and in the movies – is the idea of the architect as a person of marked creativity, creativity so strong it can seem a primal or religious force, allowing the architect to envision what does not yet exist, and so fundamental to [her or] his identity that others cannot help but acknowledge it, with various degrees of admiration, awe, envy, and fear." It is the potential for the creativity of the architect – design innovation, unconventional language, or dress – to be converted into capital that makes it valuable in the age of neoliberalism. Here a unique building design, language used by the architect, or dressing of an architect can create marketing capital for architect and client alike.

According to the sociologist Richard Biernacki (in Deamer ed. 2015, p. 40): "Economics instrumentalizes [sic] creativity as a factor of production." Architect Manuel Shvartzberg (in Deamer ed. 2015, p. 181) sees that 'creativity,' 'innovation,' and 'disruption' have become imperative in neoliberal societies and are essential to maintain a competitive market position. It is because of the ability of "creativity [to] ma[k]e new worlds out of nothing" and to "measure … that productivity as a kind of surplus value relative to other inputs" (Biernacki in Deamer ed. 2015, p. 40) that economists such as Richard Florida (2004) have defined the value of the 'creative class' in which architects, though more so avant-garde architectural designers or 'starchitects,' sit comfortably. According to Florida (2004, p. xiii), "Human creativity is the ultimate economic resource."

Nowadays the architectural 'creative class' commodifies design labour through product innovation and marketing, a topic discussed later in this chapter. Design as "immaterial labour gets categorized, spatialized, and monetized [sic]" (Deamer in Deamer ed. 2015, p. xxxiii) – the extent of which depends on the degree of 'innovation' performed by the designer within the market. The intelligence and business savviness that commodifies a design idea in architecture, or in fact any field, is enacted by the French philosopher, Michel Foucault's *homo oeconomicus* (or economic man or economic woman). The *homo oeconomicus* architect has specific character attributes and lives a particular lifestyle. To play the game of life of an architect under neoliberalism it is important to understand *why homo oeconomicus* makes his or her life choices and critically analyse *how* those choices are available, or not, to people of different gender, race, or ethnicity, class, and age. Whether working in the university setting or architectural practice, in any country in the world that follows a neoliberal agenda, *homo oeconomicus* has become an extremely useful economic commodity because of their ability to generate capital.

Foucault's *homo oeconomicus* is competitive, driven, and singularly-focused on the economisation of their labour through his or her *total* commitment to their work life. In her reflection on Foucault's lectures and theories, political scientist Wendy Brown (2015, p. 33) argues that under neoliberalism's free market advocacy, economic man and economic woman "takes its shape as human capital seeking to strengthen its competitive positioning and appreciate its value." They can commercialise and capitalise on every design idea they have but they also are able to devote all their time to work and *only* work. *Homo oeconomicus* can work hard for long hours and consequently can potentially take on more work and be more productive in their paid labour. *Homo oeconomicus*, who is free of family, can choose to devote more time to their professional life since their personal commitments do not require that their time be compromised for use in other ways. American sociologist, Arlie Hochschild (in Hochschild with Machung 1989, pp. x–xi) argues in her Preface to *The Second Shift: Working Families and the Revolution of Home* that women who have a career and family and are primary carers, "Seeing that the game is devised for family-free people, …[can] lose heart."

Being "family-free," however, does not always mean that an economic man or economic woman is without their own family. *Homo oeconomicus* can be married or not, partnered, or have children. If they do have children, their freedom comes from not having primary care responsibilities, thereby giving them more time to work. Economic man and economic woman with a child or children or others to care for can be "family-free" because their partner, a nanny, an au pair, a boarding school, care home, cattery, dog sitter or dog hotel, etc., takes primary care responsibilities away from them and diverts them to other workers who are either paid or unpaid for that care work. It is argued here that for architects who have care responsibilities, being able to make the choice to be "family-free" or not depends to some degree on the gendered division of labour at work and home. As Weeks (2012, p. 9) writes, "To say that work is organised by gender is to observe that it is a site where, at a minimum, we can find gender enforced, performed, and recreated." This contrasts the widely-held belief that upward mobility, through entrepreneurism, is equally attainable, for instance, for white American economic men and white American economic women. The issues of race/ethnicity, class, and age add additional stereotyping to gendered work.

There are other gendered factors, however, such as the desire or ability to engage in entrepreneurism, that can also contribute to professional career mobility and impact on how well men and women play the business game in architecture. Not everyone wants to be a businessperson or salesperson having to sell their architectural ideas, but success requires (the individual or one of the partners in the office) to have that skill. Women and men architects who don't want to buy into selling their persona and designs as an architect have a lesser chance to succeed in the game. For the economic man or economic woman who is happy to or can naturally play entrepreneur, an exceptional design idea with global market gravitas is what an architect contestant would need to sell to Sir Sugar on *The Apprentice*.

Homo oeconomicus is entrepreneurial, using their creativity and all their available time to produce sellable, unique products to gain a market edge in the global economy. Market forces allow 'the creative class' to operate as entrepreneurs to increase their market share because the Unique Selling Point (USP) of their product creates global demand able to increase revenue generation. With each new idea that transforms into architecture comes the potential for neoliberal business growth and expansion. However, the entrepreneur who is focused on monetising his or her ideas, skills, or wares, has specific personality attributes that allow them to optimally compete in the market. Those personality traits mostly relate to business management and communication, risk-taking, and competitiveness to win in the game of the global business markets of architecture and design. Nowadays, it is becoming increasingly common for the global elite in architecture schools or practices to employ vocabulary gleaned from 'new discourses of management' (Thrift 2009) for marketing 'the new.' That language uses acronyms (to save time because time means money), catch phrases, brand jargon, short pithy slogans, etc., to market the world with their entrepreneurial idea, many of which follow an American-style publicity and business speak and which everyday people do not commonly use to communicate with. (Fugere, Hardaway and Warshawsky 2005) Entrepreneur architects seek to capture new market opportunities in the game of selling their brand of design.

Entrepreneur, meaning 'to capture' or 'to take' what is 'between,' comes from the 13th century French masculine verb *entreprendre*. Due to its use in *Principles of Political Economy* by the English philosopher and political economist, John Stuart Mill (in Laughlin ed. 2009) it became popular in the late 19th century onwards when it was used to describe an entrepreneur as both a businessperson and a risk taker. This definition has remained ever since. Sociologist, Zulema Valdez (2016, p. 1) defines "entrepreneurs as creators who bring new ideas to the market, develop new products or provide new services, and seek to maximize profits and grow their businesses." Taking the lead from the German economist Joseph A. Schumpeter, Valdez (2016, p. 3) explains that "entrepreneurs are often described as possessing characteristics that encourage business ownership, including being hard-working, risk-taking, optimistic, creative, and … [have] a 'problem with authority'." Under 'liquid modernity,' entrepreneurship is often attributed to a more 'positive ideology' than steady, stable long-term employment. (Valdez 2016, p. 3) Valdez (2016) also connects *Entrepreneurs and the Search for the American Dream* because entrepreneurism can offer a primary pathway to improve status and wealth towards realising the American Dream. All over the world, no longer reliant on family, 'old' money, any architect who seeks and has the capacity to make real the American Dream has the opportunity to become, in theory, part of the architectural 'nouveau riche' by quickly jumping to a higher social and professional class.

In theory, architect-entrepreneurs can climb the social, class, and professional ladder through the standard entrepreneurial route of the "the pursuit of opportunity beyond resources controlled." (Stevenson quoted in Eisenmann 2013 in Valdez 2016, p. 6) Architecture values entrepreneurship and the history of great architects, their buildings, theories, practice, and monopolies spring from the architect's ability to take advantage of an 'opportunity' – returning to the origins of the word *entreprendre* – 'to capture' or 'to take' new architectural markets 'between' the existing markets through design and product innovation. Knowing how to create an opportunity for market advantage is a fundamental aspect of all business game-playing, whether in architecture or not.

The parallel between the entrepreneur who has a "problem with authority" (Valdez 2016, p. 3) aligns with the history of famous architects too. Like Roark, many want to defy systems of conformity. There have always been architects who were and are contrary and unconventional in every aspect of their lives and who often parallel the life model of an eccentric artist. Architectural unconventionality generally aligns with unconventional behaviour and is one way in which an architect consolidates their brand as an artist-designer who has no limits. For example, the desire to not lead a 'normal life' – happily married with a family and monogamous – choosing instead marriage *and* lovers and children inside and outside marriage, or no marriage or children at all, are ways to resist gendered and social conventions for USP.

The wearing of unconventional clothing or dress can also signify a desire to challenge societal conventions. Whether architects wear black to stand out or not, be 'stylish,' flattering, or for other reasons, unconventional dress is a phenomenon employed by the 'creative class' architect. Think first of Wright with his broad-brimmed hat and signature cape or the flamboyant apparel of Iraqi-born British architect, Dame Zaha Hadid.

Hadid recognised that her wanting to "wear unconventional clothes" paralleled her "not at all conventional behavior [sic]." (Holub 2016) Hadid's dress image as a 'creative professional' was bold, playful, entirely original, and exclusive, just like Hadid's one-off building designs. Since 2006, Hadid wore for special events the custom-made designs by German fashion designer, Elke Walter, whose designs are inspired by nature and architecture. Mostly black, Walter's garments created a sculptural form around Hadid's body, paralleling Hadid's sculptural architecture. Prada and Yohji Yamamoto also designed one-off pieces for Hadid, "and her closet was packed with Miyake, Gigli and Miu Miu." (Holub 2016) Hadid established and performed her difference, her (literal) exceptionalness, as a personal brand which contributed to her construction as a creative genius and her elite designer authorship. It is the very nature of many elite architects that they grow from a

FIGURE 2.2   Iraqi architect Zaha Hadid in her London office U.K., circa 1985. Hadid
designed architecture, furniture, and other products. Photograph by
Christopher Pillitz/Getty Images. Editorial # 106423266, Hutton Collection.
Date created: 01 January, 1985.

mythological narrative and are obliged and rewarded for reinforcing that myth. While most elite architects choose not to wear unconventional clothing, it is this extreme obsessive designer behaviour to design every aspect of their image and that of their clients by Wright and Hadid – who both designed fashion themselves and Wright for his clients (Gorman 1995) – that comes to reiterate their architectural excellence. As part of neoliberal celebrity marketisation, whether purposeful or not, Hadid's bodily image reiterated the unique product brand of *everything* designed in her company name.

Publicity and the Architect's Brand Identity

Image-making for publicity is a fundamental feature of capitalism. Capitalism is dependent on the continuous production and consumption of images of new products. As the American writer, filmmaker, and philosopher, Susan Sontag (2008, p. 178) notes, "A capitalist society requires a culture based on images. It needs to furnish vast amounts of entertainment in order to stimulate buying …" Nowadays, architectural education uses the relentless production of rebranded university buildings, websites, architecture shows, and associated catalogues and books to promote themselves. In architectural practice, architecture and design cultures are driven by the relentless production of images made to buy and sell the practice's architecture, designer products, and design culture and designers.

While architects in some countries are not legally able to publicly 'advertise' their services, there are subtle ways that architects develop world renown and increase their market share through branding. These include building brand *personality*; marketing an architectural signature, celebrity brand; creating 'icon (brand) projects' in brandscapes; and spinoff products designed using the unique signature architect brand which ties the architect's name to their other designer product ranges.[6]

Brand *personality* refers to a group of characteristics that a human has that are attributed to a brand name. A brand *personality* allows a consumer to relate to the product range, which always display consistent product traits. In 'Architectural Branding,' Canadian American architect, educator, and writer, Withold Rybczynski (2008, p. 279) describes how architects build an architectural brand *personality* as they build consecutive buildings, sometimes in a distinct house style, but not normally so. Brand *personality* goes hand in hand with company slogans, making it easy to remember a product's USP in a few words. (Norman) Foster and Partners' international brand *personality* is "Innovative Solutions to Complex Problems." (Rybczynski 2008, p. 279) The Renzo Piano Building Workshop's (RPBW) brand *personality*, "which conveys a sense of bespoke elegance, is something like Stylish Solutions to Any Problem" (Rybczynski 2008, p. 280) and Hadid Architect's brand *personality* has been defined as feminine-inspired curvaceous architecture. (Holub 2016)

The performativity of femininity by women for market advantage, defined by Critical and Cultural theorist, Robin Truth Goodman (2013: 3) as 'professional femininity,' uses woman, and in this instance the woman architect and her architecture, for market advantage. In the case of Hadid, this includes her creative outputs in architecture, product design, and visual arts, all of which increase marketisation. The construction of femininity as a unique identity is transformed by neoliberalism "into marketable commodities" (Goodman 2013, p. 3) and can be used to create a unique marketable brand.

Marketing a brand culture and identity in architecture relies on publicity of an architect's buildings and theories disseminated through public lectures, exhibitions, interviews, news stories, books, architectural magazines and journals, websites, documentaries, and office openings, etc., which all contribute "to the construction of an architect's public image." (McNeill 2009, p. 59) If the architect is a proficient writer, they have the advantage of being able to self-publicise rather than rely on others to do so.

In an example of this self-publication through writing, Le Corbusier carefully planned and wrote over 40 books in his lifetime (De Smet 2015). Rem Koolhaas too, is a prolific self-publicist, having published a profuse number of books to date – sometimes in collaboration with others and/or through the OMA (Office for Metropolitan Architecture) research, branding, and publication studio, AMO which skilfully blends playful graphic design advertising with architectural history and theory. The trend for architects to consolidate their brand through their use of mass media, which began in the modern early 20th century (Colomina 1996; Moreno and Lubell ed. 2018) is a crucial way that contemporary architects advertise their product range. Mass media allows architects to develop and promote a competitive edge in reputational and economic world markets through instantaneous global publicity. Nowadays, achieving celebrity status in architecture demands continuous marketing from firms to sustain dominance in the market. It is increasingly unlikely that success in the game of architecture will come about without self-promotion. This is something a young generation of mostly male architects have become experts at; take for example the Danish architect, Bjarke Ingels from BIG (Bjarke Ingels Group) who is a 'Baby Rem.' (MacLeod 2015)

With access to new media becoming easier and more accessible, architects are using online publishing and social media platforms to control and market their brand and image making, selling themselves through a 'flow of images' and 'flow of words' (Ingels in WHATA 2009). Expanding to video animations, documentaries, blogs, and archicomics (Troiani 2018), etc., some architects become famous before they have built their designs. For example, being young and aggressive within the architectural market today is noted by Franco Ghilardi (in van der Hoorn 2012, p. 135), who, referring to Ingels and BIG, acknowledges how the "Dane personifies the unbridled marketing orientation of the younger generation of architects." Ghilardi (in van der Hoorn 2012, p. 136) explains:

The idea that you build up a reputation, you do an amazing building and then people get to know you, is a bit outdated. There is a shift in speed: people coming right out of school are already famous, or even earlier. Younger generations are very busy with how they sell themselves.... They get their hands on whatever media they can to be faster, more direct, more efficient and to reach more people in more different countries. And of course, if you do a comic, maybe 500,000 people will read it, whereas if you do a text with a black cover, maybe 50,000 will read it.

Like many big brand architectural firms, BIG exploits the visual imagery of their designs using the latest digital technologies. Clients and a public who are titillated by an increasing entertainment-experience economy validate the production of an abundant and happy 'flow of images' from comic strip to video animation to celebrity lecture. The advantage of this, as Donald McNeill (2009, p. 72) notes in *The Global Architect* is that; "Visual images often travel before or with the architect's name or personality."

'A-list architects' are not only seen to add 'design value' but they also add celebrity cachet because "their names are so well-known to the public that they have achieved the status of brands." (Rybczynski 2008, p. 279) For 'big brand' international architectural firms, the constant promotion of the architect and their buildings before, while, and after they are built also happens through real estate property and city marketing. Rybczynski (2008: 279) explains that the names of famous starchitects – Richard Meier, Daniel Libeskind, and Jean Nouvel, to list but a few – have all "featured in advertisements for high-end residential properties." While architectural design and the architect's name have been at "the service of commercial real estate" since the 19th century, real estate developers have, since the 1970s, been commissioning 'A-list architects' to produce "class-A buildings"; value-adding because of the already prestigious design and name value of the world-known architect. (Rybczynski, 2008, p. 279)

The cachet of the architect celebrity has become a draw card for cities and cultural institutions who commission the design of an iconic building. In such cases, the city or cultural institution sells itself through association, through the value inherent in the iconic piece of starchitecture that attracts tourists, and the association to the starchitect. Rybczynski (2008, p. 281) explains that in 2008, Canadian-born American architect, Frank Gehry had "perhaps the strongest architectural franchise in the world today." Completed in 1997, Gehry's Bilbao Guggenheim Art Gallery in Spain's Basque country is arguably a seminal turning point in consolidating the Gehry franchise because the building created a 'Bilbao effect.' The 'Bilbao effect' is the phenomenon that can come from a signature building used for "deeply politicised place marketing, the architectural branding of an aspirational art institution, and the worldwide projection of … [the architect] as a celebrity brand." (McNeill 2016, pp. 81–82) More and more cities worldwide that want to improve or consolidate their status invite a signature architect or architects to design a landmark building in their city for tourist spectacle and entertainment. London, for example, boasts an icon building (or two) designed by Fosters and

Partners (30 St. Mary Axe, nicknamed 'The Gherkin' [or Pickle], 2004); Richard Rogers (Lloyd's building, Lime Street, nicknamed 'The Inside-Out Building,' 1986); Renzo Piano (The Shard building, Southwark, nicknamed 'The Shard' or 'The Shard of Glass,' 2012); Rafael Viñoly (20 Fenchurch Street, nicknamed 'The Walkie-Talkie,' 2015); Richard Stirk Harbour + Partners (The Leadenhall Building, 122 Leadenhall Street, nicknamed 'The Cheesegrater,' 2014), etc. Beijing has iconic landmark architecture designed by OMA (China Central Television (CCTV) Headquarters, nicknamed 'Big Pants,' 2008); Herzog de Meuron with Li Xinggang (Beijing National Stadium or the National Stadium, nicknamed 'The Bird's Nest,' 2008); Zaha Hadid Architects (ZHA) (Wangjing SOHO, based on the idea of 'Dancing Chinese Fans,' 2014); and the dragon-inspired Beijing Capital Airport (Terminal 3) by Foster and Partners, etc. Much like the Golden Arches logo for McDonalds, many of the buildings are given a nickname and a simple graphic advertising symbol that acts as a logo for easy brand recognition.

Since the Canadian author and social activist, Naomi Klein published in 1999 *No Logo: Taking Aim at the Brand Bullies* – later renamed *No Logo: No Space, No Choice, No Jobs* (Klein 2005) – there has been a steady shift under neoliberalism to *Go Logo!* (Cato 2010) Many starchitects are happy to identify with and be in the privileged position to participate in the reaffirmation of urban corporate advertising. Signature architects are city-brand image-makers that create building logos for cities. So, just as Rand saw the Manhattan skyscraper as the symbol of American freedom and aspiration, contemporary iconic buildings have become corporate city advertisements that contribute to creating iconic cityscapes that brand a city.

Unlike earlier periods of metropolitan development, brandscapes tie physical urban landscape development to corporate value systems. According to Anna Klingmann (2007) in the 21st century, cities are no longer only skylines, but they are brandscapes and buildings are not objects, but advertisements for corporate companies and institutions. They are destinations that offer sensations in an experience economy that incentivise consumption of a particular city. In the new environment of brandscapes, buildings are not only about where we work and live, but they signify what image a city wants to project of itself through its monopoly corporations and corporate architects.

However, while architectural branding has benefitted cultural institutions and cities all over the world in drawing in tourists from far away to experience icon architecture, the correlation between the value of an architectural brand, an icon building, and its value-adding for commercial viability or profit-making are not always a certainty. (Rybczynski 2008) What is certain though is that the more 'icon projects' a corporate brand architect can produce, the stronger their capacity is to build a global brand identity to their designer market inside and beyond architectural design.

For instance, through inventive business entrepreneurship, ZHA created a market share in architecture, furniture, product, fashion, and jewellery design that employed Hadid's brand *personality.* (Figure 2.2) In addition to the ZHA business, Zaha

Hadid Design (http://zaha-hadid-design.com/) sells Hadid-designed merchandise including chess sets, candleholders, platters, vases, dinnerware, cup and saucer sets, ties, scarves, placemats, coasters, glasses, mugs, books on her work, her lithographs, a shelving system, chandeliers, and stools. Costing up to £9,999 per item, the designer objects are produced in limited and numbered editions, directed at a collector market. ZHA designed sets for the Pet Shop Boys; collaborated with Karl Lagerfeld to design fashion installations, namely the Mobile Art Chanel Contemporary Art Container; and designed furniture such as the Iceberg bench for Z-Scape Collection for Sawaya & Moroni. Hadid designed handbags for Louis Vuitton, and collaborated with Brazilian shoe designers to produce the Melissa shoe range and with Pharell Williams for Adidas. Between 2005 and 2008, ZHA designed the Z. Car with Kenny Schachter/ROVE, a two-person, hydrogen-powered city car with zero emissions. All these products, and more not listed here, contributed to Hadid's vast wealth.[7] ZHA continues its global enterprise profitting postumously from ZHA's brand identity.

"In globalized [sic] practice," starchitects have the market advantage of using "the phenomena of celebrity—capitalized [sic] upon by architectural media and the profession alike—[to] assign identity to the work as commodity of cultural capital, as branded talent." (Owen 2016, p. 62) In order to become an equal competitor at the highest level of global architectural production in a neoliberal age, celebrity architects develop their brand and product identity through increasing their global market capture. This requires extensive globe-trotting, in person or virtually, and the trait of never saying no to a potentially good project, no matter how busy you are.

Globalisation and the Architect as *Yes Man*

As Michel Crozier pointed out a long time ago, being free of awkward bonds, cumbersome commitments and dependencies arresting the freedom of manoeuvre, was always a favourite and effective weapon of domination... Speed of movement has today become a major, perhaps the paramount, factor of social stratification and the hierarchy of domination.

(Bauman 2000, p. 151)

Architects have always globe-trotted around the world "designing structures for distant lands, getting the designs approved, and overseeing construction" (Davis in Owen ed. 2009, p. 122); their "fame travelling before" them. (McNeill 2009, p. 1) American Professor of Philosophy, Michael Davis notes, however, that there are key differences between architectural business globe-trotting in times past and architects' globe-trotting in the 21st century. Previously, architects operated mostly within a few empires, not worldwide, and this meant that while they might have been importing one empire's architecture to another country, they "did not worry about 'globalization [sic]'," (Davis in Owen ed. 2009, p. 122) preferring instead to focus on their designs. Nowadays, however, the large signature practices have international offices dotted worldwide in locations to capture market opportunities anywhere and everywhere, because as one nation's economy declines, there is another market seeking architectural modernisation elsewhere in the world.

As American architectural educator and urbanist, Ellen Dunham-Jones (in Deamer ed. 2014, p. 150) notes, "Equating capitalism with modernization [sic] and change, Koolhaas identified early on how global capitalism created dynamic, highly speculative urban conditions that were transforming the contemporary city." For Koolhaas (1996a, pp. 232–239; Koolhaas 1996b) new global markets provide architects with both destablilisation and liberation. In *Architecture, Ethics and Globalization*, Graham Owen (2009, p. 1) quotes Koolhaas who explains, "It seems clear that somehow we [architects] should be able, when given the impossibly difficult problem of designing in two weeks a city for three million people, to respond with vigor [sic] and skill." Koolhaas's writings on architects engaging with big business and big urbanism is a logical next step towards global, corporate architectural practice. Indifference for the sake of building allows select architects to depoliticise and promote neoliberal ideology, which asserts that "free markets … result in the most efficient and socially optimal allocation of resources" and that "economic globalization [sic] … spurs competition, increases economic efficiency and growth, and is generally beneficial to everyone." (Korten 1996, p. 184)

When discussing the "interesting topic, [of the] economics of architecture," Koolhaas (quoted in Lubow 2000) argues that architects should take on as many commissions as possible because "you can never say no, because there is someone behind you who will say yes." This philosophy of always saying yes to secure an architectural commission has been expanded by Ingels' (2009) reflections on the architect as 'Yes Man' (or woman) in *Yes is More*. Here the identity of the architect is seen to intertwine the image of Roark, the idealist artist architect, with that of Keating, the business-oriented architect. What is key to 'Yes [wo]Man' behaviour is that once there was a distinction between an architect who, for their own ethical reasons, says 'no' to a commission and the architect that always says 'yes', but nowadays practice is enacted in a spirit of optimistic 'yesism,' a culture that neoliberalism has favoured because it has the capacity to depoliticise or ignore politics, ethics, etc., in the name of commerce. This can result in some architects creating rhetoric to promote and win a commission.

In *Yes is More*, Ingels (2009, p. 15) advocates; "An architecture that allows you to say yes to all aspects of human life, no matter how contradicting! An architectural form of bigamy, where you don't need to chose [sic] one over the other, but you get to have both." Premised on the need for constant change, adaptability, and flexibility within the marketplace – fundamental components of competitive neoliberal-driven architectural practice – Ingels presents to the reader his oeuvre of designs all over the world in comic strip format. Ingels (2009, p. 26) explains that it is only through "random opportunities and chance" that the architect can realise his/her career and because a career cannot be planned, the architect today needs to, "respond to accidental challenges through opportunistic improvisation, mutation and migration of ideas" sold to clients as "a product of post-rationalization [sic]." Architect and editor, Jeffrey Inaba (2007) explains how the 'Yes' philosophy reframes service delivery:

> The term Yes Man once referred to the spineless corporate crony, but today it means something else. Bjarke Ingels is a Yes Man. He says 'yes' to just about any demand, reasonable or otherwise. It fuels his ambition to accept all the political interests surrounding a project and absorb them into back-bending forms that disarm the opposition and that eventually populate areas of Scandinavia (and beyond).

Architects of different generations differ in opinion on taking on every commission they are offered. Unlike BIG who support a Yes philosophy, many other architects can develop an image of them, or their practice, that is not always market palatable and this choice is one that can disable an architect's practice and progression, short or long-term. Take for example, the early ZHA during the period when Hadid was, like Roark, deemed uncompromising. Architecture critic Herbert Muschamp (2004) saw that failing to build the Cardiff Bay Opera House prompted Hadid to change her behaviour from being difficult and self-defeating, and that this brought her more supporters and clients. In terms of changing her image, it could be argued that Hadid altered from being the frustrated architect of design integrity who could not get her designs built to getting them built. When Hadid shifted to computational methods of drawing production, ZHA developed a marketable brand of computer-generated curvaceous architecture and simultaneously increased productivity to expand their global market, a topic discussed later in the book.

As a consequence of her change in behaviour, Hadid began to build and expand her business and brand to take a share of what was otherwise "a white, male business." (Moore 2013) However, while the image of the globe-trotting architect can be seen as glamorous and aspirational to some, there can be negative consequences for the architect who chooses to take on projects in foreign lands. Later in the book, it is argued that there can be ramifications on the body of the celebrity architect practicing across countries simply through travelling and working continuously through time zones that run on a 24/7 market. Only certain types of architects choose to and can engage in a frenetic global life in architecture; and are typically some of the best-known architects in the world.

For less well-known architects the relationship of home life and work life can be compromised by the demands of frequent or continuous work and travel, and this limits those with domestic care responsibilities when they cannot defer them to others. The image of the not 'family-free' architect who is unable to commit totally to work and travel, who splits their time between work and domestic family life, is problematic for architects who do not fit the mould of *homo oeconomicus* and will now be discussed. Chapter 3 considers how diversity including gender, race/ethnicity, class, and age can advantage or disadvantage an architect, which in-turn affects fulfilment in life.

Notes

1 Martha "Mamah" Borthwick Cheney was the wife of Wright's client, Edwin Cheney. Wright designed the Edwin H. Cheney House in Oak Park, Illinois, U.S.A. for the couple in 1903. Borthwick later became Wright's mistress.
2 Dominique Francon is the wife of Paul Keating. In the movie, Francon cannot resist falling in love with Roark's heroic persona.
3 Adler was a key player in moving the American Institute of Architects (AIA) towards a stronger business-oriented focus (Saint 1983, p. 172, Footnote 55).
4 Saint writes: "Excoriating the slavishness of past American architects in a lecture in 1931, he [Wright] approved a sharply contrasting stance [of holding out]: … A tale is told of Louis Sullivan has the lady come in and ask for a colonial house—'Madam' said he, 'you will take what we give you.'"
5 Noteworthy is that while creative starchitects can and do achieve wealth, they are by no means the richest firms. The American multinational firm Gensler for instance has repeatedly been the wealthiest practice worldwide. Gensler are recognised for delivering quality well-designed buildings on time and on budget and have created a large global client portfolio of mainly other multinational corporate firms who return to Gensler time and time again as repeat clients.
6 Similar marketing strategies are employed by universities and architecture schools, but they are not being discussed here, as the body of the architectural worker not the body of the university is the focus on this book.
7 At the time of her death, Hadid had a total fortune worth £67,249,458. Of this she bequeathed to Patrik Schumacher (£500,000), her four nieces and nephews (£1.7 million), employees and office holders of the companies, and the Zaha Hadid Foundation, which was set up to promote architectural education and exhibitions of Hadid's work, and other charities. (Booth 2017) Her architecture practice, ZHA, of which she was sole owner, was left in trust. "In the [fiscal year ending] April 2015, Zaha Hadid Ltd turned over £48m and employed 372 people" (Booth 2017).

References

Bauman, Z. 2000. *Liquid Modernity*. Cambridge: Polity Press.

Biernacki, R. 2015. The Capitalist Origin of the Concept of Creative Work. In Deamer, P. ed., *The Architect as Worker: Immaterial Labor, the Creative Class, and the Politics of Design*. London: Bloomsbury Academic, pp. 30–43.

Booth, R. 2017. Zaha Hadid Leaves £67m Fortune, Architect's Will Reveals, The *Guardian*, January 16, 12.49 GMT. https://www.theguardian.com/artanddesign/2017/jan/16/zaha-hadid-leaves-67m-fortune-architects-will-reveals Accessed November 06, 2023.

Brown, W. 2015. *Undoing the Demos: Neoliberalism's Stealth Revolution*. New York: Zone Books.

Cato, M. 2010. *Go Logo! A Handbook to the Art of Global Branding: 12 Keys to Creating Successful Global Brands*. Beverly: Rockport.

Colomina, B. 1996. *Privacy and Publicity in Architecture: Modern Architecture as Mass Media*. Cambridge, Mass: The MIT Press.

Cullen, J. 2003. *The American Dream: A Short History of an Idea that Shaped a Nation.* Oxford; New York: Oxford University Press.

Davis, M. 2009. Has Globalism Made Architecture's Professional Ethics Obsolete? In Owen, G. ed. *Architecture, Ethics and Globalization.* London; New York: Routledge, pp. 121–132.

De Smet, C. 2005. *Le Corbusier, Architect of Books.* Zurich: Lars Müller Publishers.

Deamer, P. ed. 2015. *The Architect as Worker: Immaterial Labor, the Creative Class, and the Politics of Design.* London: Bloomsbury Academic.

Deamer, P. 2015. Introduction. In Deamer, P. ed., *The Architect as Worker: Immaterial Labor, the Creative Class, and the Politics of Design.* London: Bloomsbury Academic, pp. xxvii–xix.

Durham-Jones, E. 2014. Irrational Exuberance: Rem Koolhaas in the Nineties. In Deamer, P. ed. *Architecture and Capitalism: 1845 to the Present,* London; New York: Routledge, pp. 150–171.

Florida, R. 2004. *The Rise of the Creative Class: And How it's Transforming Work, Leisure, Community and Everyday Life.* New York: Basic Books.

Fugere, B., Hardaway, C., and Warshawsky, J. 2005. *Why Business People Speak like Idiots: A Bullfighter's Guide.* New York: Free Press.

Goodman, R. T. 2013. *Gender Work: Feminism after Neoliberalism.* New York: Palgrave Macmillan.

Gorman, C. R. 1995. Fitting Rooms: The Dress Designs of Frank Lloyd Wright, *Winterthur Portfolio: A Journal of American Material Culture,* 30 (4) (Winter 1995): 259–277.

Higgin, H. Dir. 1928. *Skyscraper.* United States: Pathé Exchange.

Hochschild, A. with A. Machung. 1989. *The Second Self: Working Parents and the Revolution of Home.* London: Piatkus.

Hochschild, J. 1995. *Facing up to the American Dream: Race, Class, and The Soul of the Nation.* Princeton: Princeton Architectural Press.

Holub, D. 2016. Zaha Hadid's World of Fluid Freedom. May 31, 2016. www.designersatelier. co.uk/dagmars-articles/zaha-hadid-s-world-of-fluid-freedom/ Accessed on November 06, 2023

Inaba, J.and Ingels, B. 2007. Ambition, *Volume Magazine* 13, October 2007. http://archis. org/publications/volume-13-ambition/ Accessed November 06, 2023.

Ingels, B. 2009. *Yes is More: An Archicomic on Architectural Evolution,* Köln: Taschen.

Ingels, B. WHATA. 2009. WhATA Interviews Bjarke Ingels from BIG. March 20, 2009.

Jameson, F. 1992. *Postmodernism, or, the Cultural Logic of Late Capitalism.* London: Verso.

Klein, N. 2005. *No Logo: No Space, No Choice, No Jobs.* London: Harper Perennial.

Klingmann, A. 2007. *Brandscapes: Architecture in the Experience Economy.* Cambridge, Mass.: MIT Press.

Koolhaas, R. 1996a. Architecture and Globalization. In Saunders, W. ed. *Reflections on Architectural Practices in the Nineties.* New York: Princeton Architectural Press, pp. 232–239.

Koolhaas, R. 1996b. Understanding the New Urban Condition: The Project of the City, *GSD News* (Winter/Spring 1996).

Korten, D. C. 1996. The Mythic Victory of Market Capitalism. In Mander, J. and Goldsmith, E. eds. *The Case Against the Global Economy.* San Francisco: Sierra Club Books, pp. 183–191.

Levison, N. 2000. Tall Buildings, Tall Tales: On Architects in the Movies. In Lamster, M. ed. *Architecture and Film.* New York: Princeton Architecture Press.

Lloyd Wright, F. 1931. *Two Lectures on Architecture,* Chicago: The Art Institute of Chicago.

Lubow, A. 2000. Rem Koolhaas Builds, *The New York Times Magazine*, July 09, 2000. www.nytimes.com/2000/07/09/magazine/rem-koolhaas-builds.html, Accessed November 06, 2023.

McLeod, F. 'Baby Rems' and the Small World of Architecture Internships, *Arch Daily*, July 09, 2015. https://www.archdaily.com/769864/baby-rems-and-the-small-world-of-architecture-internships, Accessed November 06, 2023.

McNeill, D. 2009. *The Global Architect: Firms, Fame and Urban Form*. New York; London: Routledge.

Mill, J. S., and Laughlin, J. L. eds. 2009. *Principles of Political Economy*. New York: Project Gutenberg e-book. First published in 1884.

Moore, R. 2013. Zaha Haid: Queen of the Curve, *The Guardian*, September 08, 2013.

Moreno, J. author, and Lubell, C. ed. 2018. *The University is now on Air, Broadcasting Modern Architecture*. Heijningen, The Netherlands: Jap Sam Books.

Muschamp, H. 2004. Woman of Steel: Getting Her Architecture Built Was Zaha Hadid's Most Formidable Challenge, *New York Times*, March 28, 2004.

Owen, G. ed. 2009. *Architecture, Ethics and Globalization*. London: Routledge.

Owen, G. 2016. 'I Have No Power': Zaha Hadid and the Ethics of Globalized Practice, *Candide: Journal for Architectural Knowledge*, 10, (2016 December): 41–64.

Ralston, R. E. 2006. Publishing *The Fountainhead*. In Mayhew, R. ed. 2006. *Essays on Ayn Rand's The Fountainhead*. Lanham, Maryland: Lexington Books, pp. 65–76.

Rand, A. 2007. *The Fountainhead*. London: Penguin.

Rank, M. R. 1994. *Living on the Edge: The Realities of Welfare in America*. New York: Columbia University Press.

Rank, M. R. 2004. *One Nation, Underprivileged: Why American Poverty Affects Us All*. New York: Oxford University Press.

Rank, M. R. 2011. Rethinking American Poverty, *Contexts*, 10: 16–21.

Rank, M. R., Hirschl, T. A., and Foster, K. A. 2014. *Chasing the American Dream; Understanding what Shapes our Fortunes*. Oxford: Oxford University Press.

Rifkin. J. 2005. The European Dream. How Europe's Vision of the Future is Quietly Eclipsing the American Dream, Lecture at Vortrag an der Humboldt-Universität zu Berlin, April 18, 2005. https://www.rewi.hu-berlin.de/de/lf/oe/whi/FCE/2005/rifkin.pdf Accessed November 06, 2023.

Rifkin, J. 2004. *The European Dream: How Europe's Vision of the Future is Quietly eclipsing the American Dream.* New York: Penguin.

Rybczynski, W. 2008. Architectural Branding. *Appraisal Journal,* 76 (3): 279–284.

Saint, A. 1983. *The Image of the Architect*. New Haven; London: Yale University Press.

Schleier, M. 2009. *Skyscraper Cinema: Architecture and Gender in American Film.* Minneapolis: University of Minnesota Press.

Shvartzberg, M. 2015. Foucault's 'Environmental' Power: Architecture and Neoliberal Subjectivization. In Deamer, P. ed., *The Architect as Worker: Immaterial Labor, the Creative Class, and the Politics of Design*. London: Bloomsbury Academic, pp. 181–205.

Sklair, L. 2017. *The Icon Project: Architecture, Cities, and Capitalist Globalization.* New York; Oxford: Oxford University Press.

Sontag, S. 2008. *On Photography*. London: Penguin Books.

Thrift, N. 2009. The Rise of Soft Capitalism, *Cultural Values* 1 (1) (March 01 2009): 29–57.

Troiani, I. 2012. Zaha: An Image of 'The Woman Architect,' *Architectural Theory Review*, 17 (2–3), 346–364. Republished as Troiani, I. 2014. Zaha: An Image of 'The Woman Architect' In Stead, N. ed. *Women, Practice, Architecture: 'Resigned Accommodation' and 'Usurpatory Practice.'* London: Routledge, Chapter 10.

Troiani, I. 2018. Neoliberalism, Architectural Design and the Happy 'flow of images': Reading BIG's Archicomics. In Dougan, B., Mitchell, K., and Watson, G. eds. *The Process and Practice Across Disciplines (PPADD) 2018 AUS Conference Proceedings*, February 2018, American University of Sharjah, pp. 53–59.

Valdez, Z. 2016. *Entrepreneurs and the Search for the American Dream.* New York; London: Routledge.

Van der Hoorn, M. 2012. *Bricks & Balloons: Architecture in Comic-Strip Form.* Rotterdam: 010 Publishers.

Vidor, K. Dir. 1949. *The Fountainhead.* United States: Warner Bros Pictures.

Weeks, K. 2011. *The Problem with Work: Feminism, Marxism, Antiwork Politics and Postwork Imaginaries.* Durham; London: Duke University Press.

Zaera-Polo, A. and Abascal, G. F. 2016. Architecture's 'Political Compass': A Taxonomy of Emerging Architecture in One Diagram, December 16, 2016.https://www.archdaily.com/801641/architectures-political-compass-a-taxonomy-of-emerging-architecture-in-one-diagram Accessed November 06, 2023.

3

STARTING FROM A DIFFERENT POSITION

Architect as *Femina Domestica*

FIGURE 3.1 Single mother architect Melanie Parker (played by Michelle Pfeiffer) juggling care of her son, Sammy Parker (played by Alex D. Linz) from *One Fine Day* (Dir. Hoffman 1996). Photograph: Photo 12/Alamy Stock Photo.

DOI: 10.4324/9781351199834-4

Architecture, Diversity, and Cumulative Inequality

As discussed in the previous chapter, it is commonly accepted that "The American Dream is portrayed as attainable, as long as we commit ourselves to hard work and perseverance in striving toward our goals." (Rank et al. 2014, p. 2) It has "ultimately been about the manner in which our lives unfold and the ability of the individual, no matter where he or she comes from, to exert considerable control and freedom over how that process occurs." (Rank et. al. 2014, p. 2) The landscape of opportunity is changing under neoliberalism, however. This is because neoliberalism can accentuate inequality rather than its promise for greater equality because "… Inequality, not equality, is the medium and relation of competing capitals." (Brown 2015, p. 35) While everyone working the neoliberal marketplace, including architects, imagines that their trajectory can be dictated by the career they work towards, it cannot be personally dictated or controlled because the opportunities available are not equal for all. The lack of a "level playing field" in the way "the economic race … [is] run" (Rank et al. 2014, p. 107) affects the ability to achieve work-life ambitions. As architects come to the profession with differing pre-existing advantages and disadvantages, they are not all starting at the same point of the game of life in architecture. 'A landscape of opportunity' (Rank et al. 2014, pp. 67–83) to achieve our hopes and dreams for the future is not equitable for all architects because our familial, social, or economic status can be an advantage or disadvantage in the architectural gamespace. In addition, there are not an equal number of opportunities for everyone; not everyone can make it to the top.

In earlier research on poverty and underprivilege, Rank (1994; 2004; 2011) uses the analogy of playing "musical chairs to illustrate the mismatch between opportunities and the pool of individuals in search of such opportunities." (Rank et al. 2014, p. 68) The game of life as an architect is dependent on many factors including economic, social, and cultural background as well as our gender, race/ethnicity, class, and age. These factors, and others, can have a large bearing on the opportunities made available to some and not others at different stages of life. They relate to one's biology, enactment of gender stereotyping, origins, and how one is socially produced to not be able to play (at all or properly) or play to win or lose at the game of an architecturally successful life. The ability to profit in life socially and professionally is tied to theories of economic growth.

First published in 1955, *The Theory of Economic Growth*, written by the African American industrial economist W. Arthur Lewis (2003, p. 84), considers economic growth in relation to intersectional characteristics, such as race, class, and religion, for example, and 'vertical mobility.' The ways in which intersectional characteristics and 'vertical mobility' enable or are restricted in growing economic capital are key factors that can impact on satisfaction at work or outside work and career progression.

Lewis contends that while economic growth does not guarantee happiness, the wealth it generates enhances social status and power. Individuals with more energy and the disposition to work harder than others have the greater potential for economic growth in their lifetime than others. A common feature held by wealth accumulators is 'the spirit of adventure' which relates to the willingness to "manoeuvre economically." (Lewis 2003, p. 42) The willingness to operate outside conventional rules and taboos, be a risk-taker, or move from one place or job to another as required – as entrepreneurism prescribes – exemplifies an adventurous spirit that can allow economic and career manoeuvrability. (Lewis 2003, pp. 42–43) Moving jobs, occupation, or residence, etc., are ways in which wealth can grow. Lewis (2003, p. 49) contends that "growth constantly demands movement of this kind…" but notes that "While it is true that the individual is more likely to succeed if he is willing to be mobile, it is not necessary to economic growth that everyone should be mobile." (Lewis, 2003, p. 51) Unlike the neoliberal promise that all entrepreneurism will deliver rewards, Lewis (2003, p. 51) recognises that not all economic growth requires innovation and nor will all innovators be able to create economic growth since it depends on 'an adequate supply of innovators' (though not too many), which are acculturated in a social environment that gives them the scope and opportunity to do so. In the case of an architectural worker, there may be willingness to take risks or move but this is not available to all.

A high degree of 'vertical mobility,' (Lewis 2003, p. 84) both upward and downward, is associated with economic growth. The ability to create economic growth in a business or in a worker depends not only on their 'qualities' but also what they learn from the cultures in which they develop, namely what is learnt at school, from parents, family, and friends. Lewis (2003, p. 85) notes that "who … [your] parents are" is a key contributing factor. While new types of economic activity are pioneered by rising social class, there is no evidence of an historical pattern to suggest that class structure and mobility correlate to economic growth rising. (Lewis 2003, p. 87) More common is that economic growth "creates or expands the middle classes, mainly by recruitment from below, and is not to be expected in societies which place obstacles in the way of upward mobility." (Lewis, 2003, p. 88)

More "'sensible' aristocracies" allow only the minimum, necessary amount of 'vertical mobility' within their organisation to allow those "people of superior talents to rise, and people of inferior talents to fall…." (Lewis 2003, p. 89) "At the same time, social peace is easier to maintain if it is clear that the most clever Jews or Negroes or working class boys [or girls] will not be prevented from reaching the highest rungs of the ladder, even though they are only a negligible proportion of their class, and even though the great majority of average people in their class are kept firmly 'in their place'. Nevertheless, however 'sensible' the aristocracy may be in tolerating these exceptions, a community must be depriving itself of opportunities for growth if it restricts the opportunities for vertical mobility." (Lewis 2003, p. 89) It is noteworthy that discrimination and restriction of opportunity in society can be a positive driver of the will to increase wealth for some; while for others having no opportunities or protection from moving downward, can create a cycle of 'cumulative disadvantage.' (Rank et al. 2014, p. 107) In terms of market positioning, Lewis (2003, p. 143) explains that:

> change reinforces itself cumulatively. Once economic growth has begun, institutions change more and more in directions favourable to growth, and so strengthen the forces making for growth. Alternatively, if the rate of economic growth begins to decline, institutions become less favourable to growth...
>
> Cumulative forces work in the same way if the change starts not in the economic opportunities but in the institutions themselves. For then the very fact that people become more willing or have more chance to seize opportunities will itself either create or reveal new opportunities to be seized; and the emergence of new opportunities will in turn reinforce the changes in beliefs and institutions.
>
> *(Lewis, 2003, p. 143)*

Importantly, "The proximate causes of economic growth are the effort to economize [sic], the accumulation of knowledge, and the accumulation of capital." (Lewis 2003, p. 164) The relationship between an individual's identity is crucial to whether advantage or disadvantage accumulates.

An individual architect's identity forms over their lifetime and is connected to their ability or inability to choose, create, and sustain that identity or not. A biographical narrative in architecture is the vehicle through which an architect constructs their professional image. Choosing where to study architecture, who to be taught by, who to work for – whether a global corporate practice or a small architectural practice –, who to marry, where to buy a house, whether to have children, etc., all contribute to the evolution of a certain kind of professional and personal architectural life narrative and life path in which luck and skill play a part, but in which the overall game's outcome is predicted from where each person is able to start. Rank et al. (2014, p. 107) defines this overall pathway as "cumulative inequality, or cumulative advantage and disadvantage" where early advantages or disadvantages can result in further advantage or disadvantage that multiplies over a lifetime.

Diversity among architects (Wilkins 2016) and cumulative advantage and disadvantage are directly related in architectural practice. Four areas that have historically illustrated cumulative inequality in architecture are gender, race/ethnicity, class, and age. While the landscape of equal opportunity is evolving and changing to varying degrees in these areas in different countries, each of the four will be discussed here because of their effect they have on the ability to play the game of architecture.

According to Professor of Gender, Sexuality and Feminist Studies, Kathi Weeks (2011, p. 10), "...Gender identities are coordinated with work identities in ways that can sometimes alienate workers from their job and other times bind them more tightly to it." In architecture the architect has historically been identified as male. However, as female architects are increasing in number, and themselves transforming into architect-*homo oeconomicus*, it is important to understand how *homo oeconomicus* is socially being produced differently. This means reflecting on the social economic role and labour of (unpaid) *femina domestica*. Traditionally, *femina domestica* (or domestic woman) typically refers to a partner, wife, mother, aunt, etc., who undertakes either a part of or all the domestic labour – child rearing, housework, and 'emotional work.' Included in the definition here are also those lesser-paid (mostly) female workers who domestic labour is outsourced to when familial support is not available, namely nannies, cleaners, child carers, etc. It also includes surrogate mothers. Building on the definitions of labour by Friedrich Engels, chemist, Margaret Benston (1989) refers to domestic labour as 'unproductive labour' or 'reproductive labour' rather than 'productive labour.' The link between gendered labour, social role, and social positioning is important to consider here.

German-British sociologist, Ralf Dahrendorf (1973, p. 17) argues that "To every social position there belongs a social role." The limits of social roles including *homo oeconomicus, homo politicus, homo sociologicus, femina domestica*, etc., is changing for men and women in neoliberal societies because of women's entry into the 'productive labour' market which has meant that men have begun to enter the 'unproductive labour' market. So just as *homo oeconomicus* has a female form, *femina domestica* has a male form. These can include a male partner, husband, father, uncle, etc., and the male nanny, cleaner, child carer, etc. Although the male version of *femina domestica* are far fewer in number, their numbers are growing. Women and men can be both *homo oeconomicus* and *femina domestica* if they so choose or if they are needed to be. Regardless of which gender is undertaking 'productive labour' or 'unproductive labour,' *feminina domestica* in its feminine or masculine form allows the greater income-earning *homo oeconomicus* to be optimally productive in their paid work. This is because as Benston (1989) argues 'unproductive labour' is essential to the flow of 'productive labour' for capitalist production. Since it is only recently, beginning in the late 1800s, that women have entered the 'productive' architectural labour market, there is substantial ground to be gained to first, find their equal place in architecture and second, address the fluid and changing space between their and men's 'productive' and 'unproductive' labour.

Femina Domestica: Economics, Gender, Marriage, and Family

While women have always worked, and had influence, in architecture and construction, only in the last 100 years have they been accepted into professional bodies. In 1888, Louise Blanchard Bethune became the first female associate of the American Institute of Architects (A.I.A). Ten years later, in 1898, Ethel Charles became the first Royal Institute of British Architects (R.I.B.A) registered woman architect in the U.K. In 1923 in Australia, Florence Mary Taylor became the first woman to be a full member of the New South Wales (NSW) Institute of Architects and Chinese born Lin Huiyin (known as Phyllis Lin or Lin Whei-yin when in the U.S.) is known to be the first female architect in modern China, having helped establish the Department of Architecture in Northeastern University in Shenyang in 1928.

Since women only entered the professional architectural market a century ago and remain lower in number, there is a smaller but steadily-growing body of literature recording their achievements. Since the late 1980s research has been undertaken on women in architecture (Walker 1997; Toy 2001; Stead ed. 2014; Darling ed. 2017; Espegel Alonso 2017; Hartman 2022, to name but a few) to mostly make visible women architects who have made important contributions to the field; to showcase them as role models. Still, in most of that literature rarely, or if ever, is the conundrum of work-life balance discussed. Women architects who are married or who have a family rarely discuss the complexities of being both *homo oeconomicus* and *femina domestica*, instead preferring to sometimes suggest that there is no difference between men and women architects (and their bodies), asking instead to be considered an 'architect' rather than a 'woman architect.'

The Hollywood romantic comedy, *One Fine Day* (directed by Michael Hoffman in 1996) tells the story of two single working parents, workaholic architect and divorcee, Melanie Parker (played by Michelle Pfeiffer) (Figure 3.1) and journalist Jack Taylor (played by George Clooney), who juggle caring for their children, 5-year-old Sammy Parker (played by Alex D. Linz) and Maggie Taylor (played by Mae Whitman) respectively, with their demanding jobs when they miss catching the bus for a school trip. Sammy comes to the office with Melanie, who is pressured to do her work while caring for him. They travel together with a model of an architectural design in the back seat of a yellow cab. Exhausted from the demands of work and care responsibilities, the movie concludes with Melanie and Jack falling asleep on the sofa, their children happily looking on. As a single working mother, Melanie represents the architectural worker of any sex who is stretched both at work and at home.

Being a woman or a man architect working in a demanding work environment is challenging, and being a woman or a man architect with demanding work *and* domestic labour responsibilities presents additional problems and compromises. Whether working full-time or part-time women and men who are not 'family-free' can suffer stresses from working in both domains if they cannot afford to outsource some of their work. To date, women undertake more part-time or casual work in architecture than men. Like women, more men are choosing part-time work as a lifestyle choice (Moulds 2014), changing "the myth of masculinity" through their changing of commitments to family and work. (Gerson 1993, Chapter 9) However, the decision to work part-time or casually has implications on the ability of men and women architects to make money and can disadvantage their career progression. To avoid this, the profession must begin to take responsibility to share more than just biographical work narratives to emerging architects but also share biographical work-homelife narratives about women's and men's experiences.

Although a growing number of women architects are beginning to gain public recognition, the most famous architects in the world are, and have always been, men and so most literature in architecture is on artistic- to business-oriented images of male architects, as discussed in the previous chapter. Changes to how gendered labour and masculinity for male architects has changed is an under-analysed topic. *Stud: Architectures of Masculinity* (Sanders ed. 1996) presents a range of essays which open up discourses about the homoerotic gaze and homosexuality. There is an expanding body of literature on queers and architecture (Betsky 1997; Cook 2014; Gorman-Murray and Cook 2017) but the way in which male architects – heterosexual or homosexual – deal with other commitments associated with marriage, family, and care commitments is little discussed. Arguably, this is because economics has failed to recognise and factor in domestic labour, instead choosing to exploit it to improve male positioning.

In *Who Cooked Adam Smith's Dinner? A Story about Women and Economics*, bestselling author on woman and innovation Katrine Marçal (2015, p. 30) notes that "even though the word 'economy' comes from the Greek *oikos*, which means home, economists have long been uninterested in what exactly happens at home." While it briefly changed in the 1950s when sociologist and economist, Gary Becker, and other researchers in the economics department at the University of Chicago created a branch of family home economics that sought to incorporate domestic labour into an economic model (Marçal 2015, p. 32), overall 'productive labour' is more socially valued because of its monetary generation. The main economic system that drives neoliberalism relies on cheap or, in this case of unpaid or lesser paid, 'unproductive labour' by mostly women (who are housewives). This traditional gender-divided social system that supports the gender-divided economic system takes away from *homo oeconomicus* the domestic work and its emotional demands and stresses associated with family and home, in order for them to be less encumbered.

In his *Theory of Moral Sentiments*, Scottish economist and philosopher, Adam Smith (1759, p. 82) acknowledges that individuals are unquestionably self-interested: "Every man is, no doubt, by nature first and principally recommended to his own care; and he is fitter to care of himself than of every other person ...." Marçal (2015), however, reveals that in order to write his 1776 economic treatise *The Wealth of Nations* (Smith 2008), which has formed the foundation of the modern economic system, unmarried Smith was dependent on the care of his mother, Margaret Douglas, with whom he lived for his adult life until her death, and thereafter on his cousin Janet. In a review of Marçal's book, American writer and editor, Danya Evans (2016) sums up; "Adam Smith developed the idea of the success of self-interest in the free market. Margaret Douglas cooked his dinner. Margaret Douglas may have been forgotten by history, but Adam Smith would not have existed without her." Neoliberalism would not exist had it not been for the tireless invisible labour of the women who supported Smith.

The philosophy of self-interest in a free-market economy leading to economic wellbeing relies on exploitation of labour. This happens in both the public and private spheres. According to Nobel economist, Joseph Stiglitz (2009, p. xxxix), market efficiency relies on Smith's "invisible hand theorem" in which "in the competitive market economy, individuals, and firms in pursuit of their self-interest are led, as if by an invisible hand, to economic efficiency... It was not until 175 years after Smith's 1776 *Wealth of Nations* that [economists, Kenneth J.] Arrow (1951) and [Gerard Debreu] (1954) ... showed that competitive markets lead to *Pareto efficiency*, in other words, no one can be made better off without making someone else worse off." As Stiglitz (2009, p. xlvi) explains "... Smith's invisible hand only said that markets would lead to an efficient allocation of resources; no one, in defending the market economy, ever claimed that it would lead to a distribution of income consistent with principles of social justice."

In the case of private life, in the traditional nuclear family the higher-paid person (formerly typically the male breadwinner) is supported by and supports an unpaid or lesser-paid person, with marriage or living together being the most common institutions through which this social contract is validated. Mothering can involve sacrificing work to ensure the family's economic efficiency. In the case where both members in the marriage or partnership are working, however, the outsourcing of domestic labour – cleaning, cooking, parenting – as a business transaction to optimise efficiency at home is a common choice under neoliberalism. Just like many working parents today who outsource care of their children at some or all stages of their child's life, Thatcher outsourced the care of her own twins.[1]

Neoliberalism can intensify traditional gender stereotypes in these forms of social partnership because the paid primary-breadwinner husband/father and unpaid housewife/mother, who has persistent responsibility of provisioning care of every sort (babies>children, parents, homework, classes after school, pets, etc.), is the most economically efficient model. Men profit from unpaid or lesser-paid women's or men's work and capitalism is sustained as a system because of the uneven gender power relations. While the money might be shared between husband and wife or partners living together (whether women or men choose to stay at home with children), the differential power hierarchy remains.

Nowadays, Brown (2015, pp. 104–105) argues that women occupy two roles within the neoliberal world; "Either women align their own conduct with this truth, becoming *homo oeconomicus*, in which case the world becomes uninhabitable, or women's activities and bearing as *femina domestica* remain the unavowed glue for the world whose governing principle cannot hold it together, in which case women occupy their old place as unacknowledged props and supplements to masculinist liberal subjects." In playing the game of life in architecture, the first choice for women is that of a traditional architectural path based on a masculinist model of *homo oeconomicus*, mimicking the primary breadwinner model. Architectural writer, Rochelle Martin (in Berkeley and McQuaid eds. 1989, p. 232) describes the path as one where "a young man works long hours at the beginning of his career to establish his reputation and gain necessary skills and knowledge." The traditional focus is on the architect self only, "on his career, often to the exclusion of family and personal life." (Rochelle Martin in Berkeley and McQuaid eds. 1989, p. 232) While this is changing, Martin (in Berkeley and McQuaid eds. 1989, p. 232) contends that, "A woman with a family is usually not free to follow this pattern and she suffers by seeing herself, as well as being seen, as not quite a "real" architect'." For the woman architect-*homo oeconomicus* there is usually a purposeful choice to be "family-free" either by not choosing to marry/partner or have children or if they do have children, to not have primary care responsibilities.

Take for example the Iraqi-born British architect, Zaha Hadid, who purposely chose not to marry or have children. When queried at age 58 about her private life sacrifices Hadid maintained it was through her free will that she devoted her life to work. "I don't think one has to get married. Nor are you obliged to have children if you don't want them." (Hadid in Hegde 2016) "You should only have children if you can give them time. If I'd stayed in the Middle East, I could have done it. The family relationships there make it easier to look after children." (Hadid in Holub 2016) Being 'family-free' allowed Hadid to become Brown's female *homo oeconomicus*, devoting *all* her time to her career without distraction. Interestingly, Fred A. Bernstein (2016) notes that while "Hadid never married; [Hadid's long-time business partner, Patrik] Schumacher .... married the Korean architect Eunsil Yang, but he is so private that most of his colleagues, when asked about his personal life, assumed he was single." In "Architects in Skirts: The Public Image of Women Architects in Wilhelmine Gemany," Canadian-born architectural historian Despina Stratigakos (2001, p. 90) examines "the tension between cultural conceptions of femininity and the social constructions of the architect as a masculine figure." From her research on women architects in the period, Stratigakos (2001, p. 98) concludes that "to make herself over in the image of the architect was to dislodge the self that was rooted in cultural notions of femininity. ... Becoming an architect meant surmounting the social construction of a 'lady'. At the same time, this feminine identity was also considered desirable. Negotiating these contradictory images was the inescapable fate of the woman architect." Stratigakos notes that while women architects in Wilhelmine Germany embraced both the feminine and masculine, women commentators downplayed their gender. Like Hadid who preferred to be considered an architect not a woman architect, Emilie Winkelmann (quoted in Trost 1919, pp. 598–599), the first woman to study architecture in Germany and who ran her own architectural office in Berlin, was quoted in a 1920 article as stating: "I think it is wrong to lay stress on the work of the woman in the building traces; all that matters is the quality and the evidence that with an equal education a woman accomplishes the same as her male colleague."

Even today, 'the independent woman' without husband, partner, or children is atypical for architects. When, in 1949, Simone de Beauvoir wrote *The Second Sex*, she set out the conundrums for 'the independent woman.' "There are... a fairly large number of privileged women who find in their professions a means of economic and social autonomy.... [As] a minority; they continue to be a subject of debate between feminists and anti-feminists." (De Beauvoir 1997, p. 691) While Hadid never claimed to be a feminist, the relationship between capitalism and feminism established in the latter half of the 20th century is important to understand here because the freedom for women to choose work *over* family or work *and* family impacts on career progression and gendered power relations in the workplace.

The second path a woman architect can take is becoming both *homo oeconomicus* at work and *femina domestica* at home with their partner, husband, and/or family. The choice to marry and have a family can dramatically affect women's career progression and wage-earning capacity but still many women purposely choose both. This is because, as American sociologist, Robin W. Simon (2008, p. 41) notes, "In the Joys of Parenthood, Reconsidered" that culture presents "Parenthood … [as] pivotal for developing and maintaining emotional well-being … Even more than marriage and employment, our culture promotes the idea that parenthood provides a sense of purpose and meaning in life, which are essential for good mental health." Even though parenting can come with significant emotional and financial stresses many women and men architects still choose a traditional home life, choosing marriage, partner/husband/wife, and children. Love, marriage, and motherhood still have a strong allure regardless of knowing how children impact on economic wellbeing.

In *Why Gender Matters in Economics*, Canadian economist, Mukesh Eswaran (2014, p. 10) notes that while "marriage is a universal institution," "the social, psychological, and economic conditions of married people differ to those of unmarried people." On the matter of the way in which working women manage their work and personal lives, sociologists Margaret M. Poloma and T. Neal Garland (1971, p. 538) recall in "Married Professional Woman: A Study in the Tolerance of Domestication" the words of de Beauvoir: "Desire for a feminine destiny – husband, home, and children – and the enchantment of love are not always easy to reconcile with the will to succeed." Their research on high status professional women in heterosexual-couple households shows a tolerance by working professionals for "domestication in order to mesh the roles of career woman with marriage and a family." (Poloma and Garland 1971, p. 538) From their research, and their noted surprise, Poloma and Garland (1971, p. 538) found that women in the study from all age groups – 25 to 30 or from 50 and over – did not object to this noting "they expressed great satisfaction in being able to combine marriage and a career, with the family role as the salient one and the professional role as supportive in the role hierarchy." Their explanations for this, regardless of the pursuit of women's emancipation, is the different "socialization [sic] process between men and women, a long-standing tradition of unequal opportunities for women, the psychological process of cognitive dissonance, as well as a genuine liking for the situation the way it is." (Poloma and Garland 1971, p. 538)

Even if the marriage route is chosen, it is because of what Zygmunt Bauman (2000, p. 147) describes as the replacing of 'long-term' mentality with a 'short-term' mentality, "… marriages 'till death us do part' are decidedly out of fashion and have become a rarity." It is not uncommon for people to divorce or have multiple 'short-term' partnerships, whether bearing children or not. For male architects, these kinds of very 'fluid' and flexible relationships have been historically validated, particularly for the heroic artist type (discussed later), with women partners taking on childcare for the children they have born. "Fleeting forms of association are more useful to people than long-term connections" (Sennett 1998, p. 24) and allow for more flexible work-life opportunities for the partners without care responsibilities. The disentanglement from personal private associations, not professional ones, can facilitate greater work opportunities through providing autonomy and personal freedom to move (on to something better).

Arguably, still nowadays, 'traditional' alpha males are raised from childhood to be more self-confident and better trained than some women to see future opportunities and to 'disentangle' themselves in personal associations. Lower confidence and a sense of expectations, goals, and ambitions leads some women not to challenge the norms associated with their work and home lives. (Ely and Padavic 2007, p. 1125) Regardless of this, it is not only women of all ages who are modifying their behaviour to suit a work life but young males too. Men and women in architecture, and in the mostly male-dominated construction industry, are having to modify and negotiate gender difference more and more. "… Men in the [construction] industry regarded as the gatekeepers are now finding ways to respond to and make sense of a changing workplace, and the realities that women are now actively encouraged to participate, legally protected against discrimination … All players are trying to negotiate ways to integrate each other into a new environment in a manner which allows them to comfortably reconcile issues of gender." (Agapiou 2002, p. 697) Working women and men are both in phases of transition having to reinvent through different journeys their former relationship between work and life (Rossetti 2015) and gender performativity.

The performativity of masculinity and femininity is related and unrelated to biological gender and sexuality. (Kuhlmann 2013, p. 35) As Robin Ely and Irene Padavic (2007, p. 1128) note in their studies on organisational labour; "Although they are not biological, masculinity and femininity are incarnated in bodies as well as in belief systems [but] neither the masculine nor feminine domain is unitary (Connell 1987;1995; 2002)." "Masculinity and femininity each contain multiple forms, and the dominance of one form or another depends on the historical and social context." (Ely and Padavic 2007, p. 1128)

Less commonly discussed in architecture is how gender is constructed and transforms socially as "a stylized repetition of acts" (Butler 1988, p. 519) *across* the home and architectural workplaces including the male-dominated construction site and over a lifetime. It is not the sex that one is born with that can dictate one's career path but the way gender stereotypes are performed or not through one's architectural life.

Butler's (1990) theory of the enactment of gender, developed in *Gender Trouble*, detaches the identity of a woman or man from their biological sex and proposes that the performativity of gender can be masculinised or feminised or ungendered according to *how* and *where* a woman or man 'practices' their sexuality in everyday life. How and where a female or male architect practices femininity or masculinity affects their social and professional positioning. A woman architect can convey attributes of the architect who 'wears a skirt' (Stratigakos 2001) and 'wears the trousers.' For instance, Hadid was presented to the public as a 'nice' 'earth mother' who could transform, because of her commitment to the highest quality of production in her office, into a "Queen of Hearts screaming, 'Off with their heads.'" (Hattenstone 2010) The ability to perform a nurturing versus aggressive persona as required for good business brings into question the image of the woman architect (Troiani 2012; 2014) practicing under neoliberalism.

Management, leadership, and business savviness by women does not always replicate that of men. In the guide, *Hardball for Women: Winning at the Game of Business*, Pat Heim and Susan. K. Golant (2005) contend that because women entering business are adapting to formerly male only workplaces, they need to learn to decode male business culture or learn how to 'lean in.' (Sandberg 2015) However, for everyday women architects who choose to perform a mixture of traditional and untraditional roles, the most obvious being to marry and have a family, being a fluid worker is less easy or, arguably, achievable. The decision to conform with or against gender stereotypes can have a significant effect on an architectural career. Identification with a gendered sexual identity (lesbian, homosexual, bisexual, transgender, and heterosexual) can be advantageous or disadvantageous depending on the architectural social circles in which one moves. Choices of personal or professional partnering (male–male, female–male, female–female) can impact on the potential to accrue social and reputational capital. The performativity of singlehood, motherhood, or fatherhood can also be key factors influencing career progression. In neoliberal countries, where identity choices are presented as infinite, gender stereotypical behaviour – in architectural life and everyday life – is collapsing so that what was formerly traditional masculine or feminine behaviour, both or neither, as Butler argues, requires purposeful performativity. Under Bauman's (2000) 'liquid modernity,' women and men and the family have transformed into fluid entities.

In "The Good Architect and the Bad Parent," Despoina Stratigakos (2008) notes that there is a pervasive theme in modern architectural history that many famous male architects who have a family tend to sacrifice it for career. In the case of the American architect, Louis Kahn, who had three families from a wife and two mistresses, his relationship with his children was often compromised in pursuit of architectural success (and the juggling of the three families). The characteristics that make a good male architect may mean they make a 'lousy father.' (Stratigakos 2008, p. 283) Stratigakos (2008, p. 284) contends from her research that the required characteristics that make for a good architect and a good parent are "opposing and contradictory …, it was said, and success in one endeavour meant necessary failure in the other." Many renowned architect-fathers can be seen by their children to sacrifice fathering for fame. For elite male architects who travel extensively as global practitioners or educators, fathering is further compromised because they just aren't always around for their children. Due to the problem of having to compromise their time, some famous architects including Le Corbusier (Charles-Édouard Jeanneret) married but purposely chose not to have children to better pursue architecture (and a life with a wife or lovers).

The way that an architect struggles with 'the family-individual conundrum' (Brown 2015, p. 103) is universally subverted in architectural discourse because the profession compels itself to only address architecture's public images rather than present the private, sometimes entangled, images. (Colomina 1999) These aren't separate worlds, however, in fact they are intrinsically intertwined affecting our capacity to succeed or not in either the domestic or work domain. As neoliberalism values selfhood over citizenship, it can be difficult for men and women architects to negotiate between gender stereotypical and non-stereotypical behaviour at home and at work. The shifting space between paid architectural work and unpaid domestic household labour is transforming for men and women today, both of whom have always worked but in different domains and for unequal economic reward, with many women historically always being generous in their domestic and emotional labour and subsequently being disadvantaged economically.

While women have always untaken unpaid work in the home, it is only in the last decades that that they have changed jobs, moving from working in the home to taking up paid work in the (business) market. (Marçal 2015, p. 4) Aside from the problems they can experience with work-life balance, many women architects have suffered and continue to suffer from discrimination in the workplace.

Architecture, more than some other professions, has moved slowly to accommodate its own increasing number of women practitioners. (Fowler and Wilson 2004) Since the 1970s when the African-born, American architect, Denise Scott Brown (in Berkeley and McQuaid eds. 1989, pp. 237–246) published "Room at the Top? Sexism and the Star System in Architecture" and other commentators started to ask about the place of women in architecture (Berkeley and McQuaid eds. 1989), histories of sexism, discrimination, exclusion, and obstacles for women obtaining positions of power in the architectural workplace are abundant and continue to be uncovered. While the situation is improving in some countries, there are uneven levels of change worldwide in the rates of progression of and promotion for women working in architecture. The formerly slow but improving rate to obtain gender balance in architectural education and practice is in part due to the link architecture has to "a specific historical and cultural construction of masculinity and a masculinist vision of professional work." (Davies 1996, p. 661) This, combined with what remains, even today in the most progressive developed countries, a heavily male-dominated architectural and construction industry means women suffer considerably from a deeply embedded culture of dominant male social networks, which sustain a "soft, chummy violence [that]... circulates within ... the spaces of institutions." (Bloomer 1993, p. 19) Institutional violence, endemic in many architecture schools and offices and the construction industry at large, needs to be constantly exposed through formal complaint in order to improve the situation for women and minority architects. Some headway has been made by organisations such as the

Chartered Institute of Building (C.I.O.B.), the Royal Institute of British Architects (R.I.B.A.), and the Royal Australian Institute of Architects (R.A.I.A.) to name but a few, but more needs to be done.

A U.K. report documenting women's membership into the CIOB (1995) entitled *His House or Our House?* (Lowe and Byrne 1993) revealed that while women were increasing in numbers in the construction workplace, they were simultaneously suffering discrimination that inhibited their ability to work happily. Funded research by the R.I.B.A. entitled *Why Do Women Leave Architecture?* (De Graft-Johnson et al. 2003) and by the R.A.I.A. entitled *Parlour: Women, Equality, Architecture* (Stead et al. 2014) have exposed continuing acts of professional everyday discrimination against women – and more recently male architects – which has inhibited their career progression. For both genders, inflexible workplaces restrict career progress for those who seek work-life models other than the traditional male career path. For women architects to be able to play the game of architecture in a neoliberal society is it vital that all architects in positions of power resist the urge for competitive play and create collaborative and supportive work environments that develop alternative work-life lifestyles by engaging with, rather than silencing, feminist critiques. Even though feminism too has been co-opted as a marketable commodity under neoliberalism it is essential that women and men architects seeking change challenge the status quo.

In *Working the Spaces of Power: Activism, Neoliberalism and Gendered Labour*, Professor of Social Policy, Janet Newman (2012, p. 151) discusses the "coincidence between feminism and global capitalism." Newman (2012, p. 151) draws out two discourses on the topic in feminist scholarship, the first being "how processes of 'mainstreaming' served both to acknowledge and depoliticize [sic] feminist claims; and second, how neoliberalism appropriated identity politics." Newman (2012, p. 150) contends that through its ability to commodify everything and everyone for reasons of increased marketisation, feminist activism has been shunned and diminished. Under neoliberalism working women seek to be equal players in the marketplace. As additional 'human capital' they become a productive economic market opportunity within the enterprise culture. (Newman, 2012, p. 153) According to American philosopher and critical theorist, Nancy Fraser (2009), feminist critiques of patriarchy opened up women to new forms of exploitation, in which women's emancipation was tied to the engine of capital accumulation. As example, American sociologist, Arlie Russell Hochschild (2013) notes in "The Outsourced Self: Intimate Life in Market Times" how the mothering self (and the over-worked couple) has been outsourced and laments that the dream that feminists once had of mothers being paid, even in part, to care for their children has vanished. Still, if we accept neoliberalism as a system that we cannot currently change, it is vital that we construct third-wave feminist strategies towards a more inclusive and balanced relationship between gender, labour, and economics in architecture.

In "Architecture, Gender, Economics," Architectural writer and editor, Justine Clark (2012) contends that statistics of a survey undertaken of Australian architects at the time pointed to women architects being poorer, as a group in full-time, part-time, and casual work, in part because women do not ask to be paid more. Clark argues for the "business case" for gender pay equity sought for women architects. Clark presents to architectural employers that their business will be better off if they better remunerate and retain the best women architects and provide more flexible work environments, thereby reducing the cost to find other employees of the same quality. It is clear from literature in almost every field that "gender matters in economics" (Eswaran 2014), in part because, as is the case in women acquiescing to domestication when working, women often cannot or do not demand promotion and pay rises in the manner in which many men do. Playing the game of promotion for increased remuneration for architectural work remains another area for change in the profession.

Eswaran (2014, p. 5) maintains that "… Women may not make it to the top, not because they lack the skills, the drive, or the creativity but simply because they do not care for the means employed to select the winner." Due to stereotypical "gender differences in competitiveness and cooperativeness, both within single-sex groups and within mixed-sex groups," women's disengagement with winning at work can "lead to asymmetric economic outcomes." (Eswaran, 2014, p. 5) Many women can have the equivalent, or sometimes more, relevant work skills including education, experience, and ability as their male counterparts but due to lack of confidence or competitive drive or discrimination, they can be disadvantaged in promotion. Steady, non-risky work practices differ to the economic potential offered by risky entrepreneurism. As Eswaran (2014, p. 8) notes; "One of the most noticeable aspects of gender differences in the economic sphere is in the realm of entrepreneurship …[where] a far higher proportion of entrepreneurs is male than female." Entrepreneurship in architecture – usually related to starting your own practice/brand – offers the potential to make more money than salaried employee positions. In addition, marriage may be a factor that is economically disadvantageous to all sexes. "Married men are known to earn higher incomes than their unmarried counterparts with similar qualifications. Is marriage responsible for this income difference?" (Eswaran 2014, p. 10)

In the early 20th century, economists agreed that women – who work full time and have the same education, skill level, and on-the-job training, etc., as their male counterparts – earned less than men do in most fields of labour. (Jacobsen in Moe ed. 2003, p. 161) Joyce P. Jacobsen (in Moe ed. 2003, p. 161) asserts that the concept of human capital offers a partial explanation for the gender gap in earnings. While there are many definitions of human capital, the meaning most accepted by economists follows that of Smith (1776 II.I.17, 1991) presented in *Wealth of Nations* in which a worker chooses to acquire talents "during his education, study, or apprenticeship," which "as they make a part of his [or her] fortune, so do they likewise of that of the society to which he belongs." More recent definitions expand human capital to include attributes of healthiness (mental and physical) which can facilitate increased energy for productivity. (Hamermesh and Rees 1988, p. 63;

McConnell, Brue, and Macpherson 1999, p. 614) Jacobsen (in Moe ed. 2003, p. 161) notes that "Generally, people with more human capital would be expected to be more productive and therefore to earn more per unit of time than people with less human capital, all else equal." However, because of the persistence of gender pay inequality in many professions, gender is seen to be a factor that can affect human capital investment and remuneration. Due to the glass ceiling effect, "subtle discrimination" can prevent women from achieving equal returns to those of men as they reach the higher levels of human capital within a given occupation or industry. (Jacobsen and Levin 2000) It is essential that women (and men) who hit 'glass ceilings' look at ways to move sideways to gain promotion, rather than stay in positions that demean their esteem.

Coined by Marilyn Loden in 1978, but also used by Marianne Schriber and Katherin Lawrence at Hewlett-Packard in the same year, the glass ceiling was defined as discriminatory promotion patterns in which the written promotional policy is non-discriminatory, but in practice denies qualified women promotion. (https://en.wikipedia.org/wiki/Glass_ceiling) The more recent phrase 'bamboo ceiling' has been coined to define the obstacles East Asian-Americans face in advancing their career but the phrase 'glass ceiling' is used for both the barriers to equal promotion and pay for women and minority groups of different race/ethnicity and class.

Race, Ethnicity, and Class in Architecture

Five years before the release of *One Fine Day*, American director, Spike Lee (1991) produced the romantic drama film, *Jungle Fever.* The film's protagonist is the successful, sole black architect in his office, Flipper Purify (played by Wesley Snipes). Purposely dealing with issues of race, class, family, and background, *Jungle Fever* – defined as an attraction borne of sexualised racial myths rather than love – recounts the story of the extramarital affair Purify has with his American-Italian temp assistant, Angie Tucci (played by Annabella Sciorra), whose employment Purify initially challenges, although he is told the appointment is not based on race but ability. (Figure 3.2) While the film centres predominantly on the consequences of the interracial relationship in the office and on the private lives of both architect and his assistant, it gives one example of how race and class can be factors which create professional and personal cumulative consequences in an architect's career.

Black and Asian architects entered the architectural profession much later than white women architects in the United States and United Kingdom. In 1923, 35 years after Louise Blanchard Bethune became the first white female associate of the American Institute of Architects (A.I.A), Paul Revere Williams joined the Southern California chapter of the A.I.A., having become the first African-American architect two years earlier. Following Williams, Norma Merrick Skalarek became the first black woman to be licensed as an architect in New York in 1954 – 66 years after Bethune became an A.I.A. member. In the U.K., Ghanaian-British

FIGURE 3.2 Successful black architect, Flipper Purify (played by Wesley Snipes) is introduced by his bosses, Jerry (played by Tim Robbins – in suit) and Leslie (played by Brad Dourif), to his temp secretary Angie Tucci (played by Annabella Sciorra) in *Jungle Fever* (Dir. Lee 1996). Photograph: Photo 12/Alamy Stock Photo. Photographer: Archives du 7e Art Collection, Image ID: B7TN0W.

architect Sir David Adjaye made history by being the first black male architect to win the R.I.B.A Royal Gold Medal in 2021. In 2016, Iraqi-born British architect, Dame Zaha Hadid was the first West Asian woman to be awarded the R.I.B.A Gold Medal. Minnette de Silva was the first Sri Lankan woman to be trained as an architect in London and the first South Asian woman to be elected an associate of the R.I.B.A in 1948.

Race[2] and ethnicity[3] differ in that race is seen as a narrower category based on similar physical and biological traits, whereas ethnicity is broader, based on a person's place of origin and cultural expression. Just as some argue that architecture in some countries remains 'a white gentleman's club,' architects of different race and ethnicity, including black and brown architects, are underrepresented in both the academy and practice and literature, but this representation is growing – including in literature. (Williams 1937; 1986; Adams 1991; Weiss 1994; Hudson 1993 to name but a few) Unlike gender and architecture which has been in institutional limelight for longer, the relationship between race, ethnicity, class, and architectural advancement and design (Tauke, Smith, and Davis eds. 2015) are fields that are scantly represented but emerging. American Professor of Architecture, Kathryn H. Anthony (2001) examines the relationship between gender, race, and ethnicity in the architectural profession in her book, *Designing for Diversity* and the journal article of the same title. (Anthony 2002) Anthony argues that different aspects of architectural practice can hinder or support the full participation of women and persons of different race and ethnic background. Anthony contends that at the turn of the 21st century, women architects were often positioned in interior architecture, African-American architects were pigeonholed into government architectural offices, and Asian-American architects worked more in computer-aided design. Gender and racial stereotyping can underpin stereotyping of professional labour division.

While African-American architects are growing in number in the U.K., U.S.A., and elsewhere, establishing their own practices and thereby increasing racial diversity in the profession (Travis ed. 1991; Feldman and Travis 1993; Wilkins 2016), racial and ethnic discrimination remains in academia and practice. In a survey of architects from Black and Minority Ethnic (BAME) backgrounds working in the U.K., it was reported that architecture is "a profession struggling with unacknowledged racism where architects from … (BAME) backgrounds feel the colour of their skin hinders their career." (Waite and Tether 2018) However, the colour of an architect's skin, just like their gender, is only one variable. If an architect is of race and of an ethnic minority but from a wealthy background, privilege can accrue further architectural privilege and distinction.

Corporate financial analyst, Victoria Kaplan's (2006) book, *Structural Inequality: Black Architects in the United States* – based on her PhD (2004) – gives a deeper insight into the relationship between race and business entrepreneurship. Kaplan's research examines how a black man's experience "had shaped his life…. the triumphs and tribulations he had experienced as the sole owner of an architectural firm." (Kaplan 2006, p. 5) In the Foreword to the book, R. K. Stewart (in Kaplan 2006, p. xi), Gensler partner and 2007 president of the American Institute of Architects (A.I.A.), recognises the additional barriers faced and explains, "The everyday challenges all architects face become huge *barriers* to the success of black architects as well as other architects who are not white males."

As 'a social construction' the concept of race has evolved over time as socio-political and cultural climates have altered although "Economic disparity remains a barrier to the ability of blacks, of any socioeconomic class, to achieve their full potential." (Kaplan 2006, p. 11) Kaplan (2006, p. 11) asserts that as long as there is a wealth disparity between black families and white families, there will be remain social and economic inequality for blacks.

Kaplan builds upon African-American Professor of Sociology, Melvin L. Oliver and Professor of Sociology, Thomas M. Shapiro's (2006) *Black Wealth/White Wealth: A New Perspective on Racial Inequality*, first published in 1997, which examines the relationship between private wealth and racial inequality. The thesis presented by Oliver and Shapiro is "that wealth brings advantage – in housing, education, health care, and generally in a sense of security." (Kaplan 2006, p. 11) Importantly, Kaplan (2006, pp. 11–12) recognises that 'the wealth gap' between blacks and whites "creates limits for black architects, and other business owners of color [sic], in part by limiting their access to investment capital, social networks, and other assets that would facilitate the success of their firms." Understanding class structural inequality, therefore, requires an analysis of wealth and social networks. (Kaplan 2006, p. 12; Barabási 2003)

Professor of Sociology, Dalton Conley (1999) in his book, *Being Black, Living in the Red: Race, Wealth and Social Policy in America*, studies how race and class affect the economic disparity between blacks and whites in the U.S. at the time and how this affects 'access to opportunity.' (Kaplan 2006, p. 12) Conley (1999, p. 52) writes that "Wealth, not occupation or education, is the realm in which the greatest degree of racial inequality lies in contemporary America" and this in turn relates to the opening up of commission opportunities. The patronage system that supports architects winning commissions relies on personal relationships to broaden contacts. However, being able to build social networks starts with hiring. Of the black architects Kaplan (2006, p. 12) interviewed, she concludes "Not only have blacks been limited in their ability to create those contacts... but as many... told me, 'People hire architects who look like themselves.'"

As an elite profession, architecture remains superfluous and set apart from the everyday lives of most people. Only the wealthy or those able to access wealth can appoint an architect. As a formerly 'white gentleman's profession' where white educators taught white architects, it is essential that black architects, and those of other race and ethnicity, have access to university education. Unlike the U.S. with its Historically Black Colleges and Universities (HBCUs) which were established in the South, architecture schools in the U.K. implement their own equal opportunity policies, guided by government and accreditation bodies, to ensure racial and ethnic diversity in their student cohorts, which, like tailored mentoring of black students from primary school onwards by black architects, will increase representation in the profession. (Kaplan 2006, p. 21, 32) Making female and male black architects visible in the media and through personal contact offers role model examples for others. The way in which architectural curricula are embedding wider literature beyond a Western, Eurocentric framework is a key area in which change can support racial and ethnic diversity. "Allowing other, different voices has the potential to challenge the status quo in the field." (Kaplan 2006, p. 58; Refer Sutton 1991)

Referring to French sociologist Pierre Bourdieu's theory of social capital (discussed in Chapter 1), Kaplan (2006, p. 150) sees that:

> The ability [for architects] to get customers, obtain funding, and have access to professional services and clients is often dependent on both behavior [sic] and connections; competence is relevant only if you do not have it, or if, on the basis of ethnicity, you are *perceived* not to have it. Appropriate behavior [sic], or what Aschaffenburg and Maas refer to as being able to 'decode the implicit "rules of the game," ' can often be invested in other ways…. Knowing and abiding by the rules often results in more invitations to play.

Building upon the writings of Pierre Bourdieu (1986), in his study of the process of acquiring architectural distinction, Garry Stevens briefly examines the relationship between social networks and class structure in architecture. In *The Favored* [sic] *Circle: The Social Foundations of Architectural Distinction*, Stevens (1998) identifies that the Marxist definition of class is tied to means of production and relates to identity, whereas the Bourdivin definition of class "is a group of people occupying similar positions in social space." (Bourdieu 1987) Stevens (1998, p. 65) notes that "Classes are defined relationally, as being above or below each other in terms of the capital they have." Since the desire is always to build capital, choices are often made to improve social class, moving from a *subordinate class* (those who value cultural capital including "intellectuals, artists, professionals") to a *dominant* class (those who can acquire the "most economic capital—entrepreneurs, managers and so on." (Stevens 1998, pp. 65–66) Stevens (1998, p. 66) contends the *dominant class* are responsible for the production of symbolic goods whereas the *subordinate class* are involved in the production of material goods.

As will be seen in Part 2 of this book, social class distinctions defined before choosing to study architecture have the capacity to create architectural class inequality. Students studying at the better schools can be advantaged so that they are subsequently accepted to study in better architecture schools. Just as private (public, in the U.K.) and independent schools incorporate different classes, so too do fully-private to semi-private architectural schools. Class inequality in architecture, which appears most markedly as a dominant 'starchitect' creative class in contrast to a subordinate not-starchitect class (or what is referred to an everyday architectural class), reiterates the theory of "cumulative inequality, or cumulative advantage and disadvantage" (Rank et al. 2014, p. 107), where early advantages or disadvantages can result in further advantage or disadvantage that multiply over a lifetime. Under capitalism, large corporate offices create capital through using the labour of cheaper paid employees. Although it claims to aim to dissolve them, neoliberalism is based on the need to sustain class distinctions (differences in wealth and labour enactment) and in architecture this refers to a privileged architectural class and less-privileged architectural class. The privileged architectural class often win the largest, most prominent commissions with the wealthiest clients, reiterating Reinhold Bentmann's and Michael Müller's (1992) study of Palladian villas linked to the rise of the wealthy Italian merchant shipping class. A wealthy, privileged client class transfers wealth to a privileged architectural class. The architectural market is controlled by affluent classes of architects and their patron clients.

To continue using Hadid as an example; she was from an upper-class family (her father was from an upper-class Iraqi family). She was well educated, attending an international school for women and then one of the best architecture schools in the U.K. at the time, the Architectural Association (A.A.), from which she built her reputational capital. While there is substantial literature on her being a woman architect and how that affected, or did not affect, her practice, there is almost no discourse about the effect of her being an Arab Muslim woman on her career progression. While Hadid worked for clients all over the world and was known to complain that the British architectural establishment could be exclusive, operating as an 'old boys club,' she stated that she did not experience discrimination because of her gender or race in other countries. She was able to produce a range of projects for wealthy clients all over the world. Cultural differences are not necessarily discriminatory if an architect comes from an elite architectural class, but they can detrimentally affect architects who are not.

Just as Hadid was able to study in the U.K. as an overseas student in the early 1970s, only becoming a naturalised British citizen in 1980, students of all nationalities from wealthier backgrounds and with the ambition to expand their global knowledge and life experiences are studying in countries other than their country of birth. The ease of movement under globalisation is one way that facilitates trans-national knowledge exchange. Depending on the economic wealth and opportunities made available to students in different countries, there is a global racial exchange in architectural education worldwide. How students and architects trained in one country negotiate work-life balance in other countries in which they choose to work is complex and will become a growing area of focus. This is because of the distance from family and friends at home (in one's home country).

Gender, race, ethnicity, and class can or cannot become ways in which architects identify themselves, i.e., define their identity. The neoliberal global marketplace chooses to either neglect difference to flat line work cultures, so an architect can become ungendered and un-acculturated, in order to simplify production, or it can exploit difference for market advantage. While there have been significant audit and policy changes in U.K. academia (through the implementation of the Athena Swan and EDI (Equality Diversity and Inclusion) Strategies) and practice (through the

R.I.B.A and ARB's guidance for architecture practices on closing the gender pay gap, as part of its commitment to support a diverse and inclusive profession) there remains gender and racial inequality. How an architect identifies their self in relation to their gender, race, ethnicity, or class, or not, is important in how they play, or are able to play, the game of life in architecture. The rules of the game play are historically different for men and women architects, for architects who are white, black, or brown, or who are of lower or higher economic background. The rules of play and goalsetting depend too on age and the generation in which one is born.

From Generations Z, X, Y to Baby Boomers

No matter how contrasts between generations have been created, one fundamental fact of life remains true in the United States: Generations matter. To understand other people, and even to fully understand ourselves, we must consider generational identity at least as carefully as we consider any other social characteristic.
Quotation from the sociologist, Elwood Carlson (in Sollohub 2019, p. ix)

In the 20th century, generations started to change in their overall way of life. American economic and social theorist, Jeremy Rifkin (2009, p. 388) notes that for instance 'the new concept of adolescence' emerged between the 1890s and 1930s. It equated women and men in a phase "devoted to developing one's personality, discovering one's interests... [etc.]" (Rifkin 2009, pp. 388–389) and changed the consciousness of young middle-class women and men giving them more time to socialise (because they entered the workforce later), more time to "think about 'careers' and the kind of life they would like to live" with more "emotional and mental luxuries" available to them than earlier generations. This shift transformed focus to 'good personality' rather than 'good character.' "Individuals became less concerned about their moral stature and more interested in whether they were liked by others... To be personable was to exude charisma, to stand out in a crowd ...." (Rifkin 2009, p. 391) A narcissistic element in personality "became fodder for an incipient advertising industry that played off personal insecurities...." (Rifkin 2009, p. 391) For the generations that followed, this dramatic change in human consciousness, purpose, and life ambition is tied to the American Dream, although older generations can be more ideologically driven than younger generations (Rifkin 2009, p. 505) even if they are all in the property rat-race.

The exact generation you were born in can be a significant contributing factor affecting the way you play the game of life in architecture under neoliberalism. This is because different generations – from Generations Z, X, Y to Baby Boomers – have different characteristics and aspirations for life, because of the social, cultural, political, and economic context in which they were born and grew or grow up in and their response to the lifestyles and aspirations of a previous generation/s. Consequently, different generations of architects play for different stakes and goals and often play to different rules. Some, mostly older, generations arguably play more by the 'old' established rules of the game, while other, mostly younger, generations are happy to play by the new rules of the neoliberal game. As 'neoliberal subjects' (Brown 2015, p. 33) younger generations tend to focus more on selfhood, quick fame, and careerism. Rather than adhere to organisational structures, they prefer to challenge them through disruption (Sollohub 2019), particularly since neoliberalism demands greater productivity and outputs in a more liquid and 'flexible' mode of work.

Many famous architects are renowned for having long careers, working well into their old age or until their death. (Stevens 1998, p. 134) For instance, American architect, Frank Lloyd Wright practiced architecture for some 70 years until his death at 91. In 2022, Frank Gehry (born 1929) was 94 years old; Dutch architect, Rem Koolhaas (born 1944) was 79 years old; and Bjarke Ingels was 49 (born 1974). All were at the time working and running large global multinational practices. However, each generation of architect can be seen to approach working within a capitalist and celebrity-focused system differently.

For instance, the Post-War Cohort in the U.S. and Canada, in which Gehry sits, was born between 1928 and 1945 and came of age between 1946–1963. While there are variations, as a cohort they are recognised to have had strong job and education opportunities after the war ended and the post-war economic boom and to "value security, comfort…" (Schroer c. 2004), something shared in most other developed countries.

After the Post-War Cohort were the first generation of Baby Boomers or Boomers I, born between 1946 and 1954, and who came of age between 1963 and 1972. Koolhaas is born at the cusp of these two generations. Boomers I were born through the period of assassinations of John F. Kennedy and Martin Luther King, the Civil Rights movement, and the Vietnam War. In the U.S., "Boomers I had good economic opportunities and were largely optimistic about the potential for America and their own lives, the Vietnam War notwithstanding." (Schroer c. 2004) This equivalent generation in China were born around the time Mao Zedong proclaimed the foundation of the People's Republic of China (PRC) in 1949 and grew up under the single-party state Communist Party of China (CPC). This generation experienced extraordinary transformations in political and economic circumstances.

Born between 1955 and 1965 are Baby Boomers II (Boomers II), or Generation Jones, named after their competitive 'keeping up with Joneses' approach to life. Born with high expectations, Generation Jones's came of age between 1973 and 1983 and had to face other harsh governmental realities. In America, they were the post-Watergate generation who lost "trust in government and optimistic views (that) the Boomers I maintained. Economic struggles including the oil embargo of 1979 reinforced a sense of 'I'm out for me' and narcissism and a focus on self-help and skepticism [sic] over media and institutions is representative of attitudes of this cohort. While Boomers I had Vietnam, Boomers II had AIDS as part of their rites of passage." (Schroer c. 2004) Due to long periods of unemployment as a result of de-industrialisation in the 1970s and 1980s, American Generation Jones did not have the same work, housing rights, or opportunities as the generation before them and, like Generation X after, have suffered. (Schroer c. 2004) With the turn of other countries including the U.K. to neoliberalism, as already outlined in Chapter 1, Boomers II in the West began to increasingly shift, as Rifkin (2009) notes, from more socially-oriented community imperatives to economic 'me' imperatives.

Born between 1966 and 1976, everyday American Generation Xers are understood to be a 'lost' generation due to being in outsourced childcare, exposure to divorce, and increased economic pressure, mostly associated with the global rise in American Dream aspirations. "Gen X is often characterized [sic] by high levels of skepticism … but they are arguably the best educated generation with 29% obtaining a bachelor's degree or higher (6% higher than the previous cohort). And, with that education and a growing maturity they are starting to form families with a higher level of caution and pragmatism than their parents demonstrated. Concerns run high over avoiding broken homes, kids growing up without a parent around and financial planning." (Schroer c. 2004)

In *Generation X: Tales for an Accelerated Culture*, Canadian novelist, Douglas Coupland (1992) argues that the British generation X is recognised to have been so bound to the need for private property ownership that they sacrifice all, including their personality, to pay off their home mortgage and become locked into jobs they can sometimes hate because of it. They crave any form of entertainment that distracts them from the tedium of monotonous work tied into daily routines. Celebrity culture takes hold day and night with increased access to more images and more information about everyone and everything through the mainstream use of the internet 24/7. However, Chinese born in this generation are playing a different game, which one might argue is a positive reaffirmation of the American Dream – beginning almost at the cycle equivalent to the Post-War Cohort in the U.S. and Canada. Filled with hopes and opportunities for increased wealth created through Deng Xiaoping's 'reform and opening-up' policy the Chinese Generation X (if it can be called that) believes in building stable and economically-strong models through increased access to education, saving, and expansion into private property portfolios. Accessibility to the internet and opening up to foreign cultures and investment increases a fascination with celebrity culture. Ingels was born in Generation X.

Generation Y, Echo Boomers, Millenniums, or Millennials are born between 1977 and 1994 and, in the early 2020s, are the main generation of graduate architects all over the world today. In the West, they are the largest generation since the Baby Boomers. Gen Y 'kids' are known to be technologically savvy, because they grew up with it and have been exposed to it since early childhood. "Gen Y members are much more racially and ethnically diverse and they are much more segmented as an audience aided by the rapid expansion in Cable TV channels, satellite radio, the Internet, e-zines, etc." (Schroer c. 2004) They are less brand loyal and their access to the internet has allowed them to be more flexible in their favouring of quickly-changing fashion trends in any industry including architecture. They are recognised as having been raised more in dual-income families or single-parent families and are the largest generation that has "a credit card co-signed by a parent." (Schroer c. 2004)

In neoliberal countries, Millennials who are funded by family wealth are, particularly in the U.K. (Lund 2019), the new generation who will likely never be able to own their own home – opting instead for owning a digital version in *The Sims* or another equivalent video gamespace. They have been/are prone to being addicted to Instagram, Facebook, WhatsApp, etc., and can worry more about how they, their social network, lunch, holiday stories, architectural successes, or failures, etc., look on social media websites. (Dobson 2017) Raised under a deeply entrepreneurial publicity culture, many of the more confident Generation Xers open their architectural practice as soon as they graduate. This generation of *Microserfs* (Coupland 1995) are conditioned to live in a 24/7 digital workspace. Some argue their conditioning to work for free (as interns) or for less, being debt-riddled (because of their education), poorer, and a more medicated generation is counterbalanced by their being better educated and hard-working than some earlier generations. (Harris 2017) Millennials can be stereotyped as being uncritical because of the bombardment of information they are constantly exposed to but others argue they are more aspirational than other older generations. (Kalpathi 2016; Harris 2017) While they might be conditioned to 'a laptop lifestyle,' they are keen to explore alternative modes of work beyond those they were raised to expect to do. (Ramachandran 2015)

Generation Z are those born between 1995 and 2012 who came of age between 2013 and 2020. While university and market analysts know less about their attributes, the environment they are growing up and studying in is highly diverse and competitive. "Generation Z 'kids' or the Playstation generation will grow up with a highly sophisticated media and computer environment and will be more Internet savvy and expert than their Generation Y forerunners." (Schroer c. 2004) In the West, many Generation Z students are adept at complaining about their student satisfaction with their architecture school and teaching and their customer-user experience is one contributing factor to rank architectural education in universities world-wide. Overseas students studying in architecture schools elsewhere vary from being critical or not of their education environments. Overall, though most of the Generation Zers are being educated in environments to enter industry with entrepreneurial and digital skills of fast production.

Clearly generations from Z, X, Y to Baby Boomers are not so distinct, stereotypically exhibiting instead overall behavioural trends. There are also overlaps between value systems and aspirations amongst members of all generations. However, generations choosing to, studying, or working in architectural academy or practice, in the current neoliberal context – where all generations of architects working at high or low levels of reputational capital – are playing the same monetary game worldwide and are mostly serving a system of capital production. (Deamer 2014) Some distinct generational differences that affect work-life balance include the ability to work with ease with digital technologies; family size and support networks; and optimism toward being able to achieve goals in the future.

Distinct generational differences can exist between those that are 'digital natives' or "N-[for Net]-gen or D-[for digital]-gen" – who having grown up within high digital technology environments –and those that are 'digital immigrants' – who was born or brought up before the widespread use of digital technology. (Prensky 2001, p. 1) American education theorist, Marc Prensky (2001, p. 1) defines 'digital natives' as "all 'native speakers' of the digital language of computers, video games and the Internet" with 'digital immigrants' being less comfortable or capable of speaking a contemporary global digital language. Perhaps the generation gap suggests that 'digital natives' are simply a different type of learner and speaker, however. (Prensky 2001, p. 3) Putting this question aside, the generation gap between 'the rise of the Digitals' versus the postmodern generation (Luther 2009) can present associated advantages or disadvantages in the architectural workplace that become cumulative.

Where engagement in capitalism has been fast-tracked, as is the case of China since the 1980s, and where family sizes have changed from being large to being small to non-existent, generation gaps are more pronounced. (Lei 2013; Sun and Cheng 2018) There can be workplace advantages to a cultural trend for familial social responsibility. Whereas in the West, many dual-income couples with children must outsource care and domestic responsibilities, in China there remains a healthy system of familial support inside and outside the family, which can ease work-life pressures.

Perhaps the most distinct difference between generations is their sense of being able to achieve life goals, both in terms of ownership and status. The children of the 1970s had different access to the property, job, and labour markets locally, nationally, and internationally than younger generations did or do. (Andres and Wyn 2010) Some argue that the benefits provided to earlier generations such as the Baby Boomers took opportunities from their children's generation. (Willets 2019) Shifts in belief and trust in some governments has affected attitudes to money and borrowing such that the saving mentality of generations can be vastly different. Younger generations may also see the financial obstacles ahead of them so insurmountable such that they give up trying.

In terms of structural equality, distinct gaps remain in society. While the feminist and activist movements of the 1960s sought quick change in equality for all regardless of gender, race, ethnicity, class, and age, it appears some 60 years later that social progress is much slower than envisaged and more complicated to achieve across all demographic spectrums. Issues of identity tied to success have become more pronounced than for pre-WW2 generations, such that neoliberalism offers everyone no matter what gender, race, ethnicity, class, or age the promise of success. Managing the expectations for success of the Millennial generation can relate to learning or being taught that *Not Everyone Gets a Trophy*. (Tulgan 2016) There are also clashes in multi-generational attitudes (Grubb 2016) to opportunism that need to be negotiated in architectural workplaces. "Different generations not only have their own distinct worldview, but their own way of working and preferred methods of communication … Business managers have their hands full trying to negotiate the psycho-social quirks of … different generations." (Roos Unknown) The shift from Gehry to Ingels, from a slowly-developed architectural oeuvre and career to establishing a career before graduating from architecture school shows distinct changes in playing the game of architecture. Differences in generational work practices in a global workplace, where architecture is produced in a 24/7 real and digital realm, is an area that has not yet been researched in depth in regard to labour practices in the profession.

To summarise, just as the American dream allows for migrants to jump up a class, entrepreneurial African-Americans, and Chinese entrepreneurs in the U.S.A. (Valdez 2016, pp. 25–26), are able to, theoretically, achieve success when formerly unsuccessful. So, just as a nouveau riche class can quickly acquire economic capital under healthy capitalist and neoliberalism to match the old establishment class, architects of different gender, race, ethnicity, class, and age also able, theoretically, to achieve architectural fame and notoriety. Gender, race/ethnicity, class, and age stereotypes can be shed if a woman architect, architect of colour, or working-class architect chooses to play, gamble, and get lucky in the architectural gamespace. What is agreed by many critics to be the key to architectural success is one essential feature: the power of the creative imagination of the individual in architecture over the collective. (Schieffer 1984, p. 16) Though why would/does someone choose architecture over other creative industries or other professions? In Part 2 of the book, 'Gameplay Moves: Become an Architect (or not),' choosing another design profession or an architectural life in academia or practice are discussed in light of the question of work-life balance.

Notes

1 While Thatcher was married with twin children (Carol and Mark, born in 1953, 26 years before she became prime minister), she was, according to Carol Thatcher (in Walker, 2013), an 'absentee mum' who was devoted entirely to her political working life. Thatcher was privileged and wealthy enough to have nannies care for her twins, allowing her to pursue her career.
2 Race is defined in the Cambridge Dictionary online (2022b) as "one of the main groups to which people are often considered to belong, based on physical characteristics, that they are perceived to share such as skin colour, eye shape etc."
3 Ethnicity is defined in the Cambridge Dictionary online (2022a) "a large group of people with a shared culture, language, history, set of traditions, etc., or the fact of belonging to one of these groups."

References

Adams, M. 1991. Perspectives: Historical Essay, Black Architects: A Legacy of Shadows, *Progressive Architecture*, pp. 85–87.

Agapiou, A. 2002. Perceptions of Gender Roles and Attitudes toward Work among Male and Female Operatives in the Scottish Construction Industry, *Construction Management & Economics*, 20 (8), (November/December 2002): 697–705.

Andres, L. and Wyn, J. 2010. *The Making of a Generation: The Children of the 1970s in Adulthood*. Toronto, Canada: University of Toronto Press.

Anthony, K. H. 2002 May. Designing for Diversity: Implications for Architectural Education in the Twenty-first Century, *Journal of Architectural Education*, 55 (4): 257–267.

Anthony, K. H. 2001. *Designing for Diversity: Gender, Race and Ethnicity in the Architectural Profession*. Urbana, IL: University of Illinois Press.

Arrow, K. J. 1951. An Extension of the Basic Theorems of Classical Welfare Economics. In J. Neyman ed. *Proceedings of the Second Berkeley Symposium on Mathematical Statistics and Probability*. Berkeley: University of California Press, pp. 507–532.

Aschaffenburg, K. and Maas, I. 1997 August. Cultural and Educational Careers: The Dynamics of Social Reproduction, *American Sociological Review*, 62: 573–583.

Barabási, A.-L. 2003. *Linked: How Everything is Connected to Everything Else and What It Means for Business, Science and Everyday Life*. New York: Plume.

Bauman, Z. 2000. *Liquid Modernity*. Cambridge: Polity Press.

Benston, M. 1989. The Political Economy of Women's Liberation, *Monthly Review*, 41 (7): 31–43.

Bentmann, R. and M. Müller. 1992. *The Villa as Hegemonic Architecture*. New Jersey, London: Humanities Press.

Berkeley, E. Perry ed. and McQuaid, M. assoc. ed. 1989. *Architecture: A Place for Women*. London: Smithsonian Institution Press.

Bernstein, F. A. 2016. How Patrik Schumacher Will Keep Zaha Hadid's Name On Top, *W Magazine*, November 3, 2016, https://www.wmagazine.com/story/how-patrik-schumacher-will-keep-zaha-hadids-name-on-top/ Accessed November 06, 2023.

Betsky, A. 1997. *Queer Space: Architecture and Same-Sex Desire*. New York: William Morrow & Co.

Bloomer, J. 1993 April. Not Now, *Assemblage*, 20, Violence, Space: 18–19.

Bourdieu, P. 1986. *Distinction: A Social Critique of the Judgement of Taste*. London: Routledge.

Bourdieu, P. 1987. What Makes a Social Class? On Theoretical and Practical Existence of Groups, *Berkeley Journal of Sociology*, 32: 1–16.

Brown, W. 2015. *Undoing the Demos: Neoliberalism's Stealth Revolution*. New York: Zone Books.

Butler, J. 1990. *Gender Trouble: Feminism and the Subversion of Identity*. Routledge: London.

Butler, J. 1988 December. Performative Acts and Gender Constitution: An Essay in Phenomenology and Feminist Theory, *Theatre Journal*, 40 (4): 519–531.

Cambridge Dictionary online. 2022a. Ethnicity (noun), https://dictionary.cambridge.org/dictionary/english/ethnicity Accessed May 12, 2022.

Cambridge Dictionary online. 2022b. Race (noun), https://dictionary.cambridge.org/dictionary/english/race Accessed May 12, 2022.

CIOB (or Chartered Institute of Building). 1995. *Balancing the Building Team: Gender Issues in the Building Professions*. Report 284. Brighton: The Institute of Employment Studies.

Clark, J. 2012. Architecture, Gender, Economics, in *Architecture Australia* as "Engendering Architecture", May 11, 2012. http://archiparlour.org/gender-architecture-economics/ Accessed May 12, 2022.

Colomina, B. 1999 September. Collaborations: The Private Life of Modern Architecture, *Journal of the Society of Architectural Historians*, 58 (3): 462–471.

Conley, D. 1999. *Being Black, Living in the Red: Race, Wealth and Social Policy in America*. Berkeley: University of California Press.

Connell, R. W. 2002. *Gender*. Malden, MA: Blackwell.

Connell, R. W. 1995. *Masculinities*. Cambridge: Polity Press.

Connell, R. W. 1987. *Gender and Power: Society, the Person and Sexual Politics*. Stanford, CA: Stanford University Press.

Cook, M. 2014. *Queer Domesticities: Homosexuality and Home Life in Twentieth-Century London*. Basingstoke: Palgrave Macmillan.

Coupland, D. 1995. *Microserfs*. London: Flamingo.

Coupland, D. 1992. *Generation X: Tales for an Accelerated Culture*. London: Abacus.

Dahrendorf, R. 1973. *Homo Sociologicus*. London: Routledge and Kegan Paul.

Darling, E. ed. 2017. *AA Women in Architecture 1917–2017*. London: Architectural Association Publications.

Davies, C. 1996 November. The Sociology of Professions and the Profession of Gender, *Sociology*, 30 (4): 661–678.

Deamer, P. ed. 2014. *Architecture and Capitalism: 1845 to the Present*. London; New York: Routledge.

Debreu, G. 1954. Valuation Equilibrium and Pareto Optimum, *Proceedings of the National Academy of Sciences*, 40 (7): 588–592.

De Beauvoir, S. 1997. *The Second Sex*. London: Vintage. First published in 1949.

De Graft-Johnson, A., Manley, S., and Greed, C. 2003. *Why do Women Leave Architecture?* Research project funded by the RIBA and match funded by the University of the West of England.

Dobson, R. 2017. *Millennial Problems: Everyday Struggles of a Generation*. London: Square Peg.

Ely, R. and Padavic, I. 2007. A Feminist Analysis of Organizational Research on Sex Differences, *Academy of Management Review*, 32 (4): 1121–1143.

Espegel Alonso, C. 2017. *Women Architects in the Modern Movement*. London; New York: Routledge.

Eswaran, M. 2014. *Why Gender Matters in Economics*. Princeton: Princeton University Press.

Evans, D. 2016. Adam Smith Isn't the Real Economic Hero — His Mother Is, *New York*, June 13, 2016. https://www.thecut.com/2016/06/katrine-marcal-adam-smith-dinner-interview.html Accessed November 06, 2023.

Feldman, R. M. and Travis, J. 1993 November. African-American Architects: In Current Practice, *Journal of Architectural Education*, 47 (2): 117–119.

Fraser, N. 2009. Feminism, Capitalism and the Cunning of History, *New Left Review*, 56: 97–117.

Gerson, K. 1993. *No Man's Land: Men's Changing Commitments to Family and Work*. New York: BasicBooks. [Chapter 9 – The Myth of Masculinity]

Gorman-Murray, A, and Cook. M. 2017. *Queering the Interior*. London: Bloomsbury Academic. (ebook)

Grubb, V. M. 2016. *Clash of the Generations: Managing the New Workplace Reality*. Oxford: John Wiley & Sons.

Hamermesh, D. S. and Rees, A. 1988. *The Economics of Work and Pay*. New York: Harper & Row.

Harris, M. 2017. *Kids These Days: Human Capital and the Making of Millennials*. Kindle Edition, New York: Little, Brown and Company.

Hartman, J. C. ed. *The Women who Changed Architecture*. Princeton: Princeton Architectural Press.

Hattenstone, S. 2010. Zaha Hadid: 'I'm Happy to be on the Outside,' *The Guardian*, October 9, 2010. https://www.theguardian.com/artanddesign/2010/oct/09/zaha-hadid, Accessed November 06, 2023.

Hegde, S. 2016. Zaha Hadid, 'Queen of the Curve' Dies of Heart Attack, April 1, 2016. https://twitter.com/sush7482, Accessed November 06, 2023.

Heim, P. and Golant, S. K. 2005. *Hardball for Women: Winning at the Game of Business*. Rev. ed., New York: Plume.

Hochschild, A. R. 2013 May. The Outsourced Self: Intimate Life in Market Times, *Theory, Culture & Society*, 30 (3): 140–145.

Hoffman, M. Dir. 1996. *One Fine Day*. United States: Twentieth Century Fox.

Holub, D. 2016. Zaha Hadid's World of Fluid Freedom. May 31, 2016. www.designersatelier.co.uk/dagmars-articles/zaha-hadid-s-world-of-fluid-freedom/, Accessed November 06, 2023.

Hudson, K. E. 1993. *Paul R. Williams, Architect: A Legacy of Style*. New York: Rizzoli.

Jacobsen, J. P. 2003. Human Capital Explanation for Gender Gap in Earnings. In Moe, K. S. ed. *Women, Family, and Work: Writings on the Economics of Gender*. Malden, MA; Oxford; Melbourne; Berlin: Blackwell Publishing, pp. 161–176.

Jacobsen, J. P. and Levin, L. M. 2000 May. The Effects of Internal Migration on the Relative Economic Status of Women and Men, *The Journal of Socio-Economics*, 29 (3): 291–304.

Kalpathi, S. S. 2016. *The Millennials: Exploring the World of the Largest Living Generation*. Gurugram, Haryana, India: Penguin Books India Private Ltd.

Kaplan, V. 2006. *Structural Inequality: Black Architects in the United States*. Lanham; Boulder; New York; Toronto; Oxford: Rowman & Littlefield Publishers, Inc.

Kaplan, V. 2004. *Against All Odds: An Ethnographic Case Study of One African American Architect*. PhD Dissertation. Santa Barbara, CA: Fielding Graduate Institute.

Kuhlmann, D. 2013. *Gender Studies in Architecture: Space, Power and Difference*. London; New York: Routledge.

Lei, W. X. 2013. *Deep Gap Between Human Beings: A Historical Perspective for Generation Gap of Chinese Society* (Chinese Edition). Beijing: China Book Press.

Lewis, W. Arthur. 2003. *The Theory of Economic Growth*. London; New York: Routledge.

Lowe, L. and Byrne, S. 1993 December. *His House or Our House?* A Report of the Women in Building Consultative Committee, The Chartered Institute of Building.

Lund, B. 2019. *Housing in the United Kingdom: Whose Crisis?* Switzerland: Springer Nature Switzerland AG.

Luther, K. 2009. *The Next Generation Gap: The Rise of the Digitals and the Ruin of Postmodernism*. Bloomington, Indiana: iUniverse.

Marçal, K. 2015. *Who Cooked Adam Smith's Dinner? A Story about Women and Economics*. London: Portobello Books.

Martin, R. 1989. Out of Marginality: Toward a New Kind of Professional. In Berkeley, E. P. and McQuaid, M. eds. *Architecture: A Place for Women*, Washington, DC: Smithsonian Institution Press, pp. 229–236.

McConnell, C. R., Brue, S. L., and Macpherson, D. A. 1999. *Contemporary Labor Economics*. London: McGraw-Hill Education.

Moulds, J. 2014. More Men Working Part-time Shows a Shift in Lifestyle Choice, August 13, 2014, https://www.theguardian.com/sustainable-business/men-part-time-work-lifestyle Accessed November 06, 2023.

Newman, J. 2012. *Working the Spaces of Power: Activism, Neoliberalism and Gendered Labour*. London: Bloomsbury Academic.

Oliver, M. L. and Shapiro, T. M. 2006. *Black Wealth/White Wealth: A New Perspective on Racial Inequality*. New York: Routledge.

Poloma, M. M. and T. N. Garland. 1971 August. The Married Professional Woman: A Study in the Tolerance of Domestication, *Journal of Marriage and Family*, 33 (3): 531–540.

Prensky, M. 2001. Digital Natives, Digital Immigrants, *On the Horizon*, 9 (5): 1–6.

Ramachandran, J. 2015. *Job Escape Plan: The 7 Steps to Build a Home Business, Quit your Job & Enjoy the Freedom*. U.S.A.: CreateSpace Independent Publishing Platform.

Rank, M. R. 2011. Rethinking American Poverty, *Contexts* 10: 16–21.

Rank, M. R. 2004. *One Nation, Underprivileged: Why American Poverty Affects Us All*. New York: Oxford University Press.

Rank, M. R. 1994. *Living on the Edge: The Realities of Welfare in America*. New York: Columbia University Press.

Rank, M. R., Hirschl, T. A., and Foster, K. A. 2014. *Chasing the American Dream; Understanding what Shapes our Fortunes*. Oxford: Oxford University Press.

Rifkin, J. 2009 *The Empathic Civilization: The Race to Global Consciousness in a World in Crisis*. Cambridge: Polity.

Roos, D. (Unknown) How Generation Gaps Work, https://people.howstuffworks.com/culture-traditions/generation-gaps/generation-gap.htm Accessed November 06, 2023.

Rossetti, L. 2015. *Women and Transition: Reinventing Work and Life*. New York: Palgrave Macmillan.

Sandberg, S. 2015. *Lean In: Women, Work, and the Will to Lead*. London: W H Allen.

Sanders, J. ed. and author. 1996. *Stud: Architectures of Masculinity*. Princeton: Princeton Architectural Press.

Schieffer, P. W. 1984 Winter. Review of *The Image of The Architect*. In *Cite*, 16.

Schroer, W. J. c.2004. Generations X, Y, Z and the Others, http://socialmarketing.org/archives/generations-xy-z-and-the-others/ Accessed November 06, 2023.

Scott Brown, D. 1989. Room at the Top? Sexism and the Star System in Architecture. In Berkeley, E. P. and McQuaid, M. eds. 1989. *Architecture: A Place for Women*. Washington, DC: Smithsonian Institution Press, pp. 237–246.

Sennett, R. 1998. *The Corrosion of Character: The Personal Consequences of Work in the New Capitalism*. New York; London: Norton.

Simon, R. W. 2008. The Joys of Parenthood, Reconsidered, *Families*: 41–48.

Smith, A. 1759. *The Theory of Moral Sentiments*. London: A. Miller, in the Strand and A. Kincard and J. Bell, in Edinburgh.

Smith, A. 2008. *The Wealth of Nations*. Radford, VA: Wilder Publications.

Sollohub, D. 2019. *Millennials in Architecture: Generations, Disruption, and the Legacy of a Profession*. Austin: University of Texas Press.

Stead, N. et al. 2014. *Parlour: Gender, Equity, Architecture*, https://parlour.org.au/about/ Accessed November 06, 2023.

Stead, N. eds. 2014. *Women, Practice, Architecture: 'Resigned Accommodation' and 'Usupatory Practice'*. London; New York: Routledge.

Stevens, G. 1998. *The Favored Circle: The Social Foundations of Architectural Distinction*. Cambridge, Mass.; London, England: The MIT Press.

Stratigakos, D. 2008. The Good Architect and the Bad Parent: On the Formation and Disruption of a Canonical Image, *The Journal of Architecture*, 13 (3): 283–296.

Stratigakos, D. 2001 November. Architects in Skirts: The Public Image of Women Architects in Wilhelmine Germany, *Journal of Architectural Education*, 55 (2): 90–100.

Stiglitz, J. 2009. *Selected Works of Joseph E. Stiglitz, Vol. 1: Information and Economic Analysis*. Oxford: Oxford University Press.

Sun, J. and Cheng, D. 2018. *China's Generation Gap* (Routledge Contemporary China Series). London: Routledge.

Sutton, S. E. 1991. Finding Our Voice in a Dominant Key. In Travis, J. ed. *African American Architects in Current Practice*. New York: Princeton Architectural Press, pp. 12–15.

Tauke, B., Smith, K., and Davis, C. eds. 2015. *Diversity and Design: Understanding Hidden Consequences*. New York: Routledge.

Toy, M. 2001. *The Architect: Women in Contemporary Architecture*. Chichester: Wiley-Academy.

Travis, J. ed. 1991. *African American Architects in Current Practice*. New York: Princeton Architectural Press.

Troiani, I. 2014. Zaha: An Image of 'The Woman Architect.' In Stead, N. ed. 2014. *Women, Practice, Architecture: 'Resigned Accommodation' and 'Usurpatory Practice.'* London: Routledge, Chapter 10.

Troiani, I. 2012. Zaha: An Image of 'The Woman Architect,' *Architectural Theory Review*, 17 (2–3): 346–364.

Trost, K. 1919. Die Frau als Architektin [The Woman as Architect], *Die Fruenfachschule*, 29: 598–599.

Tulgan, B. 2016. *Not Everyone Gets A Trophy: How to Manage the Millennials*. Oxford: John Wiley & Sons.

Valdez, Z. 2016. *Entrepreneurs and the Search for the American Dream*. New York; London: Routledge.

Waite, R. and Tether, B. 2018. Race Diversity Survey: is Architecture in Denial? *AJ: Architects' Journal*, May 10, 2018. https://www.architectsjournal.co.uk/news/race-diversity-survey-is-architecture-in-denial/10030896.article Accessed November 06, 2023.

Walker, P. 2013. Thatcher's Children: A Tale of Twins with Mixed Blessings, *The Guardian*, April 08, 2013. https://www.theguardian.com/politics/2013/apr/08/thatcher-children-twins-mixed-blessings Accessed November 06, 2023.

Walker, L. ed. 1997. *Drawing on Diversity: Women, Architecture and Practice*. London: RIBA Heinz Gallery.

Weeks, K. 2011. *The Problem with Work: Feminism, Marxism, Antiwork Politics and Postwork Imaginaries*. Durham; London: Duke University Press.

Weiss, E. 1994. Paul R. Williams, Architect: A Legacy of Style; the Will and the Way: Paul R. Williams, Architect, Review. *The Journal of the Society of Architectural Historians*, 53: 478–480.

Wilkins, C. L. 2016. *Diversity Among Architects: From Margin to Center*. London: Routledge.

Willetts, D. 2019. *The Pinch: How the Baby Boomers Took Their Children's Future - And Why They Should Give It Back*. London: Atlantic Books.

Williams, P. R. 1937. I Am a Negro, *The American Magazine* 124 (1), 59: 161–163.

Williams, P. R. 1986. Blacks Who Overcame the Odds: Ingenuity, Determination and Ability made Paul R. Williams a Nationally Recognized Architect in the '40s and '50s in Spite of Wide-Spread Racial Segregation, *Ebony* 42 (1): 148–154.

PART II

Gameplay Moves: Become an Architect (or Not)

4

THE FREEDOM TO CHOOSE TO STUDY ARCHITECTURE OR NOT

FIGURE 4.1 Neil Hughes (left) and Peter Davies playing chess in 1970, from *7 Plus Seven.* (aka14 Up!) (Dir. Apted 1970) Both boys attended the same middle-class Liverpool suburban school, and both aspired to become an astronaut. After becoming homeless, Hughes studied at university and became a councillor and preacher; Davies became a lawyer. Photograph: Everett Collection Inc/Alamy Stock. Date taken: October 20, 2006.

DOI: 10.4324/9781351199834-6

Childhood Hopes and Dreams

In 1964, the year the U.K. Conservative Party lost the election and Margaret Thatcher became spokeswoman for Housing and Land, a middle-class law and history graduate of the University of Cambridge, Michael Apted, produced what was meant to be a one-off political documentary[1] entitled *Seven Up!* but which continued every seven years, and later became the *Up* series. In the first *Seven Up!* (Apted and Almond Dir. 1964) 14 seven-year-old British Baby Boomers II (Boomers II) or Generation Jones children – four girls, 10 boys – living in different cities, ranging from the north to the south, Liverpool to London, were interviewed about their hopes, dreams, and fears for the future. They were from upper-, middle-, and lower-class families and one was an orphan.[2] Apted premised the documentary on the Jesuit motto, "Give me a child until he is seven and I will give you the man," because he already had written a thesis about social mobility in the U.K., namely that at the time, the British class system remained firmly in place. Still, there were unexpected twists and turns in the life paths of many of the children, the most notable being that of Neil Hughes. (Figure 4.1) The series reveals how factors like a child's sex race, ethnicity, and class predetermines a child's future or not. Seven of the 10 *Seven Up!* boys attended university either straight after school or later in life (some Oxbridge), but none of girls on *Seven Up!* went on to university.[3]

Since the first episode of *Seven Up!* in the mid-1960s, lives have changed to suit more 'liquid times' in which many more choices exist at all life stages for women and men. In his book, *Liquid Times: Living in an Age of Uncertainty*, the Polish philosopher, Zygmunt Bauman (2007, p. 1) argues that we are living in an unprecedented epoch because of the shift "from the 'solid' to a 'liquid' phase of modernity." As is witnessed in the lives of all the *Seven Up!* participants, institutions from marriage to workplaces are no longer stable and nor is life as predictable as it was before neoliberalism and other crises, economic or pandemic. While a life path can never be predicted, every aspect of neoliberal life that focuses on free choice means that nothing keeps its 'shape for long'; 'long term life strategies' clash with 'short term expectations.' In this climate of precarity, Bauman (2007, p. 1) argues that "the collapse of long-term thinking, planning and acting, and the disappearance or weakening of social structures in which thinking, planning and acting could be inscribed… lead to a splicing of both political history and individual lives into a series of short-term projects and episodes which are in principle infinite, and do not combine into the kinds of sequences to which concepts like 'development', 'maturation', 'career' or 'progress' (all suggesting a preordained order of succession) could be meaningfully applied. A life so fragmented stimulates 'lateral' rather than 'vertical' orientations," and this change has an enormous effect on how the game of life is played.

Living in liquid times requires that the game of life be played very flexibly. Rules are less restrictive or fixed. These align with the neoliberal deregulation in which the former rules whereby the government regulates the market are 'liquidated.' These conditions allow 'neoliberal subjects' (Brown 2015, p. 33) to embrace being liquid, flitty, flighty, and opportunist. There is no longer the requirement to stay in a job for a lifetime, in fact, neoliberalism supports changing jobs in order to move up the ladder or create new career opportunities as quickly as possible. One is always encouraged to shop around for a better job or a better partner, for instance. Playing the market, taking a gamble to build capital is at stake in every decision. This is the freedom of the neoliberal marketplace of life in which the choice of a university or degree to study is but one moment of gameplay.

Uncertain times in a global workplace require even greater agility, fluidity, and flexibility which have changed how, when, and where labour is enacted and for how long. So how can you navigate a future path of work in these 'liquid times'? What factors most influence the decision to go to university or not? Why would architecture be chosen as a course of study at university over other types of work? And how does the economic transaction of the cost of education versus potential revenue return later in life bear on that choice?

In a capitalist model of consumption and production the choice of what kind of work to undertake or which college or university to attend becomes part of an economic equation relative to the cost of that education and the predicted value of labour in the market after graduation, short and long-term. Under neoliberalism, quantitative economic imperatives of future labour profitability can heavily inform the early choice of a work career. This chapter accepts that any potential architecture student who reads this book is already considering going to university to study architecture. Still, what the chapter does, is firstly discuss free choice and being spoilt for choice in the workforce generally and in the global, neoliberal H.E. marketplace in terms of where and what to study. Related to that, second, it studies the concept of "degrees of choice." (Reay, David, and Ball 2005) It recognises that many kinds of labour can still today have previous gendered, race, ethnicity, and class associations; many, but not all, of which are changing to some degree. Still, these associations can have differing effects on career success and work-life fulfilment. Third, it sets out how to make the choice of where and what to study, with work-life balance and career fulfilment considerations in mind. It considers how architecture might be chosen over study in another design field in the creative industries because of it being a recognised profession. As the choice of what to study, if you are able to do so, is a key pinch point in most life paths, it is important to understand the implications of free choice, how neoliberalism has spoiled us for choice, and the (degrees of) freedom to choose.

The sociologist and philosopher, Renata Salecl and psychologist, Barry Schwartz study different aspects of free choice. Examined from the perspective of psychoanalysis, Salecl (2009, pp. 157–180) argues in "Society of Choice" that our contemporary world has been made to thrive on the notion of choice. According to Salecl (2009) "the ideology of choice" has fundamentally changed people from political rights-bearers to consumerist choice-makers. In *Choice*, she (Salecl 2010) argues that seeing our lives as a product of a series of free choices means that we see everything from the university we attend, to our careers, relationships, identities, etc., as being there for *our* choosing.

Schwartz examines choice from the perspective of psychology and economics, delving into the problem that affluent countries worldwide have of being spoiled for choice. He identifies a paradox. In *The Paradox of Choice*: *Where more is Less*, Schwartz (2005; 2019) argues that the extraordinary increase of the numbers of choices now available to us comes from the idea that we have all been conditioned to believe that we need to invent and reinvent through consumerism, and in continuum, every aspect of our life including our identity – which is tied both to our work and personal life. Schwartz (2005) explains, "With respect to marriage and family, there was a time when the default assumption that almost everyone had, is that you got married as soon as you could, and then you started having kids as soon as you could. The only real choice was who, not when, and not what you did after. Nowadays, everything is very much up for grabs." Additionally, because "neoliberalism literally *marketizes* all spheres" (Brown 2015, p. 31) of life so that everything-is-up-for-sale in a neoliberal mindset, with a constantly growing number of optional products and services being added to flood the neoliberal marketplace, we are now suffering from the problem of how to choose and the 'tyranny of freedom.' (Schwartz 2000) Salecl (2010) notes that the pressure of making the right choices to 'be oneself' can also bring on anxiety, guilt, or feelings of inadequacy. Schwartz (2005) sees that being spoilt for choice has negative effects on people. "One effect, paradoxically, is that it produces paralysis rather than liberation. With so many options to choose from, people find it very difficult to choose at all… The second effect is that, even if we manage to overcome the paralysis and make a choice, we end up less satisfied with the result of the choice than we would be if we had fewer options to choose from." Schwartz contends that the more options we have, the more we can regret our decision, even if the decision is a good one. This is because of 'opportunity costs,' a phrase he takes from economics, which refers to the act of comparing one option to another and seeing a missed opportunity to advance further and to optimally capitalise and maximise upon. (Cheek and Schwartz 2016) The process of being so free to choose results in the sacrifice of happiness. (Schwartz et al. 2002)

The explosion of choices of universities at which to study and courses to study requires careful decision making. However, even in a choice saturated world, the decision is further complicated nowadays by the choice of *when* to study. While it was uncommon to study late in life or at any other time other than straight after school, new neoliberal markets have opened up at undergraduate and postgraduate levels, with an enormous number of ever-growing specialised programmes to suit people of all ages who want to study full-time or part-time, in person or remotely, so as to continue working in another job or to juggle family or other commitments. No matter what age, stage of life, or country in which one might be living, however, making the choice to study at university involves agreeing to the economic burden to pay for university tuition and student accommodation, if desired or required, and this relates to research on 'degrees of choice.'

Neoliberalism blinds us to the fact that our economic and social situation determines the range of choices realistically available to us because it leads us to believe we are free to choose whatever we want regardless. (Salecl 2010) However, in "Choices of Degree or Degrees of Choice? Class, 'Race' and the Higher Education Choice Process," Sociologist Diane Reay, Jacqueline Davies, Miriam David, and Stephen J. Ball (2001, p. 855) contend that for young and mature students alike, "class and 'race' issues interrelate in their decision-making"; "various mechanisms of social closure … operate to reproduce existing inequalities within the higher education sector." While higher access and participation figures nowadays are a priority for all U.K. universities, social and racial inequalities prior to university mean that it is not universities that are always at fault for not choosing a diverse cohort student body but rather some students are self-selecting, opting out of even applying to a particular university or course because of their social and economic circumstances. Gatekeeping by a university can influence being chosen to be accepted or not.

As already stated, in *The Theory of Economic Growth* published in 1955, African-American political economist, W. Arthur Lewis (2003, p. 89) explains that "'sensible' aristocracies" "allow as much vertical mobility as is necessary for vigour," but no more than is necessary. In the U.K., the government has increased the opportunities for students to attend university, through apprenticeship courses and other initiatives, to improve social mobility. While the landscape of social mobility is changing, the aspiration to move up a class that fathers, mothers, family, or friends might project on to a child becomes a factor in nurturing a child to become an architect from birth or during their schooling. Seen as an elite and noble professional career choice for girls and boys, the pathway to choosing architecture to study is increasingly less one made by a student of architecture, and more one made by members of their family. In the American study, *The Hidden Injuries of Class*, Sociologists Richard Sennett and Jonathan Cobb (1977) analyse how the game of 'achievement' can be injurious or harmful to different social classes. There can be generational consequences for working-class children who climb the social ladder, including parental shame, embarrassment, or rejection of their parents economically-restricting lifestyle leading to "the desire for a less constrained journey." (Sennett 1998, pp.17–18) First generation children of working-class background who graduate from university can fulfil the desires of their father or mother "for upward mobility" while sometimes rejecting the ways of a parent/s. (Sennett 1998, p. 18)

Since the 1990s, it has been recognised that the 'degrees of choice' in higher education relate to the history of access to it over the 20th century (Reay et al. 2001, p. 855; Egerton and Halsey 1993) and relate to, firstly, the massive expansion in the sector; secondly, the significant decrease in gender inequality; and thirdly, that social class inequality has remained virtually the same. While a prospective student has – if they are clever enough and in principle – the option to go to any university in the world to study whatever they choose, inequalities that relate to social and economic stratification can limit the range of opportunities they see realistically available to them. Their fathers and mothers, if they are actively involved with their children's futures, can have, and are increasingly having, an impact on their children's university choices because their socio-economic identities can be intrinsically tied to their children's future success.

Parents, Money, and Pre-University Schooling

Just like the board game, *The Game of Life*'s options and choices for education can begin at birth and continue throughout one's life with a myriad of consequences. Typically, in the first phase of life from birth to late adolescence choices are made for a child by others, mostly their parents. These choices can have a major effect on the quality of the child's adult life. Choosing what school and university to go to and what to gain specialist knowledge in is the first step in a sequence of neoliberally-determined life choices. Early education game play moves that lead to choosing architecture can be influenced by parents, families, friends, and teachers with fathers and mothers often having varying degrees of influence. This life stage is beyond the control of any very young player in the game, but affects progress in later life.[4]

Fathers and mothers can affect whether their child chooses to go to university or not. Since single or coupled parents constitute a growing global middle-class who are paying for or helping support their child in their educational progress pre-university and through their university studies, it is important to understand the dynamics of father–mother–daughter–son relationships to consider how gender identities contribute to whether their child chooses university study and then chooses a male-dominated, female-dominated, or gender-neutral programme of study at university.

The history of architecture is predominantly the history of great male architects with great women architects slowly growing in number, all of whom work in a male-dominated construction industry. While we know very little about why many former architects chose architecture, we are gaining insight through biographies and autobiographies into how some architect-sons or architect-daughters follow in the footsteps of their architect-fathers, architect-mothers (or both), architect-grandfathers, architect-grandmothers, architect-uncles, architect-aunts, etc. Some examples of biological families of multiple generations of architects starting from the early 20th century include the Scott family and the family of the Smithsons. For instance, Sir (George) Gilbert Scott (1811–1878), his sons, George Gilbert Scott Jr. (1837–1897) and John Oldrid Scott (1841–1913), and his grandsons, Adrian Gilbert Scott (1882–1963) and Sir Giles Gilbert Scott

(1880–1960), whose second cousin was Elizabeth Scott (1898–1972), were all architects. Israeli Canadian-American architect and urban planner, Moshe Safdie (born 1938) is the father of San Diego-based architect and partner of Safdie Rabines Architects, Taal Safdie (featured on the book cover). British born, Brutalist architects, Alison Margaret Smithson (1928–1993) and Peter Denham Smithson[5] (1923–2003) are the parents of architect Simon Smithson.[6] In these instances, young children of architects are acculturated to architecture through their family's professional-personal social circles. In his childhood years, Simon Smithson spent weekends at the Solar Pavilion (or Upper Lawn Pavilion, Fonthill Estate, Tisbury, Wiltshire, 1959–1962) that his parents designed, lunching with friends of his parents such as the influential British art historian, critic, and engineer, Reyner Banham. (Figure 4.2)

Architect-sons and architect-daughters who are the children or grandchildren or a relative of architects are acculturated to a life in architecture well before they enter architectural studies and this exposure – which can be close or far away from the office – has the potential to carry reputational capital. These experiences can have a positive or negative effect, incentivising the architect-child to follow in their architect-family's footsteps or not depending on their perception of the real life of their architect-parent or relative. Some children of architects can still choose architecture even if what they witness first-hand is not always an easy life. In the case of Simon Smithson, coming from a two-parent architect family meant he witnessed a long work hours culture of both parents who juggled having three children in the family home that included a ground floor studio. As Simon Smithson (in Cooke 2013, p. 122 Footnote*) explains:

> We [Simon and his sisters, Samantha and Soraya] would come back from school, poke our noses round the door of the studio and then go upstairs and make ourselves some toast. At 6.45 they [his parents, Alison and Peter Smithson] would come up and make dinner, and afterwards they would read or go back to work. Up until I was about eleven there was a level of ignorance [on my part]. After that, it was traumatic because they were wildly different to other parents: the food we ate, the fact we didn't get a telly until very late, even the fact we had a dishwasher and central heating. They were architecturally politicised: they believed in the idea that architecture could improve society. So they sent me to Holland Park, the first custom-built comprehensive [designed by Leslie Martin for the LCC, Holland Park opened in 1958]. For them, it must have been a pleasure to go there. But I was very marked by it, aesthetically and culturally. It was chaos, and I was bullied. All my neighbourhood friends went to public school. Your objective [when young] is to be normal. You become very conscious of the differences. Only when you're older do you say: 'That was amazing.'

FIGURE 4.2   'Upper Lawn Pavilion, Font Hill Estate, Tisbury: the family lunching with Reyner Banham on the Patio'. Photograph by Reginald Hugo de Burgh Galwey (191701971). Image date: 1963 from RIBA Collections RIBAPIX REF No RIBA19076. [Son of Peter and Alison Smithson, Simon Smithson (top right) is seated beside Reyner Banham who sits next to Peter Smithson. Alison Smithson sits opposite.]

Many non-architect-parents wish for their son or daughter to become an architect, choosing it for their child even before birth, as is the case with American architect, Frank Lloyd Wright. In *Frank Lloyd Wright: A Biography*, American biographer Finis Farr (1962, p. 13) explains: "His (Frank Lloyd Wright's) mother wished him to be an architect … and looked at pictures of English cathedrals while carrying him before birth." Lloyd Wright's nursery was decorated with engravings of the cathedrals to encourage his ambition. (Secrest 1998, p. 58) The ambition of mothers for their sons has a long historical precedent, but as mothers move from *femina domestica* to becoming working mothers, their career influences can also change expectations for their children. Equally, as fathers become more involved in the home, the influence they have on the career path of daughters has also shifted. Changes to the work-life balance of mothers and fathers is influencing future life choices of work for their offspring or those they care for. (Fine-Davis 2004; Kaiser et al. eds. 2011)

British sociologist, Sue Sharpe undertook research on girls' expectations while at school from the 1970s onwards. Sharpe contends in her book, *Fathers and Daughters* (1994, p. 4), that while there has been considerable research on the mother–daughter relationship, little had been done up to the late 20th century on the father–daughter relationship. While there are many kinds of parents or carers, fathers and mothers who participate actively in caring for their child can strongly influence their child's ambitions and subsequent identity formation through the life choices they make for their child. This also manifests in the choices their child makes for themselves later in life through *how* they father or mother, i.e., whether they parent in stereotypical or non-stereotypical ways, and the degree to which they do so or are able to do so. This happens through a process of reproduction, or not, of identities of working or non-working women and/or men at home or work.

"In looking at the ways that girls develop feminine identity and personality, it was suggested by Nancy Chodorow [1978 in *The Reproduction of Mothering*] that there is a kind of shared identification (or 'double identification') in which mothers identify with their daughters, having been daughters/girls themselves, and their daughters identify with their mothers through being of the same sex …." (Sharpe 1994, p. 12) Mothers, fathers, and other carers who raise a child can influence the choice to go to university, or not, made by the child they care for. An increasing number of mothers and fathers (both of whom can be working inside and outside the home) encourage their daughters to have the same aspirations that were formerly only the privilege of sons. The model that men come home from work and engage with their children doing more practical and recreational activities including "bathing, playing and taking children out rather than the nitty-gritty activities of changing and washing nappies and other clothes, preparing food and administering meals" (Sharpe 1994, p. 17) has changed so that there are now more of the 'new man.' (Sharpe 1994, p. 16) Sharpe suggests that when fathering covers all activities stereotypically done by mothers, closer bonds between fathers and daughters are created. (Sharpe 1994, p.18) Non-traditional types of mothering and fathering affect "the stereotyped separation of sex roles and abilities." (Sharpe 1994, p. 20) Dismantling traditional gendered work challenges not only the stereotypical behaviours of mothers who are working parents or fathers who have always worked and who want to be more involved in at-home parenting, but also the aspirations of daughters and sons and the life choices they make about work-home life balance in the future. Single parents (male or female) or one parent families exhibit 'cross-roles' where they undertake both gender stereotypical behaviours; family life is organised differently than two parent families. Single parents can impart 'feminine' and 'masculine' skills on to their child/ren (Sharpe 1994, p. 21), although this is changing for two-parent families too. Single and two-parent families without an extended family to offer childcare support can be stretched because of the problem of juggling unmanageable workloads. Additional work (which is not factored into a paid workload plan) can include caring for the home, children and other family or friends, and pets.

"Pressuring daughters to do well" (Sharpe 1994, p. 48) academically, like sons, has been an important feature of how the identities of mothers and fathers evolve too. The expectation of parents of their daughters and sons happens in relation to their own achievements. (Sharpe 1994, pp. 50–52) However, "research has suggested that high-achieving daughters have often had a close and supportive relationship with their fathers… [Sharpe (1994, p. 52) and] that some daughters have achieved in spite of their fathers," as is also the case for sons.

As the gendered labour of working-mothers or working-fathers is changing, so are the options for their daughters and sons in terms of the formation of their identities at home and work. As fathers engage more with the care of their child and because they often "want to teach them some of the ('masculine' things that they themselves enjoyed doing when they were young," (Sharpe 1994, p. 22) daughters and sons are being conditioned to look at their possible future work life as more ungendered. Some parents want to ensure their daughter feels she can "succeed in anything they wanted" and are "determined that … [their daughter] become an able and independent young woman." (Sharpe 1994, p. 22) Daughters in these relationships develop strong confidence and self-esteem. "If it is a daughter, some fathers may invest in her all the things they may have wanted for a son … and do the same 'boyish' activities with her that they would have done if she had been male." (Sharpe 1994, p. 23) If fathers or mothers feel confident about their own self-identity that confidence can transfer positively to their offspring. (Sharpe 1994, p. 43) Not only can parents have a significant influence on the decision by their child to go to university, but they can also contribute to setting up an automatic career trajectory through the schools they chose to send their children to.

French social scientist Pierre Bourdieu devoted a considerable part of his academic life to understanding how capital and taste are accrued during schooling and these insights are useful to discuss in relation to the 'degrees of [university] choice' available to prospective students. While English architectural theoretician, Helena Webster's (2005) "The Architectural Review," *Bourdieu for Architects*

(Webster 2010), and Garry Stevens' (1998) *The Favored Circle: The Social Foundation of Architectural Distinction* apply Bourdivian theories to the discipline of architecture for critique *at* architecture school and *after* graduation, here select theories from Bourdieu are considered in the *pre*-university stage of a potential architect's life. On the subject of 'cultural pedigree' Bourdieu (1996, pp. 63–68) discusses how a school student is acculturated before entering a university education and how this can affect or affects their future ability to accrue social, cultural, and economic capital, in this instance if they choose a life in architecture.

According to Bourdieu (1996, p. 1), upbringing and education are the main factors that influence the social production of distinction in any individual. In *Distinction: A Social Critique of the Judgement of Taste*, Bourdieu (1996) contends that the degree of taste that one can accrue depends firstly on the number of qualifications gained or the duration of schooling through which "cultural practices are recognized [sic] and taught by the educational system…," and secondly on "social origin." He explains that "The science of taste and of cultural consumption begins with a transgression … : it has to abolish the sacred frontier which makes legitimate culture a separate universe, in order to discover the intelligible relations that unite apparently incommensurable 'choices'…." (Bourdieu 1996, p. 2) Bourdieu (1996, p. 2) describes this as 'aesthetic consumption' which operates within everyday life. While he orients his study toward how one develops discerning taste for quality art, the concept of 'aesthetic consumption' is expanded in meaning here to 'aesthetic university consumption,' where aesthetic refers to the palatability of the university including and beyond its spatial appearance.

In most neoliberal countries, the school system has become more polarised since neoliberalism became prominent. Rather than neoliberalism allowing more freedom of choice at school level, the comprehensive school system and public (private) school systems are increasingly more polarised, creating growing educational inequality. In the U.K., this has been heightened since grammar schools – like the one Thatcher attended and which were a key conduit for social mobility – have reduced in number. If we return to the American political theorist, Wendy Brown's (2015, p. 35) argument that neoliberalism only heightens inequality rather than eliminate it because "… inequality, not equality, is the medium and relation of competing capitals," it is apparent that the level of wealth a family (social origin) has to pay for a better-quality education can be a strong influence in potentially allowing a longer duration of education for their children. This is because "Economic power is first and foremost the power to keep economic necessity at arm's length." (Bourdieu 1996, p. 55) He explains; "Even in the classroom, the dominant definition of the legitimate way of appropriating culture … favours those who have had early access to the legitimate way of appropriating culture …in a cultured household, outside of scholastic disciplines…." (Bourdieu 1996, p. 2) What one learns, ideally as early as possible, is an invaluable ability to 'see.' He explains: "… One can say that the capacity to see (*voir*) is a function of the knowledge (*savoir*)…," (Bourdieu 1996, p. 2) which in turn builds a cultivated disposition and cultural competence as early as school age. Cultivated children benefit in having the skills to ideally and theoretically make better choices later in life because they understand the playing field better. "... Most students in their last few years at school throughout the U.K. will be exposed to a 'discourse of choice'" (Salecl 2009, p. 1) that demands that individuals attend to what Salecl refers to as their 'life-making.'

In 1960 and 1967–1968, when Bourdieu was undertaking his participant survey research in France for *Distinction*, and in the same decade *Seven Up!* was produced, the formation and reaffirmation of class differences – bourgeoisie to the working class – were intrinsically tied to the choice of school (even at seven years of age), and the economic power of the child's social origin. The level of economic power that a child's family have can support or hinder the option of going to university. A two-tier school education system, as exists in most neoliberal countries, means that a girl or boy, even at seven years of age, who attends a private pre-school system such as John Brisby, Andrew Brackfield, and Charles Furneaux did in the *Seven Up!* Series, and who might encounter obstacles later in life (as Furneaux experienced) are arguably already better prepared to distinguish future choices including studying at university and are on a potentially more advantaged life trajectory.

To choose to study architecture at university – which none of the 14 *Seven Up!* participants did – or another profession aligns with how the prospective student is already acculturated to suit the profession. So, while, as Webster (2005, p. 267) notes, "The notion that formal education is a prime site for acculturation is not particularly new or contested," the type of pre-university formal education a child has had can mean they are *already* acculturated to discern and be prepared to make more optimally capital-generating choices. That, combined with the fact that classes of work have been transformed under neoliberalism from the more long-term stable jobs in the old working class, middle-class, and upper-class categories to classes of work that are increasingly subject to precarity –which include the 'army of unemployed,' precariat class, manual workers, proficians, salatariat, and the 'absurdly rich global elite' (Standing 2016, pp.8–9) – the choice of what to study is becoming increasingly a quantitative prediction of anticipated monetary return and the commodification of the student in the global H.E. marketplace. "To gain a place at a good university, the young person must sell him/herself as a commodity in order to invest years of study (and often be financially indebted) for the sake of a commodity that is the qualification." (Rodd, Reiss, and Mujtaba 2014, p. 18) In the case of long courses of higher education for a professional qualification such as architecture, the stakes can arguably be higher than choosing other courses.

Choosing a Professional Life and Un/Gendered Types of Work

As a university or college education has only recently become more available in many countries since the mid-20th century, it is important to understand a little of the history of professionalism within Higher Education. In *The Culture of*

Professionalism: The Middle Class and the Development of Higher Education in America, historian Burton J. Bledstein (1976) notes that professions like medicine and architecture began to form, much like a sorority or fraternity in the 1820s in the United States. Professions expanded in the 19th century and in England according to historian G. Kitson Clark (1962, p. 274) the rising number of "educated and professional classes" emerged as a "new type of aristocracy." Sororities, fraternities, or professional institutions "made it possible for the individual to find both privacy in his lodging and intimacy in a small group – a second family." (Bledstein 1976, p. 254) Rising into a professional class has since been the ambition of an aspiring, growing lower- and middle-class worldwide focused on status-making. The growth in a 'credential society' (Collins 2019) has consequences for different professions.

The study of architectural professionalism emerged in the 1970s through research done by sociologists. Magali Sarfatti Larson's (1977) *The Rise of Professionalism: A Sociological Analysis* – later with the revised subheading, *Monopolies of Competence and Sheltered Markets* (Sarfatti Larson 2012) – examines the sociology of the professions of medicine and architecture. Sarfatti Larson argues that medicine is *the* premier profession but that all professions –which she sees are both professional associations of occupations of independent practitioners and bureaucratic organisations – primarily reinforce dominant bourgeois ideology and were formerly considered a masculine 'field of honour.' (Lerman in Kohlstedt and Longino 1997) Later studies which focus only on the architecture profession are by sociologists, such as Judith Blau, Robert Gutman, and Bridget Fowler and Fiona Wilson.

Through a five-year survey of 152 Manhattan architectural firms, Blau's (1987) *Architects and Firms* challenges assumptions about the motivations of architects of different levels as design professionals – with younger architects placing higher value on the humanistic and creative, rather than the economic, dimensions of architecture. Gutman's (1988) *Architectural Practice* maps the American architectural profession in the mid-1980s and identifies a demise of professional power that he seeks to bring attention to, in search of a remedy. More recently, Fowler and Wilson (2004), influenced by the writings of Bourdieu, interrogate the attributes of architecture's professional culture that contribute to the discontentment of women architects. What emerges is that architecture as a profession is not exempt from exclusionary practices because of professional fraternisation and that the profession has for some time been in decline. While it has struggled because of its shift toward privatisation, medicine on the other hand has remained a more equitable and attractive profession for women and men to enter.

Many countries have progressively veered their school curriculum more towards an academic STEM (Science, Technology, Engineering, and Mathematics) subject career path with the Humanities increasingly being considered a less attractive option, although a focus on SHAPE (Social Sciences, Humanities and the Arts for People and the Economy) is offering some opposition. The reasons for STEM subjects being favoured are numerous and complex, although most relate to industries which are envisaged as having greater economic and social influence in the contemporary global marketplace. Most STEM subjects receive larger amounts of funding from the government to support the development of the sector – and this has increased further post-pandemic – as it is seen as more essential to developing the economic wealth and physical wellbeing of a nation. The battle to find a cure for the global pandemic or to be a technology giant in the global marketplace are commonly considered labours of greater value to their countries than endeavours without immediate practical, utilitarian deliverables that benefit the widest number of people in the world and the national economy. Architecture, rather than everyday building, is also considered an elite or luxury vocation. Another factor in choosing a STEM subject career path or not relates to gendered perception of a profession.

Regardless of recent advancements in gender parity at work in modern societies, when looking at the global workforce both sociologists and economists agree that "gender is linked to career outcomes." (Reskin and Bielby 2005, p. 71) As already discussed in Part 1 of this book, the sex differentiation, stratification, and stereotyping that develop through an individual's life construct gender identity. Gender identity in turn historically constructs a sexual division of labour and sex segregation of occupations and professions due to the association with the limits of each gender's 'social mobility.' (Kilby 1999, p. 84) Choosing to study a professional STEM or non-STEM subject at university versus working in an unaccredited design job in the creative industries at university involves choosing between forms of historically gendered or ungendered labour and relies on the exhibition of personal traits and characteristics historically aligned and suited to that type of work. Sexual division of labour also relates to the future relates to the wealth making potential of different professional careers.

American social scientist and economist, Gary Becker (1964, p. 114) writes in *Human Capital: A Theoretical and Empirical Analysis with Special Reference to Education* about 'the private gain from college' education for the individual and the monetary return of different kinds of education. Written over 50 years ago, the book presents a scientific study of the relationship between human capital and economic return, focusing on the gendering of labour inside and beyond the home and labour opportunities. Education has a fundamental effect on "future well-being" (Becker 1964, p. 1) through the potential to generate capital. Women and men have different capacities to make money through different gendered career choices and the inequality in ability to generate income from paid work for the educated and uneducated classes of women, more so than men, is typically heightened through family or care demands which contribute to greater work-life imbalance.

It is well known that "one of the most powerful ways of empowering women is through education." (Eswaran 2014, p. 14) "In the developed world, the gender gap in education is almost nonexistent [sic] in the present day." (Eswaran 2014, p. 15) As women are increasing their ability to accrue capital through acquiring higher levels of education, they are better enabling their 'economic well-being.' (Eswaran 2014, p. 2) Whether single, partnered, or married, women are increasingly detaching themselves from the unpaid domain of primarily domestic, household labour to become economically self-sufficient and independent. Curiously though, while women are entering higher education in greater numbers, gender and career choice/s remain stereotypically linked.

While creativity or artistic prowess are generally considered gender neutral according to some researchers (Clegg and Mayfield 1999, pp. 6–12; Clegg, Mayfield, and Trayhurn 1999; Conor, Gill, and Taylor 2015), prospective women and men students veer towards choosing different types of career paths in design in higher education. The reasons for choosing a particular design career are often based on "perceptions of dominant disciplinary discourse" (Satterfield et al. 2010) framed within the public cultural realm. For instance, the decision to study product and furniture design (where women were previously under-represented) versus fashion and jewellery (fields previously over-represented by women) "reproduces the stereotypical dualism whereby women are associated with the body and the decorative, and men with technology and the shaping of nature." (Clegg and Mayfield 1999, p. 3; Attfield 1989) Clegg and Mayfield (1999, p. 3) assert that "there is a complex relationship between disciplinary cultures and gender." Regardless of recent advancements, some professions are seen to be more gender-neutral and gender equitable than others.

As already discussed in Chapter 2, the 'creative class' (Florida 2004) builds creative industries linked to the creative economy. According to the British author, John Howkins (2001, pp. 88–117) the creative economy comprises advertising, architecture, art, crafts, design, fashion, film, music, performing arts, publishing, Research and Development (R&D), software, toys, games, television, radio, and video games. Most modern societies see the benefit of creative thinkers and inventors to the economy in terms of knowledge and potential income generation in the arts, culture, and technology. So, to enter into one design field rather than another, e.g., to become an industrial designer for Apple computers versus an architect for a large corporate practice, affects the individual's ability to find and sustain work, generate income, or establish a 'good' career. Then there are the differences between the personal traits and characteristics and ability to make independent wealth from choosing between university studies in the building and services industries, e.g., project management or real estate versus architecture.

The American real estate architect-developer, John Portman (in Portman and Barnett 1976, p. 4) notes that "The people that are attracted to the practice of architecture have quite different temperaments from those who are attracted to real estate, and the two professions are unreceptive to the subtleties of each other's work." While this held true some 50 years ago, the distance between architect and real-estate developer (who were in the main seen as ideological enemies) has, and continues to, diminish for those who see the economic potential of mixing the two types of work in one career, as will be discussed in Chapter 6. Choosing architecture over any other types of study depends on how attractive architecture is for the prospective student in relation to how it is seen favourably or not to the public as a profession, whether in decline or not (Roiphe 2016), whether it is considered gender inclusive, and the individual's gender and un/gendered work aspirations.

As an historically male-dominated profession, architecture has increasingly become the new choice by fathers and mothers for their daughters and by young women so that in most architecture schools nowadays student cohorts are roughly gender equal. The reasons for choosing an architectural education broadly parallel the reasons for choosing a career in design. Architecture is perceived by the public, and presented to them in the media, to be a creative, professional, and noble career. It is a discipline that carries with it an image of social esteem, societal contribution, and potential professional fame. In addition, it is regarded to be practical, profit making, and will lead to secure employment, regardless of gender. The latter is often the reason that some students choose it over studying, for instance, fine arts or art history. There is a public perception that architecture offers a less gender-specific career than for instance, interior design or engineering – operating somewhere in-between and around (what are perceived to be) female-dominated versus male-dominated careers respectively. It is also considered to be a job that can be practised from home, not only the office, thereby giving a sense of perceived workplace flexibility. Public perception suggests it is a career choice where 'You can have it all.'

Women and men of different ages are having diverse work-life experiences in comparison to one another because the forms of work-home life are multifarious, changing constantly in neoliberal 'liquid times.' The shifting demands on and expectations of women and men in the workplace and at home mean they are in a state of constant transition. Whether, and then when, a point of equilibrium is reached where gender, race, and class are no longer discriminatory factors is unknown. But many agree that a more demographically-diverse group of people studying architecture are better able to design more diversely-responsive architectures for a wider public of users. (Lokko 1999; Anthony 2001; Wilkins 2016) Still, once architecture is chosen as a career path, the choice of which way to study architecture –full-time, part-time, across industry and university as an apprenticeship or remotely, and where to study can influence, to differing degrees, the potential for lifelong success and wellbeing.

Choosing How and Where to be Bred as an Architect

Since education is the primary place in which one begins to accrue taste and judgement that can be mobilised later in life, the choice of what kind of architecture programme to study and where to study are fundamental to future career opportunities in relation to capital accumulation. Bourdieu (in Richardson ed. 1986, p. 243) defines three forms of capital. They are social capital – which builds social connections, contacts, and networks; economic capital – which can convert directly into money and private property ownership; and cultural capital – a form of acculturation which has the capacity to generate income through gaining educational qualifications. The three forms of capital are interdependent because there is a continual possibility of conversion of one form of capital into another.

Social capital is typically transferred through direct acquaintance. The close proximity between a master and pupil allows maximum capital transfer. There is a time–place phenomenon that determines whether someone in the network will have the opportunity to inherit social capital as it is not always guaranteed unless it becomes a direct association. However, if there is a time–place encounter between master and pupil, it can provide a student with fertile and infinite future opportunities. As Bourdieu (in Richardson ed. 1986, p. 249) notes; "The network of relationships is the product of investment strategies … aimed at establishing or reproducing social relationships that are directly usable in the short or long term." Capital becomes "accumulated labor [sic]… which, when appropriated on a private …, exclusive, basis …enables them to appropriate social energy in the form of reified or living labor. … It is what makes the games of society—not least, the economic game—something other than simple games of chance …." (Bourdieu in Richardson 1986, p. 241)

Bourdieu (in Richardson ed. 1986, p. 243) sees that schools and universities are the sites in which cultural capital is inherited and accumulated through in-person transmission. According to Harry Lou's (2003) book, *The Game of Life: How to Succeed in Real Life No Matter Where You Land*, one key target during university studies is the making of "new friends" – teachers or students in the same field – who become one's professional family. It is important during university years to meet work-related colleagues and make social network connections from which one can profit later, so Lou (2003, pp. 18, 19) says students should "… choose wisely," and this applies to university choice.

During architectural education, capital is mainly transferred through architectural educator–architectural student or master–pupil chains. As soon as one enters an architectural school, a student becomes part of an architectural family tree or architectural genealogy. Building upon the theory of social dynamics of intellectuals presented by sociologist, Randall Collins (1987), Garry Stevens (1998) contends that in the architectural intellectual field master–pupil chains are the main social mechanism and the most renowned intellectuals are in a greater number of chains. "Masters pass down cultural capital to their pupils, colleagues or rivals. The more eminent the master, the greater the capital that can be transmitted." (Stevens 1998, p. 155) The master–pupil chain has bearing on Bourdieu's (in Richardson ed. 1986, pp. 248–249) definition of social capital, which he defines as "the aggregate of the actual or potential resources which are linked … to membership in a group—which provides each of its members with … a 'credential' which entitles them to credit, in the various senses of the word." The successful transfer of social capital from master to pupil relies on close social proximity and professional socialising, but it is not possible for all pupils of great masters since there are only an available number of 'market opportunities' in any competitive field (Collins 1987, p. 48), as will be in discussed in the next chapter.

In the real game of an architectural university life the number of available choices to choose from depends on the quality of the university attended, its history, brand, architecture and campus design, online systems for teaching, and its staff and student community, both current and alumni. The most elite schools of architecture in the world have acculturated a more highly-regarded public image, mostly through their lengthier existence. The 'best' universities or highest class of architecture schools in the world are created by and create a pedigree class. For the students who are not accepted into or not interested in applying to an elite architecture school, other options exist to study architecture in schools considered of a lesser class higher education class. Making the choice to study a long degree like architecture, which does not give immediate or even sometimes long-term high remuneration in the workplace, can be a more difficult choice for a student that is less financially well off.

Unless there are architects in one's biological family or friendship network, capital is typically carried in architecture through architectural networks encountered during university and in professional practice. It is for this reason that many students prefer to apply to the best architecture schools in the world as their entry into professional life, both because of the lineages of teaching and that their future career potentially can be enhanced by the more powerful elite university networks. The kind of architecture programme chosen and where to study can create a similar potential for "cumulative advantage … [or] disadvantage" (Rank et al. 2014, p. 107) later in life as it is the case, pre-university.

While some of the canons of architectural education have endured "in design education since the École des Beaux Arts (School of Fine Arts) in Paris in the 1890s," the framing and enforcement of them varies depending on the ethos of each school (Henderson and Till, in Parnell and Sara eds. 2007, 'Foreword'). The most elite and reputable architecture schools have created brand identities renowned for contesting norms in and systems of administration commonly used in a 'traditional' architectural education. They are recognised to, and desirable within, the H.E. market because they aim to radically reinvent the discipline through innovation. This contrasts to schools of architecture that might be described as more traditional, where architecture managers and educators, in conjunction with professional regulatory bodies, obediently define the curriculum and employ audit systems of assessment that ensure quality and compliance by students to meet assessment criteria for real-world, vocational practice. Although there are exceptions, Architecture Professor Paolo Tombesi (in Deamer ed. 2016, p. 82) notes that, on the main, "discussions around work in architecture tend to fall into two separate domains: one concerned with the theoretical, socio-cultural definition of intellectual pursuit; the other preoccupied with the operative, managerial, and eventually (under-) remunerative aspects of the metier. The difference in focus implies a different framing of the architect as the subject at the centre of the analysis: individual political agency on the one side, service provider collective on the other." Still, the service provider model is becoming more dominant, particularly in neoliberal universities everywhere.

There is enormous competition for a student to be accepted into one of the 'best' architecture schools in the world, who conversely only choose students that they regard as exhibiting capital quality from which to build further capital. Choosing to study abroad – another option in the game – involves degrees of risk-taking but can contribute to future economic wellbeing in global practice. Living and tuition cost outlays, for short or long courses, are arguably less problematic for those with independent family wealth to support their studies.

For students who are unprepared or unable to undertake a conventional architecture course or are not financially independent or able to do so, architectural apprenticeships or practice-based courses which offer a combination of university education with on-the-job training can be an attractive choice after secondary school. Working in practice while studying encourages students to get into the labour market as soon as possible and is premised on "… increase[ing] … productivity by learning new skills and perfecting old ones while on the job." (Becker 1964, p. 9) While paid apprenticeships and internships offer a foot in the door of industry, architectural apprentices or interns can sometimes be susceptible to exploitation. Women or men students who need to support themselves or others financially while they study can find this route attractive, sometimes more by necessity than choice.

In many Western and Eastern countries, women are now undertaking a vocational architectural education at university – including an undergraduate and postgraduate, Masters qualification – at mostly an equal or greater rate than men. When undertaken full-time, architectural studies typically take five to six years, with most universities requiring some practical work experience in an architectural office as an additional short spell. While architecture schools use their own internal assessments on gender split and recruitment, there has been little academic research done to assess how a prospective student's gender, race, and class influences how they choose their path of study or the conditions in which they are being offered a place or not. Nor has there been much research on the way the interview process might be affected by the interviewee and interviewer's performance or their respective gender, race/ethnicity, class, or age.

When playing the game of architecture, the choice (or ability to make a choice) as to which school of architecture/university one attends can have significant ramifications on the model of labour the student enacts both in university and afterwards, and can affect the limits of post-university graduation and long-term career ambitions. If a student is accepted, the school of architecture and university they are accepted into, and the stage of life they are at, frames expectations of their performativity as an architecture student. So, after choosing to study architecture, what knowledge and skills are required to navigate an architectural education in the world university focused on 'academic capitalism'? (Slaughter and Leslie 1997) How does the architectural design studio and curriculum acculturate architects? How is neoliberal entrepreneurism and competition heightened during an architectural education? "How do educational systems [in architecture] generate, reinforce or alter gender [race and class] divisions and what, if anything, should [and can] be done?" (Shaw 1996, p. 3) What are the mechanisms of stratification in architectural H.E. today? (Shavit, Arum, and Gomoran eds. with Menahem, 2007)

In the next chapter pedagogical practice is examined in response to these questions. While most people enter architectural studies to become a practicing architect, some choose the path of architectural educator instead. Chapter 5 discusses playing the game of life as an architectural student and architectural educator working in the neoliberal university.

Notes

1 Due to the success of the first documentary, Apted re-interviewed the children at seven-year intervals to follow their life paths.
2 Orphan, Symon Basterfield, who was from a Children's home, was the only mixed-race participant in the programme. Basterfield received no formal education.
3 The *Seven Up!* boys who went to university include John Brisby (later QC), Andrew Brackfield, Charles Furneaux, William Nicholas (Nick) Hitchon, Peter Davies, Neil Hughes, and Bruce Balden. Out of the girls, Jackie Bassett, Susan (Sue) Davis, and Lynn Johnson were all from the poor working-class end of East London, attended comprehensive or grammar schools, and did not go on to university; Suzanne (Suzy) Dewey (formerly Lusk) was from a wealthy family, attended an independent London day school, and went on to marry a solicitor but did not attend university.
4 The June 2017 board game version and the July 2016 interactive digital version of *The Game of Life* are played by children as young as five years old but are marketed by Hasbro at girls and boys eight+ years and older. Whereas once the game was pitched at an adult market, the 2017 and 2016 game versions are designed for children to play with each other or with other members of their family. In this example, children are making individual or influenced game life choices much earlier than before.
5 They also have an architect-nephew.
6 Instead, Simon Smithson has worked for Richard Rogers Partnership since 1991. He became a partner of Rogers Stirk Habour + Partners LLP in 2011.

References

Apted, M. Dir. and Almond, P. Dir. 1964. *Seven Up!* Granada Television: Manchester. Documentary 40 mins.

Attfield, J. 1989. FORM/female FOLLOWS FUNCTION/male: Feminist Critiques of Design. In ed. J. A. Walker. *Design History and the History of Design*. London: Pluto, pp. 199–225.

Anthony, K. H. 2001. *Designing for Diversity: Gender, Race and Ethnicity in the Architectural Profession*. Illinois, United States: University of Illinois Press.

Bauman, Z. 2007. *Liquid Times: Living in an Age of Uncertainty*. Cambridge: Polity Press.

Becker, G. S. 1964. *Human Capital: A Theoretical and Empirical Analysis with Special Reference to Education*. New York: National Bureau of Economic Research. Distributed New York; London: Columbia University Press.

Blau, J. 1987. *Architects and Firms: A Sociological Perspective on Architectural Practices*. Cambridge, Mass.: The MIT Press.

Bledstein, B. J. 1976. *The Culture of Professionalism: The Middle Class and the Development of Higher Education in America*. New York: Norton.

Bourdieu, P. 1986. The Forms of Capital. In *Handbook of Theory and Research for the Sociology of Education*, Richardson, J. ed. New York: Greenwood Press, pp. 241–258. First published in 1983.

Bourdieu, P. and Nice, R. (Trans). 1996. *Distinction: A Social Critique of the Judgement of Taste*. Cambridge, Mass.: Harvard University Press. First published in 1984.

Brown, W. 2015. *Undoing the Demos: Neoliberalism's Stealth Revolution*. New York: Zone Books.

Cheek, N. N. and Schwartz, B. 2016. On the Meaning and Measurement of Maximization, *Judgment and Decision Making*, 11 (2), (2016 March 01): 126–146.

Chodorow, N. 1978. *The Reproduction of Mothering*. Berkeley: University of California Press.

Clark, G. K. 1962. *The Making of Victorian England*. Cambridge: Harvard University Press.

Clegg, S. and Mayfield, W. 1999 (Autumn). Gendered by Design: How Women's Place in Design is Still Defined by Gender, *Design Issues*, 15 (3), (Autumn 1999): 3–16.

Clegg, S., Mayfield, W. and Trayhurn, D. 1999. Disciplinary Discourses: A Case Study of Gender in Information Technology and Design Courses, *Gender and Education*, 11 (1): 43–55.

Collins, R. 2019. *The Credential Society: An Historical Sociology of Education and Stratification*. New York: Columbia University Press.

Collins, R. 1987. A Micro-Macro Theory of Intellectual Creativity: The Case of German Idealist Philosophy. In *Sociological Theory*, 5: 47–69.

Conor, B., Gill, R., and Taylor, S. 2015. Gender and Creative Labour, *The Sociological Review*, 63: Issue Supplement S1 (2015 May): 1–22.

Cooke, R. 2013. *Her Brilliant Career: Ten Extraordinary Women of the Fifties*. London: Virago Press.

Egerton, M. and Halsey, A. H. 1993. Trends in Social Class and Gender in Access to Higher Education in Britain, *Oxford Review of Education*, 19: 183–196.

Eswaran, M. 2014. *Why Gender Matters in Economics*. Princeton: Princeton University Press.

Farr, F. 1962. *Frank Lloyd Wright: A Biography*. London: Jonathan Cape.

Fine-Davis, M. 2004. *Fathers and Mothers: Dilemmas of the Work-Life Balance: A Comparative Study in Four European Countries*. Dordecht; Boston: Kluwer Academic Publishers.

Florida, R. 2004. *The Rise of the Creative Class: And How it's Transforming Work, Leisure, Community and Everyday Life*. New York: Basic Books.

Fowler, B. and Wilson, F. 2004. Women Architects and Their Discontents, *Sociology*, 38 (1), (2004 Feb 01): 101–119.

Gutman, R. 1988. *Architectural Practice: A Critical View*. Princeton: Princeton Architectural Press.

Henderson, G. and Till, J. 2007. Foreword. In. Parnell, R. and Sara, R. eds. with Doidge, C. and Parsons, M. *The Crit: An Architecture Student's Handbook*. Amsterdam; Boston; London; New York: Elsevier.

Howkins, J. 2001. *The Creative Economy: How People Make Money from Ideas*. London: Allen Lane.

Kaiser, S., Ringlstetter, M.J., Eikhof, D.R., and Pina e Cunha, M. eds. 2011. *Creating Balance? International Perspectives on the Work-Life Integration of Professionals*. Berlin Heidelberg: Springer-Verlag.

Kilby, M. 1999. *Stratification and Differentiation*. London: Macmillan Press Ltd.

Kohlstedt, S. G., and Longino, H. E. 1997. *Women, Gender, and Science: New Directions.* Chicago: Osiris, University of Chicago Press.

Lokko, L. 1999. *White Papers, Black Marks: Architecture, Race, Culture.* London: Continuum International Publishing Group Ltd.

Lou, H. 2003. *The Game of Life: How to Succeed in Real Life No Matter Where You Land.* Philadelphia; London: Running.

Portman, J. and Barnett, J. 1976. *The Architect as Developer.* New York; St. Louis: McGraw-Hill Book Company.

Rank, M. R., Hirschl, T. A., and Foster, K. A. 2014. *Chasing the American Dream; Understanding what Shapes our Fortunes.* Oxford: Oxford University Press.

Reay, D., Davies, J., David, M., and Ball, S. J. 2001. Choices of Degree or Degrees of Choice? Class, 'Race' and the Higher Education Choice Process, *Sociology*, 35 (4), (2001 Nov): 855–874.

Reay, D., David, M. E., and Ball, S. 2005. *Degrees of Choice: Social Class, Race and Gender in Higher Education*, 2nd edition. Stoke-on-Trent: Trentham Books.

Reskin, B. and Bielby, D. 2005. A Sociological Perspective on Gender and Career Outcomes, *Journal of Economic Perspectives*, 19 (1): 71–86.

Rodd, M., Reiss, M., and Mujtaba, T. 2014. Qualified, But Not Choosing STEM at University: Unconscious Influences on Choice of Study, *Canadian Journal of Science, Mathematics and Technology Education*, 14 (4): 330–345.

Roiphe, R. 2016. The Decline of Professionalism. *Georgetown Journal of Legal Ethics*, 29, (2016 July 07), NYLS Legal Studies Research Paper No. 2806611.

Sarfatti Larson, M. 2012. *The Rise of Professionalism: Monopolies of Competence and Sheltered Markets.* Piscataway, New Jersey: Transaction Publishers.

Sarfatti Larson, M. 1977. *The Rise of Professionalism: A Sociological Analysis.* Berkeley: University of California Press.

Salecl, R. 2010. *Choice.* London: Profile Books.

Salecl, R. 2009. Society of Choice, *Differences*, 20 (1): 157–180.

Satterfield, D., Kang, S. R., Ladjahasan, N., Quam, A., and Bjorngaard, B. 2010. A Study on Design Careers and the Impact of Gender, *Design Research Society 2010 Conference, Design & Complexity*, 7–9 July 2010. Montreal, Canada.

Secrest, M. 1998. *Frank Lloyd Wright: A Biography.* Chicago: University of Chicago Press.

Schwartz, B. 2016. *The Paradox of Choice: Why More is Less.* New York: Ecco. First published in 2005.

Schwartz, B. 2005. The Paradox of Choice. TedGlobal X 2005 talk. July 2005. https://www.ted.com/talks/barry_schwartz_the_paradox_of_choice?language=en, Accessed November 06, 2023.

Schwartz, B. 2000. Self-Determination: The Tyranny of Freedom, *The American Psychologist*, 55 (1), (2008 January): 79–81.

Schwartz, B., Ward, A., Monterosso, J., Lyubomirsky, S., White, K., and Lehman, D. R. 2002. Maximising Versus Satisficing: Happiness is a Matter of Choice, *Journal of Personality and Social Psychology*, 83 (5): 1178–1197.

Sennett, R. 1998. *The Corrosion of Character: The Personal Consequences of Work in the New Capitalism.* New York; London: Norton.

Sennett, R. and Cobb, J. 1977. *The Hidden Injuries of Class.* Cambridge: Cambridge University Press.

Shavit, Y., Arum, R., and Gomoran, A. eds. with Menahem, G. 2007. *Stratification in Higher Education: A Comparative Study.* Stanford, California: Stanford University Press.

Shaw, J. 1995. *Education, Gender and Anxiety*. London: Taylor & Francis.

Sharpe, S. 1994. *Fathers and Daughters*. London: Routledge.

Slaughter, S. and Leslie, L. L. 1997. *Academic Capitalism: Politics, Policies and the Entrepreneurial University.* Baltimore; London: John Hopkins University.

Standing, G. 2016. *The Precariat: The New Dangerous Class*. London: Bloomsbury Academic.

Stevens, G. 1998. *The Favored Circle: The Social Foundation of Architectural Distinction.* Cambridge, Mass.; London, England: The MIT Press.

Tombesi, P. 2016. More for Less: Architectural Labor and Design Productivity. In P. Deamer ed., *The Architect as Worker: Immaterial Labor, the Creative Class, and the Politics of Design*. London: Bloomsbury Academic, pp. 82–102.

Webster, H. 2010. *Bourdieu for Architects*. London: Routledge.

Webster, H. 2005. The Architectural Review: A Study of Ritual, Acculturation and Reproduction in Architectural Education, *Arts and Humanities in Higher Education*, 4 (3), (2005 Oct 01): 265–282.

Wilkins, C. 2016. *Diversity among Architects*. London: Routledge.

5

ACADEMIC CAPITALISM AND ARCHITECTURAL EDUCATION

FIGURE 5.1 Schools US, 01 March 1946: UCLA students lying around on the campus lawn. Photograph by Ralph Crane/The LIFE Images Collection via Getty Images/Getty.

DOI: 10.4324/9781351199834-7

Changes to the Life of a University Student

In *The Game of Life: How to Succeed in Real Life no Matter where you Land*, Harry Lou (2003, pp. 15–29) discusses the potential consequences of choosing to go to college or university. According to Lou (2003, p. 15) the college path requires making the choice to "borrow... money if you decide to choose pursuing a degree in HE or go out in the world of business." Lou admits this is a gamble made on the desire to enter the money-making world sooner rather than later. "In real life though, such decisions are often made on economic status, family values, and how well you managed high school." (Lou 2003, p. 16) Lou (2003, p. 16) explains that for those who choose the university path, the goal is to "graduate with the education you want, but also with your debt in check." If you are fortunate to be granted a scholarship (in the board game or in real life) your debts can be reduced. Having a part-time job to support yourself through your studies can alleviate debt accumulation but can also create more time pressures. The discussion about the cost of Higher Education and the subsequent debt one can or will incur has become an increasingly important factor in the decision to choose to go to architecture school, and more so since the neoliberalisation of the university sector from the 1970s onwards that has transformed universities more toward businesses.

In order to provide context for the business-oriented university, I will briefly outline the fundamental changes Margaret Thatcher and Ronald Reagan made to neoliberalise the H.E. sectors in the U.K. and U.S.A. The governmental funding changes have shifted the 'premodern or medieval university' (Foucault 2002) to the world university and are accompanied by the transforming of *homo academicus* (Bourdieu 2019) more toward *homo oeconomicus.* (Foucault 2008) This has moved academic life away from being slow and contemplative. (Figure 5.1)

As already discussed in Chapter 1, Thatcher and Reagan were both intrinsically opposed to supporting H.E. intellectualism. They opposed a university culture that operated as an 'ivory tower.' Arguably, Thatcher's dislike was primarily directed to elitist education and resulted in part from her experience of studying at the University of Oxford. In contrast, Reagan's antagonism was directed toward the way in which freer, more left-wing universities in the U.S. nurtured university students who were anti-war activists, protesting against America's involvement in the Vietnam War. While Thatcher and Reagan wanted university cultures to change for different reasons, they both agreed that business culture should be absorbed into the everyday life of university students well before university graduates entered the workplace.

In *Margaret Thatcher: Power and Personality*, Jonathan Aitken (2014, p. 40) notes that Thatcher, then Margaret Roberts, was unhappy from the outset as a student at the University of Oxford, finding it 'cold and strangely forbidding,' to quote her. (Thatcher 1995, p. 35) He claims her dislike was because "she was patronized [sic] by the dons and smarter students at Somerville [in particular a Cheltenham clique of wealthier students]. She was [also] unlucky in love." (Aitken 2014, p. 41) Pauline Cowan (in Aitken 2014, p. 44), who was at Somerville College with Thatcher, recalls how Thatcher's ambition to "set her cap at a young man with money and a title [Lord Craigmyle]" fell through because "'his mother couldn't stand her." Overall "She [Thatcher] was out of sorts with Oxford, and … her personality jarred with it. This was an antipathy that later became mutual.…" (Aitken 2014, pp. 40, 41) In 1985, Thatcher was refused an honorary degree (Aitken 2014, p. 41) and even the Principal of Somerville College, Oxford, Dame Janet Vaughan (in Campbell 2008, p. 62) did not hesitate to publicise Thatcher's academic and social mediocrity describing her as "a perfectly good second-class chemist, a beta chemist" and not "very interesting to talk to, except as a conservative."

Once in politics, through her influential changes to education, Thatcher made ideological enemies at the University of Oxford because of her "ambition … to make schools and universities responsive to the demands of the free-market economy." (Atlas 1988, unpaginated) Jim Reid, a tutor in German at St. John's College was an active opponent to Thatcher's importation of "the vocabulary of business to Oxford" which redefined "Professors … [as] 'senior management,' [and] Government subsidies … [as] 'contracts'" and which invaded the 'ivory tower' with "Enterprise Culture." (Atlas 1988, unpaginated) As a politician managing the country, however, Thatcher's changes, including the dismantling of student unions, occurred with or without the consent of university dons. Regardless of student protests about student unions in the U.K., Thatcher began a process of academic monetisation that Blair continued.

In the case of Reagan, his personal antagonism was also toward the 'ivory tower,' with Regan identifying Clark Kerr, President of the University of California, as an ideological opponent. Tracey Daugherty (2015, p. 220) writes that:

> In November 1966, at a Los Angeles dinner honoring [sic] the governor-elect [Reagan,]… H. R. Haldeman, later Richard Nixon's chief of staff, toasted Reagan as "the man who will bring a big breath of fresh air to the university." Seated at one of the tables, Clark Kerr knew right away that one of the new governor's first acts would be to fire him as university president. Reagan saw him as weak for not punishing student protestors more harshly. Shortly after dinner, one of the regents whispered to Kerr … "Before this is all over, you're going to be covered in blood."

Ironically, Kerr had enemies within the academy too because he was seen to have advocated a conservative government's over-taking of the American university for economic gain. First published in 1963 from a speech delivered at the University of Harvard, *The Uses of the University* sets out Kerr's (2001) factual, and therefore perceived as non-critical, history of the modern university, which other academics considered advocated it as a "factory" that served industry interest groups and government at the expense of students and higher education. "The massive infusion of federal research funds during and after World War II ... fuelled [sic] the rise of what Kerr called the 'multiversity.' The university, he said, was no longer cloistered, but now central to society, 'a prime instrument of national purpose'" (Rosenfeld 2013, unpaginated) that was driven by the expansion of a knowledge economy.

Regardless of their political persuasion, academic intellectuals who objected to Thatcher and Reagan's changes to the university as a research university working for industry (Menand, Reitter, and Wellmon eds. 2017) were powerless. French sociologist, Pierre Bourdieu (2019, p. 38) saw that university academics were a "dominated faction of the dominant class" who struggled to make a place for themselves in a ruling class defined by the economic capital of the bourgeoisie. Not only had the uses of the university shifted toward market orientation, the very purpose of the university had ideologically changed broadly from non-materialistic to materialistic motives.

In the premodern or historical university, Michel Foucault contends people's limits were defined in relation to God or outside the living world and so materialism was not a central feature of education. Education was concerned with teaching scholars to be all-round contributors to society for civic betterment. For Foucault, after modernity, people's limits became defined within the living world and the role of scholars changed to be gatekeepers framing historical processes in relation to society through the scholar's frame of virtues and knowledge. "The state is called upon to support such institutions, and it should not expect direct economic returns, for the modern university is situated above and beyond such immediate concerns." (Allen 2011, p. 369) However, with neoliberal governance in many countries shifting away from welfare provision, universities, acting like large corporations, have had to operate in a competitive global marketplace adopting innovative entrepreneurial strategies to increase recruitment, both nationally and internationally.

Since the introduction of university tuition fees, choosing where to study a long professional course like architecture requires careful research into the options. For instance, because state funding was withdrawn in 1998, the majority of universities in the United Kingdom require students to pay, often substantial tuition fees, with international students paying substantially more than domestic students. Most universities worldwide compete in the international university marketplace to recruit and feed their architectural Higher Education system. In an increasingly competitive world H.E. sector, many formerly public universities have had to focus on marketisation (or increased market and market-like behaviour).

Many modern universities take their lead from, and become intertwined with, entrepreneurial business to create the entrepreneurial university for business. Like any entrepreneurial business, the entrepreneurial university aims to spread "throughout the world (encouraging excellence and innovation in an environment of mutual competitive rivalry)" in order to "enhance [...] their own institution" in the "global university space." (Allen 2011, p. 390) Creativity in an academic arena is co-opted by neoliberalism for university and industry revenue making. Architectural researchers and educators who are innovators and who sit comfortably in Richard Florida's 'creative class' (Biernacki in Deamer ed. 2016, p. 40) become a means through which capital and labour in the university are commodified.

Sheila Slaughter and Larry Leslie (1997, p. 4) note that during the industrial revolution, academics were able to "position themselves between capital and labor [sic], protecting themselves from the harsh discipline of the market." However 'academic capitalism' (Slaughter and Leslie 1997) – coined from 'academic capital' in Bourdieu's (1986) *Distinction: A Social Critique of the Judgment of Taste* – has dramatically changed the nature of academic labour during the late 20th century. Since then, "changes in funding [have] work[ed] to bring the university and its faculty in line with economic production and the managerial revolution taking place as a global economy develops." (Gibbons 1994 in Slaughter and Leslie 1997, p. 2)

Universities roughly follow the classification of contemporary workers set out by Guy Standing (2016, pp. 8–9), in which they progress hierarchically in level top to bottom from the elite, 'salatariat,' 'profician,' manual worker, precariat, and unemployed. In H.E, the university elite are Vice Chancellors (in the U.K.) or University Presidents (in the U.S.) for example, whose pay can or cannot match that of the corporate private sector depending on if they are managing a private university or not. The university 'salatariat' who Standing (2016, pp. 8–9) defines as being those who are in stable full-time work aspiring to become university elite include Deans, Provosts, Professors, and academics on full-time permanent salary contracts with management responsibilities. Alongside the university 'salariat' are university 'proficians' who "live with the expectation and desire to move around, without an impulse for long-term, full-time employment in a single enterprise. The 'standard employment relationship' is not for them." (Standing 2016, p. 9) These academics are typically on full-time or part-time contracts, but often are not tied to working at their university if a better offer comes along. Underneath these four groups are a university's working class who work on the teaching shop floor, and who with the loss of labour regulation is a growing university 'precariat' of workers on casual contracts or who are unemployed, often with multiple degree qualifications. (Standing 2016, p. 9) As managers and their management efficiencies drive a university's economic business health, their level in the pyramidal university management structure has the highest reputational and economic capital and with it influence on changes in the working conditions and lives of educators and students. Decisions such as deploying New Public Management (NPM) in a university has a major influence.

In the U.K. and Australia, the NPM approach was developed in the 1980s in order to make public services more like businesses so as to improve efficiency and productivity using private sector management-models. The implementation of the NPM approach means that governments require universities to fund and manage their own budgets, transacting according to a neoliberal system of consuming and producing students, staff, knowledge, and research for the purpose of improving national economies through continuous growth from the engine of entrepreneurial innovation. The demands on well-established, renowned, and reputationally well-branded universities, who have more revenue streams available to them, differ in comparison to newer, less renowned universities who are in a formative stage of university brand definition.

While this is a universal phenomenon experienced across all disciplines in the neoliberal H.E. sector, here focus is on the impact academic capitalism has had on architectural education and the bodies of architecture students and educators as products of the managerial H.E system. It focuses on the link between academic capitalism, the development of a particular set of professional architectural skills, and employability. It notes the centrality of *homo academicus* producing an increasing numbers of productive *homo oeconomicus* architects whose creativity is nurtured in order to drive competitive entrepreneurship after graduation and with it, potential nation state economic wealth. It identifies how an initially male-centred model of architect defines and limits the model of architectural education. The historical model of architectural education does not always meet the demographic limits of other identities of students and educators interested in other game goals beyond corporate practice. An increased focus on productivity within the university has altered labour enacted within it so that it has dramatically sped up. Critics such as Pier Vittorio Aureli (in Deamer 2015) and James Mayo (1991) have compared universities, or the architecture schools within them, to factories both in their spatial design and modes of production.

Here the place of production (the university at which one chooses to study architecture), the production process (acquiring an architectural education), and products/subjects (architectural students and educators) are discussed because they tie into processes of product/subject reduction, abstraction, and standardisation. For this reason, in choosing to study architecture at university it is important to understand its interior processes of pedagogical production and consumption.

Architectural Design Studio, the Curriculum, and Education Factories

Whether in the U.K. or France, university students have been protesting against changes in university education since the 1960s. From the May 1960 protests in Paris to the ongoing protests across the U.K. during the 1960s (Figure 5.2) onwards, university life has changed beyond recognition. In architectural education, where studio culture was previously artistic in orientation, the industrialised lifestyle of an architectural student and educator nowadays has little resemblance to the first architecture school formed in the 17th century.

Architectural historian, Alexander Griffin (2019) claims the first institution to be devoted exclusively to the study of architecture was the Académie d'Architecture (or the Académie Royale d'Architecture). It was founded by Louis XIV in 1671 to create architects who would decorate his royal apartments at Versailles, but was

FIGURE 5.2 Student demonstrators march through Clifton to Bristol University's Senate house administrative building at the start of a protest sit-in that began on the 5 December 1968 and continued for 11 days. The students were campaigning for a greater say in the running of the university. They also wanted the university's students' union to be opened up to students from other educational establishments in the city. Photograph: Tony Byers/ Alamy Stock Photo. Date taken: June 23, 2016.

abolished in 1673 due to the Revolution. While it was only short-lived, the Académie d'Architecture was resurrected with the formation of the multidisciplinary learned society, the Académie des Beaux-Arts or the Academy of Fine Arts. Created in 1816 in Paris, the Académie des Beaux-Arts merged the Académie d'Architecture, the Académie de Musique (Academy of Music, founded in 1669), and the Académie de Peinture et de Sculpture (Academy of Painting and Sculpture, founded 1648). In 1863, it became the École des Beaux-Arts, a name granted by Napoleon III to give the school independence from the government. Women were accepted to study at the École des Beaux-Arts in early 1897.

The Palais des Études or Palace of Studies in the École des Beaux-Arts was designed around a gallery of objects in an artist's studio space and allowed architecture students to study, through hand drawing, copies of antiques, architectural patterns, etc. The curriculum was split between the study of painting, sculpture, and architecture and focused on Ancient Greek and Roman Classical art and design. Students were required to complete a design competition for the *Grand Prix de Rome* for which scholarships to study in Rome were awarded. The pattern of an architect slowly working for unlimited, long hours as an artist in their studio space was nurtured during this time.

It was also at the École des Beaux-Arts that the concept of working *en charrette* emerged. *Charrette* in French means 'chariot' or 'cart' and *en charrette* means to work 'in the cart.' (Bonda 2007, p. 29) This is because it was common at the end of the term for architecture students at the École to work day and night right up to the deadline, when a cart would come to collect their models and drawings for review. The term *charrette* remains in usage today in the architectural design studio and is tied to working intensely.

Still today, the design studio is a critical space of pedagogical production, not only because it puts students and their educators in proximity with one another, but also because it consumes most of their time in any architectural education. Its effects on the bodies of architectural workers in the university has been heighted by the neoliberalisation of H.E. and has been described as 'the elephant in the room' of architectural education. (Troiani 2021) In virtually all reputable architecture schools, design studio is most valued because it is a form of "tacit-learning-in-action" (Schön 1983) that involves practice-based learning. It is one platform through which esteemed academics can identify potentially pedigree future architects. A design studio is still typically led by a studio 'master' (who can be female or male). That studio lead collaborates with another studio tutor or other studio tutors under them, with equal or less teaching experience. Design studio tutors were always male–male couplings, but have transitioned to male–female or female–female teams, the latter of which is slowly increasing. In more avant-garde schools of architecture, the lead tutor or two main tutors establish a focus of architectural design study and practice through a self-defined Studio Brief, which is used as a framework through which to teach and assess each student's design response to it. Design tutoring done by early career academics – female and male – allows them to work part-time or casually in order to share childcare labour and/or supplement their income, which comes from working outside the university in architectural practice or elsewhere. If they enjoy the experience, casual tutors can become more and more embedded within the school, increasing the time they are involved in teaching. If their practice work becomes (financially) healthier or working for the university becomes financially unviable for them they will typically opt out of studio teaching. Most experienced design studio teachers or teaching couplings that are more established carry more prestige or capital and are valued more because their experience offers recognised benefits to the institution. Prospective students are more likely to have to compete to be accepted to work with these elite studio teachers.

Unlike lecture courses that are delivered to a larger group of students where it is less possible for educators to get to know students personally, design studio is taught to small groups of students even if there is a large student body in the year. The more prestigious schools limit their intakes and ensure staff–student ratios are more balanced. Studio working relationships are notoriously close and personal. When students are given the option to choose their studio educators, preference favours the tutor/s who students deem more suitable to work with, is more experienced, or to whom the tutor's studio theme they are more attracted. Familiarity or reciprocity of architectural ambitions manifests differently for female and male students who identify diversely with different female or male tutors. Historical research suggests that the most powerful genealogical lineages in architecture result from identity reciprocity and shared politics through close friendship. (Troiani 2005)

However, while architecture schools and design studios were formerly small in number, economic imperatives have forced many to increase their student numbers and model of production. On this front, referring to Foucault, Aureli (in Deamer 2015, p. 107) notes the effects of industrialisation and economisation on human labour in the 19th century typology of the American factory. Coinciding with the factory mass production practices outside the university, Aureli (in Deamer 2015, p. 111) explains "with the advent of mass education, universities were designed as factories whose goal was to produce not goods but subjects." Unlike the production of commodities outside the university where the product is separated from the subjects who produced it, in neoliberal architectural education "knowledge production precludes detaching the commodity from life itself... [so that] university students learn to live, network and compete. ... The university becomes an edufactory empowered by the mass production of subjects ready to be implanted into the increasingly precarious conditions of work." (Aureli in Deamer 2015, p. 112) The analogy of the university as a factory for education is analysed here in terms of the ability of architecture edufactories to profit.

Mayo (1991, p. 81) explains that "Operating like a factory has economically served architecture schools moderately well in the past." Unlike a liberal arts education where the type of job one will get is less certain, architecture remains an attractive choice because it is professionally accredited and offers job prospects.

Due to its popularity as a professional career choice, many architecture schools (like business faculties) are seen as parts of the university that can expand production. In order to create new markets for architectural education factories, the number of undergraduate and postgraduate students has increased dramatically in many universities worldwide, because the market has been opened up due to changes made by governments so that student numbers are uncapped. Governmental changes to the university model for self-economic management and recruitment has altered the numbers of students entering architectural H.E., sometimes at a disproportionate ratio to architecture teaching staff. Changes to funding can affect student–staff teaching ratios and so many universities, like commercial businesses, propose other more economically efficient ways to produce graduates. Neoliberal-driven universities worldwide are devising new strategies to be more productive while lowering their costs of production.

Some schools have set up new courses online with little or no direct teaching contact time (diminishing or obliterating the role of the educator), or have established architecture courses in other countries that capture new markets, attracting undergraduate and graduate programmes into, or midway into, their programmes in the U.K., U.S., or Australia to name but a few. This is done through offering an architecture degree from two universities rather than one – much like the two for one model that is used to incentivise buying in a supermarket generally. Summer courses and workshops that students pay for in addition to their tuition fees, or that recruit new students, are increasingly run during non-term or semester teaching time so as to optimise space usage in the edufactory. The shift to two shorter semesters rather than three terms, or proposals to graduate from an undergraduate architecture programme in a shorter time for a cheaper fee (three years compressed into two years for instance) means less architectural tuition is required to deliver the same degree. Some new architecture programmes offer architectural education divided between the university and the architectural office as an apprenticeship, thereby reducing what the university needs to offer on its site and preparing the student for faster entry into employment through on-the-job-training. Often supported by government grants, these on-the-job training degrees are at little or no cost to the students to elect to study as apprentices. The benefits of these types of education streamlining vary from discipline to discipline but in architecture, with an already intensely pressured and full programme of study at undergraduate and graduate level, compression of programme time can add pressure to the system of production in the architectural edufactory. This situation has emerged in part because non-academic business managers are increasingly encouraged to take on leadership roles in universities rather than employ managers or leaders who are academics and researchers within the university school or faculty itself.

In order to increase revenue NPM university administrators (often with no connection with the disciplines they are managing) "work with the mentality of the managerial class" (Mayo 1991, p. 81) to increase student numbers through sourcing new national and international markets and changing the demographic of their academic workforce. In some countries, architecture academics that teach are morphing from a workforce of predominantly full-time or tenured experts into a largely part-time, casual, temporary (on-demand hourly paid 'precariat' class) staff that teach design studios or deliver lectures and seminars with fewer workplace benefits for job security and progression. Academic staff of all levels often work many more hours than they are remunerated because the machinations of the university demands more productivity from them. The job description for working in academia can be limitless, with an infinite number of tasks requiring to be done outside 'normal' contracted workhours in order to deliver prescribed daily work outputs. Casual, temporary, and hourly-paid staff often accept a contract with fewer benefits and a shorter length of appointment because it offers them, in the short term, entry into the academic world, a rate of pay (comparable or higher to the income that they are making in practice) and a supplementary income to their practice day job, and intellectual stimulation (which they might be not be getting in a practice that is driven solely on selling and building their designs with no connection to the pursuit of wider social, cultural, or political issues relating to architectural design). Casual, temporary, and hourly-paid staff see that this foot-in-the door approach can, in the long term, increase their reputational capital. This neoliberal careerist mindset seeks to take advantage of any and every opportunity in the architectural market to increase capital – economic, social, and reputational.

To quote Wendy Brown (2015, p. 198), "Younger faculty, raised on neoliberal careerism, are generally unaware that there could be alternative academic purposes and practices to those organized [sic] by a neoliberal table of values." Their labour exploitation is a key way in which schools of architecture justify their 'bang for buck' or cost-to-benefit ratio. It is becoming increasingly common that when professors or other full-time staff leave or retire they are often replaced with staff without equivalent qualifications for cost saving reasons and asked to do the same job. While the university gains from its economically-rational business model, there can be detrimental effects on the quality of teaching delivered to students. Still, this is camouflaged because the reason for an architectural education, in many neoliberal universities, is no longer directed solely to producing professionals committed to enhancing civic life (although some practices can use this as a selling point), but instead are produced to feed industry.

An architectural education in most schools of architecture nowadays focuses on the vocational goal of making students immediately employable, efficient 'factory workers' after graduation who are hardworking and productive. Free student labour used in 'live projects' for outside clients in architecture schools, seen by some as exploitative, is viewed by others as beneficial, even essential, to student learning. On the teaching shop floor in mostly non-elite schools of architecture, areas of the architecture curriculum – its liberal arts and humanities aspects, namely history and theory – that are deemed to be less obviously or directly connected with architectural business can be devalued under academic capitalism. In these architecture schools, design, technical and design science, and technology as practice-based skills that enhance revenue-generating productivity in students are given equal, sometimes greater value because they increase the chances of employability and can be seen to contribute more clearly to industry and commerce. This can have a detrimental effect on architectural education, practice, and the products of architecture because a skew towards practice-centred skills can disable a graduate's ability to be critical about architecture's cultural and social contribution, with economic agendas foregrounded.

In an entrepreneurial university environment, students are encouraged to gain employment in a firm or to start their own architectural practice as soon as possible, sometimes without having developed their own architectural position, slowly and steadily over years of practice mentoring. There is also the more business-oriented tangent that has emerged recently where one trains as an architect to become a consultant whose rate of pay is higher than that of a salaried architect. Alternatively, because of the low rate of pay in the profession in many countries (worse for women than for men at the time of writing this book), some students are veering towards starting their own entrepreneurial business that is not in architecture but which is in a related field such as a visualisation company, photography or graphic design company, to name but a few. Graduates can use their visual representation training in architecture to advertise the architecture of other larger corporate architecture practices to potentially generate more economic capital. Women architects are very slowly entering these tangential disciplinary fields. This creates a division of labour in the architectural production process prioritising the aesthetic architectural image for advertising, selling, or winning jobs rather than develop the material, social, and cultural products of architecture.

The university's administratively-heavy methods of assessment have also followed neoliberal quantitative, checking systems used in manufacturing. Mike Laurence (2009, unpaginated) argues that, "the university, like the hospital or the prison, can be understood as an apparatus of perpetual examination." Following Aureli's argument, Laurence contends that a process of standardisation or normalisation occurs to acculturate students into disciplinary norms. "The student is constantly evaluated, graded, measured, created. The abnormal is marginalized, [sic] rejected, and excluded. The human sciences develop, and the university introduces the student to a world where everything can be measured, including their imaginations." (Laurence 2009, unpaginated) The monitoring of work and disciplining of work life for students and staff comes about through a university's audit culture.

Beginning in the 1990s, the phrase 'audit culture' was defined by Peter M. Taubman (2010, pp. 60–61) as describing 'the increasing use of regulatory mechanisms, designed to monitor and measure performance, in fields other than accounting, insurance, and finance, where the mechanisms originated.' Most university audit cultures rely heavily on the increasing administration of assessing performance criteria for all workers within a university. The audit culture in a university is accompanied by new values and language, such as performance management, quality assurance, accountability, transparency, efficiency, best practices, stakeholders, benchmarking, research outputs, etc., and a long and growing list of acronyms. An audit culture employs new digital technologies and software to collect data, which is used to discipline, track, and monitor productivity in work and workers within the university at all levels.

The consequence of this "examinatorial power [on the body of the architecture student and educator] is the invention of a new type of [...] calculable individual." (Laurence 2009, unpaginated) NPM driven universities present students as consumers or 'clients' of measurable academic services and academics as providers of a service or 'service providers.' Many educators in neoliberal architecture schools worldwide openly talk about and accept this unquestionably. The shift in relationship from educator/mentor–student/mentee to educator/manufacturer–student/client-consumer has significant consequences in terms of pedagogical practice because economic returns on university investment now become part of an educator's everyday field of negotiation. National Student Surveys (NSS) in the U.K. and university rankings are the indicators of an undergraduate programme's strength, and with that the strength and quality of a school of architecture. Satisfied 'clients' in high revenue-generating universities lead to mostly good NSS scores or rankings. Due to the shift to a consumer-oriented university education, in some western neoliberal universities, students can have more influence and power to make effective complaints and have change responded to by university managers than teaching staff. The issue is not that students should be limited in their ability to make complaint, but that in some institutions 'client satisfaction' means that staff complaints are devalued or ignored and/or staff, particularly younger staff, are fearful to voice their opinions. For architecture educators who are research active with full-time and fractional posts, teaching and research are under constant quantitative surveillance through scheduled "performance reviews." Performance reviews aim to ensure productive performance of architecture students and staff through a university's audit culture.

Herbert Read (in Marcuse 2007, unpaginated pre-Contents page) defines the premise of Herbert Marcuse's *One-Dimensional Man: Studies in the Ideology of Advanced Industrial Society* as seeking to examine the "central problem of our civilization—how to reconcile orginality [sic] and spontaneity and all the creative aspects of our human nature with a prevailing drive to rationality that tends to reduce all varieties of temperament and desire to one universal system of thought and behaviour [sic]." Marcuse contends that technological rational labour that is made possible by, and manifested through, industrialisation has colonised everyday life, "robbing individuals of freedom and individuality by imposing technological imperatives, rules, and structures upon their thought and behavior [sic]." (Kellner in Marcuse, 2007, p. xiv) Processes of industrial production can diminish the possibility for critique, free thought, and experimentation. In the university context, a former domain recognised for critical thought, the effect of rational processes of production on students and educators can be profound. As the British architectural theoretician, Simon Sadler (in Deamer ed. 2014, p. 125) explains, "The model of the university as a locus of criticism within the dense relations of capitalism" is limited, so that the essential "possibility of immanent critique-on locating the contradictions in the rules and systems necessary to production" are politically dismantled. No longer is a university education about free learning, thinking, and making but, under academic capitalism, it has increasingly become a tick-boxing, form-filling exercise in efficient and compliant administrative procedures. An increasing number of assessment criteria, evaluation processes, and attendance checking within the university – that a student becomes acculturated to at the factory-school (Rifkin 2009, p. 335)[1] – affect all forms of academic labour in the university. In schools of architecture, where creativity and creative thought is a fundamental feature of the discipline, a conundrum occurs for students, educators, and researchers who are compromised and pressured into greater productivity and bureaucratisation. As more non-permanent staff are employed in architectural schools, full-time academics can be required to carry more of the (paperwork) workload that non-permanent staff are not employed to do, thereby increasing their workload.

Operating like a factory worker producing and satisfying student-clients and producing and disseminating world-renowned research that is tied to industry requires that architecture academics work such long hours that they have limited time or opportunity to slowly evolve and construct new research or knowledge. The very purpose of a university life for *homo academicus*, which formerly was to encourage critical and reflective thinking, is compromised under academic capitalism in architecture. Often the academic is given minimum time to think and to produce 'deliverables' or 'outputs' from which the university can gain revenue. Both the factory worker on the shop floor – the architectural educator as *homo academicus* – and the product they are producing – the architectural student – are increasingly being acculturated into the *homo oeconomicus* model where creativity is linked to competitive entrepreneurship and where a long-hours, high-pressure workplace culture becomes normalised.

Academic Entrepreneurism and Competitive Play

The *homo oeconomicus*-architectural educator and student in a university setting is productive, entrepreneurial, creative, and family-free – not necessarily without children or a family, but they do not undertake primary care responsibilities for them. They focus on some aspects of a working life in the university and not others. Slaughter and Leslie (1997, p. 1) argue that "globalization [sic... has created] new structures, incentives, and rewards for some aspects of academic careers and is simultaneously instituting constraints and disincentives for other aspects of careers." In alignment with Ralf Dahrendorf's (1973, p. 17) claim that "to every social position there belongs a social role," as the former social role of life shifts more towards an 'economic life' because of academic capitalism, both educators and students are morphing away from *homo academicus*, *homo sociologicus* (Dahrendorf 1973), and *homo politicus* (Brown 2015, pp. 87–99) into entrepreneurial *homo oeconomicus*.

Entrepreneurialism is one way to separate oneself to take advantage in the H.E. academic marketplace. In the university context, where new knowledge is the main field of play and where originality and innovative thinking are work goals, academic entrepreneurialism is highly valued in managers, educators, and students because it allows a university and, within it, an architecture school to set itself apart and above others through its ability to generate economic, social and cultural capital, and prestige.

In a school of architecture, entrepreneurial academic educators, researchers, their collaborators and students form the 'creative class.' Career academics – defined here as people who never leave working in the university, moving from graduate to educator – typically focus on, and construct, one area of expertise in their teaching and/or research through which to consolidate their own and their university's reputation for innovation. Creating and building a linear field of teaching or research, ideally begun as quickly as possible, is usually done in collaborative teams inside the university and outside in architectural practice and industry. Typically, only the lead academic receives recognition for that work, following a pedagogical master–pupil chain, although this is starting to change. The momentum of the combination of members in the teaching or research team can propel the status and productivity of the team to obtain more funds and prestige, thereby elevating the university's image.

In the case of educators, pressure has risen in many neoliberal-driven universities for academics to bring in external money from industry or research funding bodies, taking them out of the 'ivory tower' into commercial life. This adds to their workload the task of finding money to pay their own labour; something unrequired in the pre-neoliberal university. In semi-private or private H.E. institutions "state funding of universities is 'tied' to a set of academic productivity metrics that measure knowledge according to 'impact'." (Brown 2015, p. 23) In the U.K., there are/have been a REF (Research Excellence Framework), TEF (Teaching Excellence Framework), and KEF (Knowledge Excellence Framework) used for measuring academic performance and impact. Universities in other countries operate on other funding models that put less pressure on the academic workforce to deliver economic rationalism. The rationality of the *homo oeconomicus* architectural educators working in the university quantifies and measures outputs (funded research projects, books, refereed journal articles, etc., and students who become architect figureheads), and the numbers of people engaging with those teaching or research outputs through social media network tweets, LinkedIn followers, etc. Educators who elect not to be quantified for their 'academic credit rating,' or are unable to participate at this level, can become uncompetitive and unattractive for university promotion, publicity, or image making. This means that the entrepreneurial mastery of *homo oeconomicus* to negotiate the economic game play in an academic life is favoured within the neoliberal university setting. The ideal worker in the edufactory is encouraged to focus on developing their personal academic biographical narrative through the products of their work in the particular focus area of expertise within architecture. They are strongly encouraged to compete for, and win, external funding. Most academics whose appointments are primarily or entirely for research are able to focus all their time on that one field of research and are not compromised by having to juggle their research, teaching, administration, and service or outreach obligations.

In the case of architecture students, universities offer incentive programmes to enhance student entrepreneurship. Students are encouraged to compete with one another for university, national, or international awards, the most prestigious being those for design studio work done for open international and international competitions or in-house studio projects. While other forms of non-competitive driven teaching are emerging and present in the studio setting, the traditional design studio model nurtures a spirit of competition. Competitiveness, the keystone of neoliberalism, has been seen by the profession as a positive and enduring characteristic of any emerging architect because it shows their game-playing skills. As Garry Stevens (1998, p. 203) notes "Competition creates a whole symbolic market whereby students can show their dedication to the game."

Competition and endurance as an enactment of workplace relations within the university setting is historically and culturally embedded and gendered. "Many who start architectural school never finish. There are many reasons that people drop out, the work load and competition being among them." (Lewis 1998, p. 73) According to Kathryn H. Anthony (1991, p. 165) "the competitive model of design education is very much a male model." Before there was more gender balance in studio teaching, many male tutors and reviewers used overt and covert strategies to assert their patriarchal knowledge dominance and power over students. Students can be conditioned to cope with difficult, combative, or confrontational discussions about their work through this method of teaching; some gaining pleasure, or not, from it.

One outcome of the combative design studio model is a form of (non-sexual) 'masochism' which results in a student enjoying or being grateful to receive harsh, painful questioning because it teaches them to build a tougher resolve to respond to and cope with it. (Stead 2003) Another consideration in relation to this mode of teaching is the inability of some students to want to engage in sporting contest behaviour. As Anthony (1991, p. 165) notes "the athletic and military analogies that many design instructors routinely use[d] in design studios can be a sore spot for women students [... minorities or gays] and may offend some..." simply because they see that sporting activities are for the "develop[ment of] one's own ... abilities," not to beat an opponent. The competitive nature of design studio, enacted most extremely in design juries or reviews, where students are made vulnerable through the need to defend their design position in a more public forum, can be disconcerting for shy or sensitive students who suffer from the 'emotional toll,' which can in turn affect their confidence. (Anthony 1991, p. 165) "Competitive pressure is internal and external. Dedicated students push themselves, notwithstanding other influences, reacting to an internal need to achieve. With this comes pushing from external sources—faculty, fellow students, friends, and family—which can be relentless and unending. Some students thrive on such pressures; others feel substantial anxiety, which can affect their work." (Lewis 1998, p. 74)

Fear and anxiety experienced during an architectural education, and the pressure to achieve the best grades, can have an impact on identity formation and the setting and attainment of goals (Shaw 1995, p. 115) even though grades "neither destroy nor ensure your future career." (Lewis 1998, p. 74) Managing emotional performance under stressful situations – for instance, whether a student cries openly in front of their tutors or audience or not – involves negotiating traditional 'masculine standards' of behaviour directed towards rationality and objectivity. (Kuhlmann 2013, pp. 43–44) Design jury criticism that is flattering can be at odds with a historically-embedded pedagogical practice of negative criticism in the studio because it can be seen to be less effective in producing robust architectural graduates ready to take on any world challenges. (Stead 2003)

Surviving a life in some architecture schools can be a game of endurance. The extreme amount of content that is covered in an architectural course and the fact that radical or conventional pedagogical practice can involve unlearning everything a student formerly learned means that a student's stamina – mental and physical – is often being tested. Many architecture schools in the world advocate a long-hours work culture and students are discouraged from doing anything other than university work (even things that drew them into architecture in the first place such as painting), with design studio seen as the 'most valued' subject in which to achieve excellence. Many an architectural design studio has operated or operates "like [a] boot camp: twelve hours a day seven days a week in basic design … [where students are] more or less being broken." (Izenour quoted in Anthony 1991, p. 15) Many design studio educators agree that the best students exhibit a singular focus on their individual production and are driven to do nothing but work. They meet deadlines and perform optimally under intense pressure. They are fully committed to a career in architecture. These attributes can make them highly employable. More recently in a critique of how design studio culture can set uneven work-life balance, some design tutors including Peggy Deamer, have actively sought to challenge the long-hours work culture encouraged by educators in architecture schools. Changes such as these aim to improve the health and wellbeing of students who cannot sustain the intellectual and physical energy demanded of them and aim to resist breeding unhealthy patterns of work that can continue in work life post-graduation.

Architecture educators can be, and are, notorious for being competitive within the academy too. Many academics can be territorial of the subject of their research or teaching. The play space of the architectural academy can be highly political and emotionally or intellectually violent with factional divisions – between architectural history and theory, architectural design, design science and technology, management practice subject expertise – resulting in epistemological attacks and takeovers, ostracisation or marginalisation. Some academics are hesitant to open up their territory to collaborative teaching/research or exchange beyond their discipline. This is changing however. The Bulgarian-French philosopher, Julia Kristeva (in Coles and Defert eds. 1997, p. 6) argues that many academics guard the boundaries of their disciplinary knowledge and proposes as a solution that interdisciplinarity can be "a site where expressions of resistance are latent," although new ground may not always be broken. Working in an interdisciplinary manner can reveal exciting pedagogical potentialities or simply show the educator or researcher's inadequacies. In line with this argument, John Marshall and Julian Bleecker (in Rodgers and Smyth eds. 2010, p. 219) acknowledge that; "Undisciplinary ... work ... does not play the usual games .... It is ... an approach to creating and circulating culture that can go its own way, without worrying about working outside of what histories-of-disciplines say is "proper" work... It's an epistemological shift that offers new ways of fixing the problems the old disciplinary and extra-disciplinary practices created in the first place."

Competition also occurs between architecture schools, and the inherent structure of knowing and gaining an education at the 'best' architecture school/s in the world enables educators working in them and students attending them to build stronger influential networks to help and direct their career in the future. The most reputable architecture schools are generally the Ivy League style model that tend to attract master educators, charge the most for tuition fees, and as a consequence are the better-funded private universities. Often teachers of architecture bring their best student graduates back to teach with them so strong lines of ideology are carried through pedagogical lineages. Unlike our biological parents, ambitious architecture students can choose their biological architectural mentors to ensure their elite pedigree.

Breeding in Architectural Education for Capital Accumulation

In his critical review of the architectural studio and the profession the English architectural critic and writer, Reyner Banham (1996, p. 296) notes that there are "those who have been correctly socialised into the profession" and those who have never been "socialised in the tribal long-house." Correct socialisation in architecture or architectural breeding, at its purest level, occurs through the hereditary transmission of capital from generation to generation and continues beyond university. Bourdieu argues that an architectural education that involves contact with a master/master network operates through an invisible form of social transmission of cultural capital that censors and selects the most valuable architectural progeny. The process of selection is not conscious or deliberate however. It relies on other personal qualities of resemblance and likeness. Master–pupil chains in architectural education rely on students pleasing their tutors by reaffirming their master's values and offering the master vitality to pursue their career, resembling a 'You scratch my back, I'll scratch yours' mentality. According to Bourdieu (in Richardson ed. 1986, p. 249), in order to transmit capital 'gratitude, respect, [and] friendship' is required, but it can also involve more than that, as will be discussed later.

The question of the freedom of an architectural student to develop their own identity within a system of institutional structuration relates to the theory of 'the duality of structure' proposed by the English sociologist, Anthony Giddens in which freedom is given but limited by institutional frameworks. Giddens (1976, p. 160) proposes "the realm of human agency is bounded. Men produce society but they do so as historically located actors, and not under conditions of their own choosing." As architectural breeding relies on alliances, similarities, and replication of beliefs, not all types of students can be chosen – only those who replicate or reinstate the values of their master. Just as architecture cannot be seen as an empty entity separate from its modes of production, the role of the human agent-architectural educator in institutional structures cannot be detached from the favoured 'products' of their students. Students of architecture contain DNA (social, cultural, and economic) before they enter architecture which affects their ability to be accepted into architecture schools or to 'fit in' to the established educator models. Gender, class, and race have always been contributing factors that affects opportunity and progression during and after an architectural education.

In most developed countries, women are entering undergraduate architectural studies in greater numbers than men. What was formerly a male-dominated degree has shifted to attract more women and appears in some countries to have almost reversed so that some degrees can be female-dominated programmes. At the same time, more women are becoming architectural educators, researchers, Heads of School, and Deans. Due to these changing variables in the H.E. labour workforce, it is important when making a choice of where to study architecture at an undergraduate or postgraduate level or where to work as an architectural educator, to know the gender division/balance of its teaching and management workforce.

At the time of writing this book, women in university roles of leadership, as leads and managers of architecture schools and programmes and as educators and researchers, are less in number than their male co-workers in almost all universities worldwide. How universities and schools of architecture appoint their academic workforce depends, arguably, less on the sex of the employee (although this can be a subliminal factor) than on a synergy between the school's ethos/leaders/ the selection panel and the educator. Research, however, suggests that women educators and managers in architecture can be disadvantaged more than their male counterparts in their career path and that there is a gendered division of academic architectural labour in teaching, research, and administration. Some findings of early research indicated; "there were questions about problems women had getting promotion in certain schools and there is a perception that there is a glass ceiling." (De Graft-Johnson, Maley, and Greed 2003, p. 22) At the turn of the 20th century, Ann de Graft-Johnson, Sandra Maley, and Clara Greed (2003, p. 23) witnessed a gendered division of labour in curriculum delivery, but the situation is changing with women and men educators teaching more evenly across the curriculum.

Gender can also be a contributing factor beyond the ability to accrue professional social and cultural capital. It can affect the ability of an architecture student or educator (female or male) to accrue personal social and cultural capital, which in turn can accumulate their professional social and cultural capital. Outside but intertwined with their academic performance, two ways a student can accrue additional cultural capital during their education is through interpersonal relations developed with either another student or their studio master/another staff member (male or female). The sexual relations between students and students or students and staff (the later seen as deserved of misconduct in some universities) can influence the future careers of all involved, positively or negatively.

Students studying together and of a close/r age can form an intimate partnership during their studies. After graduation, those kinds of partnerships, begun at university, can sometimes lead to establishing a 'coupling' (Colomina 1999) in private architectural practice. In this case, the labour of architecture is enacted professionally and personally, inside and outside the university, sometimes every waking hour of the day, where work happens as much in the office as at home. Some examples of famous architecture student partnerships that have become professional partnerships include: Alvar Aalto (born 1898) who married fellow student, Aino Marsio (born 1894) in 1925 and with whom he collaborated until her death in 1949; Alison Gill [later Smithson] (born 1928) and Peter Smithson (born 1923) who met at King's College, University of Durham (now the University of Newcastle) where they were both students in different years, married in 1949, and began their architectural practice together in 1950 and; Julia Bolles (born 1948) and Peter Wilson (born 1950) who met as students studying at the Architectural Association in London and began Bolles+Wilson in 1989.

Due to the close contact in the design studio, 'master' – female or male – and student affairs can occur at university or afterwards. While this is condoned in some universities, others can see this as a reason for staff dismissal. Affairs between different generations of students and teachers appear in two forms: an occupational bonus or an occupational hazard and are reliant on social and economic potential. American sociologists Paula England and George Farkas (1986, p. 53) contend the "choice of a partner [in architecture or not] [can be seen] as a market phenomenon." When the relationship between a student and a prominent figure such as a studio master or professor is enduring, the student has the opportunity to gain optimal capital that can be carried during their career. They are able to access established social networks and contacts other students might not be privy to. If the relationship is fleeting, the outcomes for the female or male student and the tutor can be detrimental to career progression, leading to either or both experiencing a glitch in, or exit from, their study or career respectively. Educators who have affairs with students can experience a slowing down in their career progression due to the complexity brought into their professional and private life, particularly if they are in an existing relationship or with a family. Others can marry or partner to start new relationships. There are many examples of these types of master–pupil relationships that culminate in marriage and the couple working together, a few examples include: Elizabeth Diller (born 1954) who studied under Ricardo Scofidio (born 1935) when he was a tutor and Professor at Columbia University – he was 40, she was 21. They moved in together in 1979 and became professional partners in 1981; Dimitra Tsachrelia (born c. 1983) was a student of Steven Holl's (born 1947) at Columbia University GSAPP where he has been teaching since 1981. In 2019 Tsachrelia was an Associate at Steven Holl Architects (SHA) – which Holl began in 1976 – and also co-teaches with Holl at Columbia University.

Entering into an intimate architectural partnership with someone inside or outside the school of architecture can impact on the capacity of an emerging architect to create capital, particularly if they have a child/ren. For architecture-student-mothers the situation can be further complicated because having a child/ren can affect their commitment to their architectural studies which can be compromised by their commitment to childcare. Having to stay late to work in the studio, attend lecture courses, guest lectures, or participate in presentations can cause problems for students with childcare responsibilities. (De Graft-Johnson, Maley, and Greed 2003, p. 23) An architecture student who has child/ren during their university education can be forced to work harder and can be put under more pressure than their peers who are without childcare responsibilities. In the past, some schools of architecture were unsympathetic to students with childcare responsibilities, but this is increasingly changing with greater attention being made to understand student family-work life balance in the university.

Academic staff who have a family during their working life can face similar problems in balancing home-life with work-life. (Castañeda and Isgro 2013) Architect-academic-mothers are recognised as being disadvantaged more than architect-academic-fathers, generally because they tend to take time off work for maternity leave more than architect-academic-fathers take paternity leave. Time away from work can affect the ability of female- or male-parent academics to progress. The slowness of universities to factor in support for academic parents with demanding childcare responsibilities promotes a family-free *homo oeconomicus* workplace model of labour in higher education. Architecture schools that generate strategies that are empathetic to different work life patterns, i.e., taking into consideration that individuals might have other commitments and responsibilities beyond a singular vision centred on university labour, create a better workplace for women and men architecture students and educators.

Childcare demands are one of the reasons cited as to why women leave architecture. (De Graft-Johnson et al. 2003, p. 23) Having less time for (university) work can mean, but is not always the case, that they may be less productive depending on how they manage their time between domestic and work responsibilities. The hours a female or male student or staff member are able to work can set them on a stronger or weaker path for career success. It dictates the degree of their human capital – a phrase defined by the Scottish economist Adam Smith (1776 in Jacobsen in Moe ed. 2003, p. 162) where a student acquires expertise "during his [or her] education, study or apprenticeship" – which contributes to their ability to be more productive for society.

As Brown (2015, p. 107) notes, neoliberalism accentuates inequality rather than diminishes it, as it claims, all of those who, at this time, are not "socially male and masculinist within a persistently gendered economic ontology and division of labor" can be disadvantaged. To further quote Brown (2015, p. 107), "this is so regardless of whether men are 'stay-at-home fathers,' women are single or childfree, or families are queer.... With only competing and value-enhancing human capital in the frame, complex and persistent gender inequality is attributed to sexual difference, an effect that neoliberalism takes for the cause." Here women or men students, educators, and researchers in architecture, of different race, ethnic, and class background, who do not follow the traditional masculinist model can be disadvantaged too because they are not able to focus singularly on the main goal of the game of a contemporary academic life – capitalism through entrepreneurialism. Unless their university or management have policies that support and cater for their life of juggling home and work life, students and academic educators and researchers who are not 'family free' in universities can be disadvantaged by the entrepreneurial turn.

The persistent gender pay and promotion gap in the labour market attests to inequalities premised on long working hours (Jacobsen 2003, pp. 161–176) and universities are equally, if not more so, behind industry in gender pay parity. Morley (2013, p. 7) contends that women (and now men) academics with family care responsibilities are "caught between two greedy institutions – the extended family and the university... A dominant view is that time expended on role performance in one domain depletes time available for the demands of the other domain." Venitha Pillay (2007, p. 30) writes that academic mothers find it difficult to balance 'two lives' because the juggle can lead to "going nowhere slowly." She suggests that the transitional space in-between motherhood and the intellectual self is not always 'smooth.' (Pillay 2007, p. vii) Academics with family care responsibilities are pressured because "each role absorbs enormous psychological, intellectual, and emotional energy." (One mother quoted in Pillay 2007, p. 30) Academic mothers, fathers, parents, and carers have to rationalise the tasks required of them in both their domestic and professional spheres so as to "become highly efficient, serious and single minded by compartmentalising work life and family life." (Chester 1990, p. 7 quoted in Pillay 2007, p. 31)

While architecture is considered a creative gender-neutral profession, many argue that gender inequalities occur through the performativity of gender enacted through a 'hidden curriculum.' (Ahrentzen and Groat 1992, pp. 101–104) While the curriculum is evolving, it is because "women building and designing today have learned their trade from men" (Goldfrank 1995, p. 202) that an architectural education is based on a historical, 'masculine' model of academic work and behaviour favours masculinity, particularly in the theatre of the design studio.

"Genderization [sic] in architectural education" in the studio has mostly occurred through the favouring of hierarchically institutionalised stereotypical masculine traits – confidence, ambition, singular focus, competition, endurance (intellectual and physical), hard work, productivity, understanding the rules of 'how to play the game' of architectural education, and not having primary childcare responsibilities – which can impact on a student's and educator's capacity for social mobility. (Ahrentzen and Anthony 1993, p. 11) As power relations between a student and an educator – in labour and personal or sexual association – are exerted more visibly in the design studio context, the studio is the location where differences in gender can lead to unequal treatment that can have a knock-on effect later on in professional practice or academic life depending on which path is chosen.

Some scholars in architecture contend that the increase in women academics teaching in universities is one way in which to gain gender equality. (Leavitt 1991, pp. 225–248) This can be achieved when women educators resist conformity and 'identify through disidentification.' (Spaeth and Kosmala in Stead ed. 2014) Women educators who do not replicate the masculine model of education that they have experienced can be better positioned to deeply understand the obstacles that women students face. In the late 1990s, Linda Groat and Sherry Ahrentzhen (1997, pp. 271–285) argued "women faculty" or educators were the "voices of change in architectural education." As an architectural educator is not limited in how and what they teach, empathic women and men educators can design the curriculum differently for greater gender diversity and inclusion. They can champion the ideals of a liberal education; forge interdisciplinary connections; encourage experimentation; integrate different modes of thought in the studio; teach principles of visual and spatial abstraction as a connection to other disciplines; establish a communicative environment; reform pedagogical practices in the studio; encourage collaboration; and care for students. (Groat and Ahrentzhen 1997, pp. 271–285) This is already starting to happen in the academy.

A key area of future work for women and men university managers lies in their expectations of student and staff performance delivery. This relates to how much work is assigned and the audit culture that is employed to monitor the production of assigned (invisible and visible) work outputs. The "impact of audit culture and managerialism in higher education" on "new neoliberal subjects" (Archer 2008, p. 270) is a fundamental area of change in how university workers in architecture are able to play the game or not. The shift is in how much universities 'goven the soul' (Rose 1999 in Delbridge and Keenoy 2010, pp. 801–802) of their workforce. Real change is possible if the "contemporary managerial rhetorical ambition [that] now embraces '*the subject in its totality* as an object of governance'" (Costea, Crump, and Amiridis 2008, p. 670 in Delbridge and Keenoy 2010, p. 801–802) widens.

All parties in education need to value women's (and men's) labour *inside* and *outside* the university. Managers, leaders, and academic colleagues need to be more sensitive to the gendered behaviour of non-masculinist female and male students and staff who struggle to manage the stress and pressure that comes with their additional outside university workload, which is never included in their annual university workload allocation. A heightened emotional register and methods of teaching that are more accommodating of a disadvantaged or struggling student or educator need to be developed. Students – female and male – should reconsider how they 'treat their teachers' and student peers equitably, giving respect and support. (Shaw 1995, p. 144) Some men in the current new generation of students and educators are already leading the way, showing empathy and non-competitive, collaborative engagement with their peers, the consequence, some argue, of having personal knowledge of (their) working mothers who they watched struggle to balance work and home life. The change in women's working life – shared between office and home – makes the work done by working mothers more 'visible' to their children, such that sons of working mothers are "less inclined to take their mothers for granted." (Smith 1996, p. 178) Many universities and Schools of Architecture are now beginning to value a work-life balance for their staff and students. This change is a complex task for higher education institutions that are transitioning from institutions for education (Foucault's 'premodern or medieval university') to entrepreneurial businesses (the 'modern university'). Neoliberal higher education makes stronger demands on its employees and students to consume and produce in a more industrialised, efficient, and voracious manner, through a particular form of academic capitalism that differs to capitalism in the private sector. In "Future Investments: Gender Transition as a Socio-economic Event," Dan Irving "confronts head-on the demands of capitalism interested in the whole life of the employee." (in Adkins in Adkins and Dever eds. 2016, p. 4) "He is concerned, in particular, with how contemporary workplaces demand that all aspects of the lives of employees – including bodies, minds and psychic lives – are put to work in the interest of the creation of economic value." (Irving in Adkins and Dever eds. 2016, p. 4)

If we are to reformulate architectural education, we need to be critical of the organisational and value systems that underpin how it is enacted. If women and men are gendered through the performativity of their daily labour, from birth to death, then it is through the performativity of feminine and masculine labour equally shared by women and men of all classes and cultures (in all of its varied identities) inside and outside the university that a more sustainable and gender balanced architectural workforce can begin to emerge. Dominant 'hegemonic masculinity' can cripple architectural education (and the architectural profession) and needs to be resisted. (Sang, Dainty, and Ison 2014, pp. 247–264) This means that the modern university should not sacrifice human capital for economic capital. Instead, it should enable its students and educators to evolve new forms of education that are socially, economically, and ethically responsible to inform and be informed by a balanced home-work life in architectural practice.

Note

1 "It is no accident that schools were set up to resemble factories. Children learned more than their ABCs. School life was structured around key temporal and spatial constraints. Students learned to be punctual and efficient and to sit at a desk for long periods of time concentrating on work. The new routines accustomed the children to the temporal

expectations and physical conditions that awaited them in the new industrial factories and offices. They were also taught to think of learning as something one acquires and possesses. Knowledge was looked at on as power and regarded as a tool or asset one could use to advance one's interest in the marketplace. The mission of education was quite different from that of the humanist period where the focus was on philosophical and theological questions. In the modern era of public schooling, the goal set forth by the state educators was to produce batches of "'productive citizens' for the emerging national economies." (Rifkin 2009, p. 335)

References

Adkins, L. 2016. Contingent Labour and the Rewriting of the Sexual Contract. In Adkins, L. and Dever, M. eds., *The Post-Fordist Sexual Contract: Working and Living in Contingency*. New York: Palgrave Macmillan.

Ahrentzen, S. and Anthony, K. H. 1993. Sex, Stars, and Studios: A Look at Gendered Educational Practices in Architecture, *Journal of Architectural Education*, 47 (1) (1993 September): 11–29.

Ahrentzen, S. and Groat, L. 1992. Rethinking Architectural Education: Patriarchal Conventions and Alternative Visions from the Perspectives of Women Faculty, *Journal of Architectural and Planning Research*, 9 (2) (1992 Summer): 101–104.

Aitken, J. 2014. *Margaret Thatcher: Power and Personality.* London: Bloomsbury.

Allen, A. 2011. The Idea of a World University: Can Foucauldian Research Offer a Vision of Educational Futures? *Pedagogy, Culture & Society* 19 (3), 367–383.

Anthony, K. H. 1991. *Design Juries on Trial: The Renaissance of the Design Studio*. New York: Van Nostrand Reinhold.

Atlas, J. 1998. Oxford Versus Thatcher's England, *The New York Times Magazine*, (April 14, 1988) https://www.nytimes.com/1988/04/24/magazine/oxford-versus-thatcher-s-england.html, Accessed February 21, 2020.

Archer, L. 2008.The new neoliberal subjects? Young/er academics' constructions of professional identity, *Journal of Education Policy*, 23 (3): 265–285.

Aureli, P. V. 2015. Form and Labor: Toward a History of Abstraction in Architecture. In Deamer, P. ed. *The Architect as Worker: Immaterial Labor, the Creative Class and the Politics of Design*. London: Bloomsbury Academic, pp. 103–117.

Banham, R. 1996. A Black Box: The Secret Profession of Architecture. In R. Banham and M. Banham, *A Critic Writes: Essays by Reyner Banham*. Berkeley, Los Angeles; London: University of California Press, pp. 292–299.

Biernacki, R. 2016. The Capitalist Origin of the Concept of Creative Work. In Deamer, P. ed., *The Architect as Worker: Immaterial Labor, the Creative Class, and the Politics of Design*. London: Bloomsbury Academic, pp. 30–43.

Bonda, P. 2007. *Sustainable Commercial Interiors.* John Wiley & Sons.

Bourdieu, P. 2019. *Homo Academicus*. Stanford: Stanford University Press. [Trans. by Collier, P. First published in 1988.]

Bourdieu, P. 1986. The Forms of Capital, in Richardson, J. ed., *Handbook of Theory and Research for the Sociology of Education.* New York: Greenwood Press, pp. 241–258. [First published in 1983.]

Bourdieu, P. 1986. *Distinction: A Social Critique of the Judgment of Taste.* London: Routledge. [First published in 1979.]

Brown, W. 2015. *Undoing the Demos: Neoliberalism's Stealth Revolution.* New York: Zone Books.

Castañeda, M. and Isgro, K. L. 2013. *Mothers in Academia*. New York: Columbia University Press.

Campbell, J. 2008. M*argaret Thatcher, Volume One: The Grocer's Daughter*. London: Vintage Books.

Colomina, B. 1999. "Couplings," *Oase* (51): 20–33.

Dahrendorf, R. 1973. *Homo Sociologicus*. London: Routledge & Kegan Paul. [First published in 1957.]

Daugherty, N. 2015. *The Last Love Song: A Biography of Joan Didion.* New York: St. Martin's Press.

Delbridge, R. and Keenoy, T. 2010. Beyond Managerialism?, *The International Journal of Human Resource Management*, 21 (6): 799–817.

De Graft-Johnson, A., Manley, S., and Greed, C. 2003. *Why do Women Leave Architecture?* RIBA Technical Report. http://eprints.uwe.ac.uk/10298 Accessed August 12, 2022.

England, P. and Farkas, G. 1986. *Households, Employment, and Gender: A Social, Economic and Demographic View*. New York: Aldine.

Foucault, M., Davidson, A. I. ed., and Burchell, G. (Trans). 2008. *The Birth of Biopolitics: Lectures at the Collège de France*. Houndmills, Basingstoke, Hampshire [England]: Palgrave Macmillan. [First published in 1979.]

Foucault, M. 2002. *The Order of Things.* London: Routledge. [First published in 1966.]

Gibbons, M. et al. 1994. *The New Production of Knowledge: The Dynamics of Science and Research in Contemporary Societies*. London; California; New Delhi; Singapore: Sage.

Giddens, A. 1976. *New Rules of Sociological Method*. London: Hutchinson.

Goldfrank, J. 1995. *Making Ourselves at Home: Women Builders and Designers*. Wastsonville, CA: Papier-Mache Press.

Griffin. A. 2019. *The Rise of Academic Architectural Education: The Origins and Enduring Influence of the Académie d'Architecture*. London: Routledge.

Groat, L. and Ahrentzen, S. 1997. Voices for Change in Architectural Education: Seven Facets of Transformation from the Perspectives of Faculty Women, *Journal of Architectural Education*, 50 (4) (1997 May): 271–285.

Jacobsen, J. P. 2003. The Human Capital Explanation for the Gender Gap in Earnings, in Moe, K. S. ed. *Women, Family and Work: Writings on the Economics of Gender*. Malden, MA; Oxford; Melbourne; Berlin: Blackwell, pp. 161–176.

Kerr, C. 2001. *The Uses of the University*. Cambridge, Massachusetts; London; England: Harvard University Press. Retrieved April 10, 2020, from www.jstor.org/stable/j.ctt6wpqkr

Kuhlmann, D. 2013. *Gender Studies in Architecture: Space, Power and Difference*. London; New York: Routledge.

Kristeva, J. 1997. Institutional Interdisciplinarity in Theory and Practice: An Interview, in Coles, A. and Defert, A. eds. *De-, Dis-, Ex, Volume Two: The Anxiety of Interdsiciplinarity*. London: Black Dog, pp. 1–22.

Laurence, M. 2009. Reconstituting the Political: Foucault and the Modern University, Paper presented at the annual meeting of the American Political Science Association, Ontario, Canada, September 2009.

Leavitt, J. 1991. Introducing Gender into Architectural Studios, in Dutton, T. ed. *Voices in Architectural Education: Cultural Politics and Pedagogy.* New York; London: Bergin & Garvey, pp. 225–248.

Lewis, R. K. 1998. *Architect? A Candid Guide to the Profession*. Cambridge, Mass.; London, England: The MIT Press. [First published 1985.]

Lou, H. 2003. *The Game of Life: How to Succeed in Real Life no Matter Where you Land.* Philadelphia; London: Running.

Marcuse, H. 2007. *One-Dimensional Man: Studies in the Ideology of Advanced Industrial Society.* Oxon; New York: Routledge. [First published in 1964.]

Marshall, J. and Bleecker, J. 2010. Undisciplinarity, in Rodgers, P. and Smyth, M. eds. *Digital Blur: Creative Practice at the Boundaries of Architecture, Design and Art.* Faringdon, Oxfordshire: Libri Publishing, pp, 216–223.

Mayo, J. M. 1991. Dilemmas of Architectural Education in the Academic Political Economy, *Journal of Architectural Education,* 44 (2): 80–89.

Menand, L., Reitter, P., and Wellmon, C. eds. 2017. *The Rise of the Research University: A Sourcebook.* Chicago; London: The University of Chicago Press.

Morley, L. 2013. Women and Higher Education Leadership: Absences and Aspirations, *Leadership Foundation for Higher Education Stimulus Paper.* London: Leadership Foundation for Higher Education.

Pillay, V. 2007. *Academic Mothers.* Stoke on Trent, U.K.; Sterling, U.S.A.: Trentham Books.

Rifkin, J. 2009. *The Empathic Civilization: The Race to Global Consciousness in a World in Crisis.* Cambridge, U.K.: Polity, pp. 315–364.

Rosenfeld, S. 2013. Clark Kerr's Classic: The Uses of the University Turns 50, *Winter 2013 Information Issue of California,* (2013 Winter) https://alumni.berkeley.edu/california-magazine/winter-2013-information-issue/clark-kerr's-classic-uses-university-turns-50, Accessed November 06, 2023.

Sadler, S. 2014. The Varieties of Capitalist Experience, in P. Deamer ed. *Architecture and Capitalism: 1845 to the Present.* London: Routledge, pp. 115–131.

Sang, K., Dainty, A., and Ison, S. 2014. Gender in the U.K. Architectural Profession: (Re) producing and Challenging Hegemonic Masculinity, *Work Employment and Society,* 28 (2): 247–264.

Schön, D. A. 1983. *The Reflective Practitioner: How Professionals Think in Action.* London: Temple Smith.

Shaw, J. 1995. *Education, Gender and Anxiety.* London: Taylor & Francis.

Slaughter, S. and Leslie, L. L. 1997. *Academic Capitalism: Politics, Policies and the Entrepreneurial University.* Baltimore; London: John Hopkins University Press.

Smith, B. 1996. *Mothers and Sons: Truth about Mother-Son Relationships.* St. Leonards, N.S.W.: Allen & Unwin.

Spaeth, M.S. and Kosmala, K. 2014. Identification Through Disidentification: A Life Course Perspective on Professional Belonging, in N. Stead ed. *Women, Practice, Architecture: 'Resigned Accommodation' and 'Usurpatory Practice.'* New York: Routledge, pp. 27–44.

Standing, G. 2016. *The Precariat: The New Dangerous Class.* London: Bloomsbury Academic.

Stead, N. 2003.Three Complaints about Architectural Criticism, *Architectural Australia,* 92 (6) (November–December 2003): 50, 52.

Stevens, G. 1998 *The Favored Circle: The Social Foundations of Architectural Distinction.* Cambridge, Massachusetts; London, England: The MIT Press.

Taubman, P. M. 2010. Audit Culture, in Kridel, C. ed. *Encyclopedia of Curriculum Studies.* Thousand Oaks, CA: SAGE Publications, pp. 60–61.

Thatcher, M. 1995. *The Path to Power*. London: Harper Collins.

Troiani, I. 2021. The Elephant in the Room: How Neoliberal Architecture Education Undermines Wellbeing, *Charrette*, 7 (2) (2021 December–Autumn): 9–33.

Troiani, I. 2005. *The Politics of Friends in Modern Architecture, 1949–1987*. Unpublished PhD at the Queensland University of Technology, Brisbane, Australia.

6
A NEOLIBERAL LIFE IN ARCHITECTURAL PRACTICE

FIGURE 6.1 Architect Frank Lloyd Wright (left) discusses plans with William Wesley Peters while other apprentices work at their drafting tables in the drawing room of Taliesen West, Scottsdale, U.S.A. Photograph credit: Bettmann. Date created: 21 September 1945.

DOI: 10.4324/9781351199834-8

Neoliberalism and Private Architecture Practice

While the image of the architect is often framed about the 'persona' of the architect as a creative genius like Frank Lloyd Wright, (Figure 6.1) architecture is also an accredited profession. Being able to work and call oneself an architect is certified with registration boards for architects, with institutes of architects acting as optional associations for members. The professionalisation of architecture has a great many ramifications in terms of expectations of the architect's purpose and standards of work.

Architecture, like other types of professions, such as law or medicine, is defined around the idea of the profession as central to a society. This was because their expertise was seen to position the professional as the best person to "supress their own self-interest in order to ascertain and pursue the public good." (Roiphe 2016, p. 649) Professionals were important because they had a vital pastoral and social role. Law professor, Rebecca Roiphe (2016, p. 649), however, argues in "The Decline of Professionalism" that this traditional understanding of professions was lost in the 1970s when *laisse-faire* neoliberal market ideology took hold, a time when being a professional suddenly "became synonymous with the delivery of services." The decline is of a particular form of professionalism, what she terms 'social professionalism.' (Roiphe 2016, p. 651) This has resulted in a shift in professional identities, for instance in law – the profession she uses as a case study –, from 'public interest lawyering' more toward 'client-centered [sic] lawyering.' (Roiphe 2016, p. 673) To parallel Roiphe's descriptions, in architecture, under neoliberalism, professional identity moved away from 'public interest architectural practice' more toward 'client-centered [sic] architectural practice.'

Roiphe identifies the role that Baroness Margaret Thatcher and her Conservative government played in shifting from public/society-centredness to client/individual-centredness, quoting Thatcher's (1987 in Roiphe 2016, p. 663) notorious statement: "There is no such thing as society... There are individual men and women and there are families."[1] The implementation of neoliberalism in all aspects of life has had a significant effect on the society of architecture professionals, namely a shift in the types of clients and projects worked on and the heightening of a competitive environment in which architectural practice operates. External changes in the structure of everyday neoliberal life have had a knock-on effect on the everyday life of architects.

Neoliberalism offers a multitude of traditional, non-traditional, or entrepreneurial and digitally-oriented options for business models of architectural practices that one can work almost anywhere in the world after studying or graduating from architecture. This chapter first sets out the historical shift in a conventional architectural practice life – since the 1930s and focusing on the U.K. after Thatcherism – in which the majority of architects have been forced to move away from producing architecture for the state to working more for the private sector. Design product creativity, entrepreneurism, marketisation, rationalisation, economisation, globalisation, and careerism are key drivers in gaining success in a neoliberal-driven architectural practice that remains predominantly structured around hierarchical lineal corporate ladders rather than zigzag corporate lattices (Benko and Anderson 2010), and which can outsource work nationally and globally. However, because 'architecture depends' (Till 2009) on a multitude of contingent factors outside the architect's control, the practice of architecture has increasingly morphed into a more flexible type of service delivery. The division of labour in the architect's office creates a neoliberal architectural class structure from an architectural elite to an architectural proletariat class (Standing 2016) as discussed in Chapter 5. Different classes of architects have different types of daily, weekly, monthly, and annual routine and engage in work for different hours of their daily lives in their private and professional lives, with work enacted at home and in the office through being able to work remotely. In addition, because of the introduction of new computer technologies – which emerged around the same time that neoliberalism did – not all the conventional stages of architectural production are essential to deliver for every type of project any longer and nor are they deliverable in the same way. Hand drawing has been replaced by computational drawing and there are entrepreneurial advantages that have arisen for *homo economicus* from the shift from drawing board to computer drawing, modelling, visualisation, and fabrication.

Second, it discusses how an architect's pedagogical genealogy and breeding – gained from university and tied to where they studied and who they studied under, as discussed in Chapter 5 – affects the type of architect they (can) become. It refers to Reyner Banham's (1996, pp. 292–299) theory of 'architectural tribes' and sets out how starchitects have emerged as a class with higher status because of their genealogy and how that higher status can be passed on to their students or employees showing how 'capital' is accrued through that well-established 'master–pupil' 'field' chain. The chapter uses the French sociologist, Pierre Bourdieu's theories on the relationship between 'capital' and 'field' and Australian architectural theorist, Garry Stevens' (1998) application of Bourdieu's theories into architecture to show how to potentially increase the probability of building a successful working life in architecture following a traditional architectural elite career path. The chapter outlines common reasons why some employees remain unable to climb (far) up the traditional ladder while others do not suffer the same obstacles.

Third, other versions of *homo oeconomicus*-centred architectural entrepreneurship or 'archipreneurship' (Maescher 2018) are discussed and how they can offer architects who are not part of the genealogical architectural elite the ability to accrue capital. Tied to realising the (American model of the) 'architect's' dream' (discussed in Chapter 2), the architect is further encouraged to become a private developer, rather than just work for them, thereby becoming a more participatory and powerful market actor in the system of building production. Architectural competitions can also create unforeseen, previously far-fetched opportunities for architects who might otherwise become known. (Theodorou and Katsakou eds. 2019) Here focus is placed on examples of young architects in contemporary history and a growing number of architectural Millennials who have applied their 'creative' mindset to the business of architecture. By doing so, they have the possibility of obtaining architectural commissions through routes which aren't always available to lesser-known architects, and which has the potential to give them more autonomy and work in a competitive, neoliberal environment or gain other streams of income. The multitude of choices that neoliberalism has created enable new possibilities in the daily work life of 'archipreneurs.'

Fourth, the chapter discusses how an education in architecture can be applied not to a career in architecture but to a range of careers *other than* architecture. Architects can move into working in creative industries ranging from video game design, 3D visualisation and animation, production design, graphic design, filmmaking, etc. Here skills gained while studying architecture such as computer drawing, rendering, 3D visualisation and animation, VR, etc., can be applied to other types of design work. People who leave architecture (most of whom are women) can also work in marketing, public relations, or business/project management. In the latter scenario, architects can be paid considerably more for working for a building contracting company, or as a developer than work in an architect's office, in which levels of pay are notoriously low for most of the staff aside from the managerial elite.

Unlike other books or guides about a traditional career path and life as an architect, what this chapter argues is that a life in architectural practice in neoliberal times has a greater range of choices. If someone trained as an architect does not want to work as one, there are new career trajectories outside architecture that offer alternative work-life models and satisfaction. Architects don't have to take the traditional path of working in a traditional practice for their entire life/marry/ have children, then retire. With the neoliberal playing field wide open, studying architecture does not necessarily mean you become one and nor might any of the skills gained from an education in architecture be necessary or useful to gaining a satisfying work-life balance in it. Here focus will be on the work-life of a corporate architect in practice in the U.K. after Thatcherism.

The Corporate Architect's Working Life under Neoliberalism

After Thatcher died in April 2013, a selection of architects reflected on the effect of the Thatcher years in the U.K. on the type of work a professional architect subsequently does. Martin Fulcher (2013) explains in the *Architects' Journal* that "The biggest impact was the closure of the vast majority of public sector architect departments" whose "in-house council teams had employed thousands of architects across the country." One example is the Greater London Council (GLC), formerly the London County Council (LCC). Since 1933, when British delegates joined the socially driven CIAM (Congrès Internationaux d'Architecture Moderne or the International Congresses of Modern Architecture) as the MARS (Modern Architectural Research) Group (Landau 1992, pp. 40–41), LCC architects who were members of MARS – such as Leslie Martin, Alison Smithson, and Peter Smithson to name but a few – had worked to redevelop Victorian slum areas of London. That work sought to rehouse the mostly working-class or post-war immigrants in new mid- to high-rise council tower blocks or build public buildings. MARS bred a group of socially-oriented architects who, propelled by government, after World War II searched for ways of improving London for all. Social architects at the LCC 'took command' (Lang 2014) from the 1950s onward because they had "both professional power and political backing." (Glendinning and Muthesius 1994, p. 3) In-between and after the wars, these Welfare State utopian social architects designed and built 28% of new public housing in England and Wales. (Glendinning and Muthesius 1994, p. 1) The Balfron Tower, 1967 by Ernő Goldfinger and Royal Festival Hall or Southbank Centre, 1951 by Leslie Martin, Peter Moro, and Robert Matthew are a few examples of architectures for 'the common man' in British society after the war.

But as Patrick Dunleavy (1981, p. 2) notes in *The Politics of Mass Housing in Britain, 1945–1975*, government became further disillusioned with social housing after 1969 – following the partial collapse of Ronan Point in 1968. Losing the backing of the Thatcher government around this time meant these in-house state architects were made unemployable and were forced to move into competing in the private commercial architectural marketplace. British architects were now at the mercy of the global marketplace designing projects which, as explained in Chapter 2, operate to sell their own architectural brand but also the sites in which their architecture is built. In "The City That Privatised Itself to Death: 'London is now a set of improbable sex toys poking gormlessly into the air'," architectural writer, Ian Martin (2015) elaborates how Thatcher's politics privatised London's cityscape:

> Then, suddenly, architecture, like everything else, was privatised. The 1980s saw deregulation, not only of the financial markets, but also of the professions. The number of local-authority architects plummeted under a regime of cuts; the harsh winter of recession in 1990 finished them off. From now on, space and air would be shaped and primped by the private sector. Architecture was redefined: no longer frozen music, but petrified Thatcherism.

As already outlined in Chapter 1, Thatcherism created "a legacy of… steel and glass" corporate towers such as the Docklands enterprise zone because of the deregulation of the City's financial services. By vastly reducing the social housing programme through the 'Right to Buy' policy some argue neoliberalism has had 'massive impact' on the current housing crisis shortage. (Hemmingway in Fulcher 2013) Neoliberalism changed how to play the game of architecture further into the 'lively, human, social… serious (now)… fun' marketplace which Thatcher (1995, p. 566) saw that any business should be. Changing the financial rules of architectural marketplace competition was a key step in enlivening the game.

To create an optimally competitive environment, neoliberal governance dismantled the previously-controlled architectural fee structure. To support "Thatcher's free market revolution … to ensure that service providers competed on a level playing field," Fulcher (2013) explains that "for architects, this meant the controversial abolition of RIBA fee scales, a move which came about in 1982 following on-going pressure from the Monopolies and Mergers Commission that had begun in 1979," the year Thatcher became prime minister.

While some architects (Addy in Fulcher 2013) welcomed the opening-up of the architectural marketplace because "the fee scale pretty much amounted to cartel behaviour and did not guarantee quality while it was in effect," not all did. Other architects (Wilkinson in Fulcher 2013) argue that "ever since Thatcher's government removed the mandatory fee scale, fees for architectural services have been pushed down lower and lower. Many clients seem to choose the designers of their buildings far more on price than on the quality of their work or the service they offer." Other architectural practitioners (Hutchinson in Fulcher 2013) contend that creating this highly competitive fee-charging platform is problematic because the profession is still underdeveloped in terms of how to charge fees and operate competitively and "unlike lawyers… Architects still have an entirely immature attitude to fees and undercutting." Undercut fees put pressure on faster production in the architectural office, and as such increase pressure on architectural workers in the team. Hours required to deliver a project, or a phase of it, are often delivered through a longer work hours culture (that initially can begin in architectural education) that the architectural worker lower down the production hierarchy needs to bear.

Creating an accentuated neoliberal architectural marketplace has also meant that architects had to fine tune their marketing skills and principals had to sharpen how they won clients through *Apprentice*-style sales pitching of their designs to 'Alan Sugar' client project sugar daddies or mommas. The increase in focus on 'marketing and the financial side of business' has significantly changed the game of architecture nationally and internationally. As architectural critic, Helen Castle (2017) notes in "Find your inner entrepreneur' in *The RIBA Journal:*

What we perhaps forget is what game changers the U.K.'s high-tech practices – such as those of Farrell, Foster, Grimshaw, Hopkins and Rogers – were in the 1960s, with their 'deep commitment to marketing and the financial side of the business' says Terry Farrell. That approach perhaps goes some way to explaining their phenomenal success and longevity. Farrell explains: 'Two linked factors underpinned the success of these practices. First, we enthusiastically embraced the private sector, and made a complete break from the then current generation of leading practices that were almost solely reliant on the state and related cultures of the post-war Welfare State era. This influenced not only the kind of clients and projects we all undertook (warehouses, factories, offices, private houses and developer's housing), but also our approach to internal organisation, marketing, publicity and so forth. Secondly, the link to construction and the design of building components was also part of this new attitude.

Marketing, niche or otherwise, for architectural practices has become increasingly important for business success. For many starchitects, this is tied to their practice identity, logo and the style of architecture they already produce. Buildings are increasingly designed to be flexible and easily changeable to suit a more fluid neoliberal workplace environment, an issue discussed in more detail in Chapter 7.

Recent research on the profession (Iloniemi ed. 2019) has examined how the identity of an architectural practice is tied to its means of communication in a wider cultural, global context and how it increasingly relies on a heightened visual digital marketing splurge. While not specifically focused on the discipline of architecture, Naomi Klein's (2010) *No Logo: No Space, No Choice, No Jobs*, first published in 1999 and inspired by the Situationists, brings into question the relationship between multinational companies and the labour and resource practices they employ in their supply chains to create brand autonomy. Being anti-globalisation, anti-logo, anti-marketing in a neoliberal architectural marketplace has previously not been looked upon favourably but economic, environmental crises (including pandemics) have brought into question the ethics and limits of global architectural practice. The ethics of architectural practice are put under greater pressure in a *laisse-faire* global marketplace.

The RIBA aims to serve its members and society by upholding professional ethics and standards for architectural professionals and helping connect architects as service providers to potential clients. However, some practitioners question what the RIBA can offer them, because the ARB is the compulsory regulatory authority that validates the chartered architect status. British architectural critic and theorist, Jeremy Till (2009, p. 181) astutely notes that "the RIBA promises more, but delivers less."

In 1997, the ARB was established by parliament to regulate the profession in keeping a U.K. Register of Architects. Unlike the RIBA, and as a government-regulated organisation, the ARB endeavours to ensure a good standard of professional service is provided to clients and allows an architect to use the title. Its purpose is to guarantee that architects play by the rules set for professionals in practice. As such, the ARB investigates complaints against chartered architects whose conduct and competence are considered below standard, thereby managing architectural practice behaviours in an (almost) anything goes neoliberal marketplace. Maintaining professional standards of ethics in practice is becoming increasingly important in a work environment that, in a contingent market landscape, is increasingly required to be flexible and fluid.

In *Architecture Depends*, Till (2009, p. 1) examines how, regardless of "the architect's best-laid plans," architecture today is "shaped more by external forces than by the internal processes of the architect." This leaves architects with an inability to fully control the design, construction, and occupation of their designs.

(Till 2009, p. 1) This "gap between what architecture—as practice, profession, and object—actually is (in all its dependency and contingency) and what architects want it to be (in all its false perfection)" (Till 2009, p. 2) locates the architect's work between the fictitious autonomous representations of architectural practice in the media, particularly in films about architects, and the disorderly reality of a life in architectural practice where the architect is at the mercy of others. It makes architectural practice a game of chance that can affect design integrity and processes.

The services an architect can provide vary depending on the client's requirements for the project and for the architect's involvement and the size, type of, and budget for the project. Traditional architectural services broadly include project briefing – done in consultation with the client –, architectural and interior design and documentation, and contract administration. In the U.K., the 'RIBA Plan of Work 2013' defines seven stages in architectural production: Stage 0 Strategic Definition; Stage 1 Preparation and Brief, Stage 2 Concept Design; Stage 3 Developed Design; Stage 4 Technical Design; Stage 5 Construction; Stage 6 Handover and Close Out; and Stage 7 In Use. The initial stages require an architect to develop a client brief for the project, produce sketches, ascertain any necessary consents, consider costs, and project programme manage. External consultants are appointed as the detailed design evolves into tender documents – drawings from which a cost estimate of the building is ascertained. Choosing an appropriate building contract and contractor from the tendering process precedes on-site building construction supervision.

Whereas previously in a regulated market, architects undertook *all* stages of work, architects are no longer always able, or required, to provide a 'full' service. The architectural service that can or is delivered is dependent on a multitude of contingent factors, most of which are dictated by the client and the rigidity or fluidity of their budget. For small-scale projects, architects typically undertake most of the work stages, but they may seek advice from external consultants including structural engineers as required. The architect's onsite supervision at the construction stage of a small project can be optional for some clients who choose to supervise projects themselves in order to cut costs. For large-scale projects, an architect usually acts as a member of a collaborative team of consultants offering specialist architectural services. The range of consultants that can contribute to a very large project include a multitude of interdisciplinary experts. Clients for high cost, complex, large-scale projects or developments often appoint a Project Manager (PM) to manage the project and project team to keep its delivery on time and budget. The emergence of the single AEC [Architecture, Engineering, and Construction] industry, which consists of separate players who work together to bring a project to fruition, are seen by clients of larger projects as being better able to collectively deliver a project. In many cases, the architect often has limited control of the building procurement process and serves as one (not always a lead) consultant in the team.

The time to procure a project from start to completion and the construction budget are important for many clients who commission an architect; it is also a major factor in the aesthetic and structural ambition and quality of the design. Jonathan Barnett (in Barnett and Portman 1976, p. 4) contends that "Most buildings that win awards and are published in architectural magazines have been designed for situations in which finance is not the primary consideration." While select famous architects in the world have had limitless budgets and can be in high demand, since the 1970s, even "architects who are famous for their talent, and [who] will not touch a routine commission, must wait until they are called upon. Their role in shaping the environment has been a subsidiary one; they can do only what they are asked to do." (Barnett in Portman and Barnett 1976, p. 4) In a client-driven marketplace where control is given to project managers outside the architect's office, architects can be excluded from aspects of the production process, so as to guarantee time and budgetary management and that targets are met. This requires other project managerial experts to administer the workflow of all team members including the architect. In an increasingly-neoliberal property marketplace, whether the architect is working for a client who wants to occupy the building themselves or a client developer who wants to sell the property on, the 'time is money' problem can have a direct influence on the excesses relating to architectural design because of the issue of market return.

Howard Roark's noble conviction in *The Fountainhead* (Rand 2007) to produce the highest quality designs and to forego a project in order to retain his artistic integrity, as discussed in Chapter 2, is a far cry from the 'inescapable reality of the world' (Till 2009, p. 2) of neoliberal business where economic imperatives drive all forms of *homo oeconomicus* architectural production inside and outside architecture. As Michael Davis (in Owen 2009, p. 128) explains "… Architecture is a 'business' as well as a profession, and resigning commissions is not a way to stay in business." Not all architects are business savvy, however. Lidija Grozdanic (Unknown) goes further to state that:

> Architects have a reputation for being bad at business. This stereotype is not entirely unfounded: The disregard for business is systematically cultivated all through our educations and professional lives. Apart from sporadic mentions of clients at architecture schools, students are largely deprived of lessons on running enterprises and making profit. While this unfortunate state may be gradually changing, there is no way around the fact that the majority of our schools are still based on an outdated educational model that is as divorced from the reality of the AEC [Architecture Engineering Construction] industry as most mainstream architectural practices are reluctant to adjust to the cultural and technological shifts taking place in other industries.

Some graduating architects do not always graduate with the skills and knowledge they need to win commissions, detail the construction of a building, or manage the project procurement process to meet economic and quality expectations. In addition, and because of its tie to the construction industry, architecture is notoriously prone to unstable and unpredictable flows of work. The boom-and-bust construction cycle in architectural practice is something that most practitioners wrestle with at various stages in their working life. When money or access to money is readily available and there is a building flurry, architects with established or new practices are generally busier; but when access to capital dries up, projects can be stalled or stop completely, and construction sites can stagnate, being left dormant. As architecture is dependent on capitalism and because neoliberalism is a rogue version of capitalism, architecture is increasingly not as solid and stable a business as it once was.

The idealistic pursuit of architectural design perfection and autonomy – which one might argue is the ideological framework that drove and continues to drive most architectural schools before the neoliberalisation of universities for industry – is compromised by architecture's explicit relationship with business, which is fluid, slippery, and opportunistic. This means that, unlike in the movies or in the architecture academy, architects are often on the back foot, i.e., in a defensive rather than offensive gameplay position when it comes to delivering the designs they want to get built, hemmed in by and controlled by an audit culture enforced by planning and building guidelines restrictions, sometimes with economic, time, social, and ethical challenges. However, some architects, such as Koolhaas, embrace this unpredictable work landscape of production (Owen 2009, p. 1) by accepting the most unreasonable demands with 'vigor.' Till (2009, p. 34) explains that "Depending on whose argument you follow, architects are mere pawns in an overwhelming regime of power and control [Michel Foucault], or else architects are active agents in the execution of this power and control [Henri Lefebvre]. Either way, they are firmly situated in the real conditions that modernity throws up, and not to be seen in some idealized set-apart space." To cope with the range of contingent forces in global architectural practice, architects acting as 'situated people' make informed choices as to how to conduct themselves to deal with a complex and often unpredictable space of production. (Till 2009, pp. 58–60)

In terms of professional conduct, Till (2009, p. 179) argues that a common mistake in architectural practice "is to confuse professional propriety with an ethical position, as if acting in accordance with the codes of professional conduct will ensure ethical behaviour." In the ARB Code of Conduct 2017, 12 standards of professional conduct and practice need to be met by registered architects.[2] According to Tom Spector (2001, p.102) all 12 standards aim to "clarify […] the architect's responsibilities to the client." The ARB code, like the American Institute of Architects (AIA) "Code of Ethics and Professional Conduct" (2017) primarily focuses on providing a quality service to the client to protect them as consumer (of architectural services) not the building users. (Till 2009, p. 180) Till (2009, p. 180) explains that "The problem lies in the assertion that the codes provide 'ethical guidance'; they do not, often quite the opposite. A client's demands, particularly in the private sector, are often short-term, opportunist, and potentially exploitative. It takes an enlightened client to understand the long-term benefits of user well-being or environmental responsibility, mainly because the market is geared toward the maximizing of development value in the short term." "… Behaving according to professional "ethics' is not the same as behaving ethically. Indeed, they might actually be Codes of Misconduct." (Till 2009, p. 181) This suggests that playing the game of architectural practice within the rules centred on client-consumer satisfaction does not in any way guarantee professional conduct, in fact it may help nurture the opposite.

Participating in the global market economy involves architects, and the construction industry in which they operate, sometimes taking commissions from authoritarian clients, or employing workers at low rates of pay requiring them to work long hours. Even in traditional practices, architects can sometimes purposely exploit their staff, underpaying them for the long hours they are required to work. Like many other large practices that billowed in size (OMA, Norman Foster, Steven Holl, Kisho Kurokawa, etc.), conquering more and more countries with more and more branded projects, Zaha Hadid Architects (ZHA) came under ethical criticism because of Hadid's "apparent indifference to the suffering of workers and low-income residents [affected by her projects]." (Owen 2016, p. 50) Hadid's arguable 'indifference' brought into question the profession's obligation towards social justice under unfettered entrepreneurism, and with it the architect's agency. Some critics, including Guy Mannes-Abbott (2015 in Owen 2016, p. 50) of the group Gulf Labor, have stated that "Starchitects have acted with breathtaking [sic] contempt for the lives and wellbeing of the migrant workers building their spectacular culture shops, from which they profit so handsomely." On the topic of whether "globalism [has] made architecture's professional ethics obsolete," Davis (in Owens 2009, pp. 121–132) argues that the problem has arisen due to the loss of a hierarchy of ethical standards of practice that comes about from working globally in a multitude of countries with different standards of ethical practice. Many not-starchitects can also be accused of abusing labour and resources within their offices by outsourcing parts of their work to cheaper specialists working for less in other countries. The reason starchitects gain such powerful positions to cherry pick their staff and their clients and projects is because of their breeding which allows them to potentially create more social, cultural, and economic capital, but which comes with an often life, focused almost entirely on nurturing their architecture persona at the expense of their outside-architecture persona.

Breeding Pedigree *Homo Oeconomicus* Architects and Getting a Life

How great architects are bred and how they can breed other great architects has been subject of research in sociology, art history, and architecture. Australian architectural critic, Stevens (1998, p. 3) expands Bourdieusien sociological theory applied to architecture in *The Favored Circle: the Social Foundations of Architectural Distinction* and argues that for famous architects "their success owes *at least* as much to their social background and to the social structures within which they are embedded as it does to their native talent (or, as Bourdieu puts it, as much to the unchosen determination of their social milieu as to the undetermined choosing of the application of their gifts)." As an architect and architectural educator, and a professional insider who was outside the dominant media circles at the time, Stevens (1998, p. 36) had a unique position from which to examine architectural culture using what he terms "the sociological toolkit of Pierre Bourdieu" – built upon Bourdieu's definition of the 'capital' and 'field' – which emerges from Karl Marx's writings. As David Swartz (1998, p. 40) notes: "Bourdieu's concept of the field functions as a mediation area between the infrastructure and superstructure where cultural producers and their institutionalized [sic] arena of production reunites the two instances that Marxist theory separates. Bourdieu seeks to write a general science of practices that combines both material and symbolic dimensions and thereby emphasizes [sic] the fundamental *unity* of social life." In this sense, Stevens, through Bourdieu's sociological framework, begins to unite social life (and the way it can socially engineer) with the production of architecture. In so doing, Stevens begins to prise out some of the social systems within architecture that can lead to an architect having differing ability to gain international renown during their career. Understanding the association between the accruing of educational, social, and professional reputational capital through personal networks is a fundamental feature of successfully playing the game of life in architecture. In understanding how social capital can build reputational capital in art and architecture, some academics (Grenfell and Hardy 2007) have built upon the theories and modified diagrams produced by Bourdieu (1993) in *The Field of Cultural Production* and *The Rules of Art* (Bourdieu 1996) first published in 1992. Others have constructed a broader understanding of unacknowledged contributors with or without referring to Bourdieu's 'field' and 'habitus' theories; some wanted to expose those who were part of powerful elite networks but not recognised. Lack of recognition, regardless of the work produced, can be the fate of architects who do not mix in elite social circles, but can also be the fate of those who work in the shadow of starchitects and whose contribution is not made apparent because glory goes to the starchitect. The former is arguably easier to rectify for theoreticians and historians who work to make visible influential architects who have formerly been hidden in the background, so that some lesser-known architects working with starchitects can gain fame and recognition before, but usually after, their death.

The way in which personal and professional life overlap in elite art and architecture circles was the subject of research during the 1980s and 1990s. It was mostly produced by feminist theoreticians who were often themselves affiliated with powerful Ivy league American universities or elite British universities and some of whom whose reputational capital was mutually transferred through their own personal partnerships and the elite social circles they were a part of. Stevens's research into professional marginality due to architectural breeding, and those inspired by him in Australia (Troiani 2005), differed in that the writers were fringe rather than central players in architectural discourse. Still, female and male writers were seeking to understand the social systems that underpin acquiring architectural success – tied with professional inclusion versus professional exclusion. This involves breaking professional secrecy by making public the very personal and intimate social relationships underpinning collaborative labour at the elite level. They were also breaking architecture's 'black box.'

In his essay, "A Black Box: The Secret Profession of Architecture," the architectural historian and engineer, but not a trained architect, Banham (1996, pp. 292–299) describes the architectural profession as a pedagogical tribe, acculturated into a specific ideological discourse that is unlike any other design discipline. Banham (1996) contends that the architectural profession closes ranks on outsiders and entails a code of secrecy for its exclusionary practices. The architectural profession consists of not one architectural tribe but many throughout the world. These are generally initiated in elite universities by significant male architect-educators, and a small number of newly-emerging dominant female architect-educators who acculturate followers in the architecture schools or practices in which they work. Their movement is transnational, occurring through the movement of individuals through the mostly-prestigious architecture schools in the world, primarily in the U.K., Europe, and North America. What is fundamental to this elite circle of architects is their ability to internally produce who can or can't be considered another elite architect through 'master–pupil' or 'master–employee' chains.

Janet Wolff's (1993) *The Social Production of Art*, first published in 1981, set out the sociology of art and questioned the singular authorship of great artists. Through studies of the machinations of architectural production, select architectural scholars have revealed the specific contribution unknown women and men architects, clients, etc., played in the production of mostly seminal pieces of 20th century architecture and their great (not so singularly heroic) male architects. They exposed how, and named the unnamed architects who, as personal friends, sometimes lovers, partners, husbands/wives, clients, or consultants, had collaborated and contributed to or were not credited in the production of select infamous pieces of architecture. Spanish-born, American architectural theoretician, Beatriz Colomina's (1999a) "Collaborations: The Private Life of Modern Architecture" and "Couplings" (Colomina 1999b), and American art historian, Alice T. Friedman's (1998) *Women and the Making of the Modern House*, along with more recent books like *The Collaborators: Interactions in the Architectural Design Process* (Herbert and Donchin 2013), expose unnamed players who collaborated in the design process of a range of projects and accentuate the complex process of collaboration that underpins architectural production as a socio-political and multi-disciplinary profession. In the main, the architecture profession has aligned and recognised a style or ideology with *an* architect and their followers and sees that there are evolutionary trees – like Charles Jencks's (2000) "Evolutionary Tree of Twentieth Century Architecture"[3] – through which architectural excellence is transferred. Most scholars refrain from digging deeply into the social backstories of "En%abling architecture" (Koolhaas 1997) and architects.

However, by detaching art and architecture's professional practice life from the personal biographical histories of those in the dominant social networks, it is never possible to see how social capital is carried professionally into practice through personal associations or to ascertain how important the friends one makes and keeps can be tied to other powerful professional or social networks. As already discussed in Chapter 3, choices of personal and professional friendship and partnering (male–male, female–male, or female–female) can impact on the potential to accrue social and reputational capital. Recently, the deeper, more personal stories of the accumulation of social, cultural, and economic capital through genealogical architectural family trees of elite architects has been diagrammed in lineal architectural 'sequences' (Rodell 2008) and in architectural genograms. (Troiani 2010) While Rosalind Krauss's (1986) "Sculpture in the Expanded Field" points to how styles are reproduced in postmodern art and questions the originality of avant-garde design as such, Joe Day (2009) contends that the capacity of the work of Jencks' evolutionary tree and Krauss's contestation of how originality operates in architecture is that it allows for disciplinary futures to be predicted through a mapping of the past and to see a cycle of reproduction of ideologies. Still, emerging architects might learn of discernible patterns which could be reproduced later, reinvigorating former ideologies to suit future life.

The diagrams never show who is excluded from these influential groups of powerful architectural players however, nor do they represent all the creative work produced at any one time or in any one place, just those in the elite circles that control architectural knowledge and its publicity. Some genealogical diagrams represent ideological competitors, and the breadth and expanse of elites grows as unmonitored media access and publicity increases. Still, even if architects create powerful groups in one country, their architectural family roots usually need to be from a famous (biological or non-biological) architectural mother or father, grandmother, or grandfather, etc., for validation by the elite. This means that how one is bred in architectural practice is fundamental to how the discipline itself – not necessarily the public but this usually follows – recognises excellence. This means that the friends or enemies one makes inside architecture and outside architecture influences the potential an architect has to gain commissions, build buildings, and accrue social, economic, and cultural capital.

In 2016, Architect theoreticians, Alejandro Zaero-Polo and Guillermo Fernandez Abascal produced a diagram to represent the greater and more varied types of architectural practices throughout the world at the time. Their diagram included in "Architecture's 'Political Compass': A Taxonomy of Emerging Architecture in One Diagram" (Zaero-Polo and Abascal 2016) is a variation of Charles Jencks's "Evolutionary Tree of Twentieth Century Architecture." Unlike other diagrams, Zaero-Polo and Abascal identify a broader range of players;

ranging from the international mainstream architectural elite who are fully engaged in global architectural capitalism to a diverse range of non-mainstream forms of architectural practice who purposely aspire to disengage themselves from, or go beyond, neoliberal economies. As previously referred to, the categories of practice defined by Zaero-Polo and Abascal (2016) are based on seven political positions:

> [1] The *"Activists,"* who reject architecture's dependence on market forces by operating largely outside the market, with a focus on community building projects, direct engagement with construction, and non-conventional funding strategies; … [2] the *"Populists,"* whose work is calibrated to reconnect with the populace thanks to a media-friendly, diagrammatic approach to architectural form; … [3] the *"New Historicists,"* whose riposte to the "end of history" hailed by neoliberalism is an embrace of historically- informed design; [4] the *"Skeptics,"* whose existential response to the collapse of the system is in part a return to postmodern critical discourse and in part an exploration of contingency and playfulness through an architecture of artificial materials and bright colors; [5] the *"Material Fundamentalists,"* who returned to a tactile and virtuoso use of materials in response to the visual spectacle of pre- crash architecture; [6] practitioners of *"Austerity Chic,"* a kind of architectural "normcore" (to borrow a term from fashion) which focuses primarily on the production process, and resulting performance, of architecture; and finally [7] the *"Techno-Critical,"* a group of practices largely producing speculative architecture, whose work builds upon but also remains critical of the data- driven parametricism of their predecessors.[4]

Defining the growing number of groups of architectural practitioners with different ideological positions and modes of architectural procurement and practice was growing in interest well before Zaero-Polo and Abascal's efforts to diagram dominant paradigms. In *Spatial Agency: Other ways of Doing Architecture*, architecture academics Nishat Awan, Tatjana Schneider, and Jeremy Till (2011), with colleagues at the Sheffield School of Architecture in England, sought to explore alternative architectural practices through roundtable discussions and other discursive events. For Awan, Schneider, and Till (2011, p. 31) 'the dialectic of agency and structure,' which underpins stereotypical representations of the architects like Roark, only represents the work of an elite circle of privileged architects. In response to a desire to "avoid on the one hand the ineffectual individual solipsism of individual agents or on the other hand despair in the fact of overarching structures," Awan, Schneider, and Till (2011, p. 31) argue that agency and structure should not be considered dualistic opposing forces. Instead, they propose that alternative architectural practices draw together human agency and structure through "choosing spatial agency." Spatial agency, as represented by the 136 examples showcased in the book, sees that the consequences of architecture are being primarily bound to wider social networks rather than "the objects of architecture."

This sharing of the process of architectural production that sees the architect as a collaborator in a societal collective, and that also shifts the objects of architecture away from the central focus of practice, removes the notion of singular authorship and undermines the egotism that can be seen to drive stereotypical elite architectural practice.

While these seven categories of types of 21st century architectural practices set out by Zaero-Polo and Abascal (2016) and the 136 examples of spatial agency showcased by Awan, Schneider, and Till (2011) respond with other ways of doing architecture in the neoliberal marketplace, there are a multitude of other architectural practitioners that operate independently of any political compass or societal motivation. If one surveys the top 150 architecture practices annually in the world, in terms of revenue turnover, it is more often the case that multinational business-oriented architects rather than the elite starchitects dominate the top ranks. As Reinier De Graaf (2017) argues in *Four Walls and a Roof: The Complex Nature of a Simple Profession*, from the extra-large, large, medium, small, to single-person practices, architects with a strong moral architectural compass instilled during their architectural education or early practice life can find themselves in a perpetual conflict between their ideological genealogical beliefs and the need to critique practice and every business of architecture in neoliberal times. If an architect is unable to gain notoriety from their novel designs, elite architectural breeding can instead lead to ongoing professional imbalance – ideologically, morally, emotionally, and financially. Due to an ongoing tussle between professional and ideological quality of architectural production and the realities of the construction and property markets, many architects find it an easier more satisfying life to abandon their professional responsibilities to quite simply just stay afloat or to make money. For those whose education is less architecturally puritanical and for a growing number of younger architects operating in an increasingly-competitive marketplace, creative archipreneurship – which requires taking risks and thinking 'outside the box' to generate a new marketplace for architectural procurement and production – becomes more a game of architectural survival. This approach can have the positive result of allowing potentially greater autonomy and professional diversity, but comes with neoliberal conditions including short-termism, heightened marketisation, and competition.

The Creative Archipreneur

The problem of how to secure work, and with it a flow of income, is and has been an ongoing concern for architects of all generations although the problem, arguably, has been compounded by the uncertainty experienced in times of crisis during which the amount of clients with money to fund projects is diminishing. As the number of students who graduate from architecture degrees increases, there is an equal increase in the number of young, chartered architects entering the workforce worldwide so that there is greater competition for projects. This needs

FIGURE 6.2   Architect and real estate developer, John Portman in front of One Peachtree Center, part of a 19-building complex. Photograph credit: Suzanne Opton/ Getty Images, Editorial # 50428592; The Chronicle Collection; Date created: 01 January, 1995; Barcode & Object name: 1028313.

to be understood in consideration of there being a limited number of clients who "can afford good design and pursue jobs [as patrons] that will provide maximum creative freedom and exposure" (Grozdanic Unknown) or which match an architect's skillset and practice agendas. Architects who are entering practice do not always get the same kinds of broad experience to understand the machinations of how to run an architectural business; nor do all of them have the time or desire to spend "years, decades even, working for others, gaining no significant insight into how companies operate, attract clients and negotiate." (Grozdanic Unknown) Architectural mentorship inside many architectural practices is changing in form, mostly decreasing or diminishing as time restrictions related to efficient productivity increase. Architects are often required to be more creative regarding how they approach gaining commissions in practice and optimise their project teams to deliver a project.

Different generations of 'neoliberal subjects' (Brown 2015, p. 33) have varying expectations and capabilities to achieve a successful, fulfilling life in architecture. The variations between the career expectations of less experienced and more experienced generations of architects can sometimes relate to the speed at which they want to, expect to, or feel they are owed or deserve promotions, commissions, etc., to build a higher profile or reputation inside or outside their office. As already explained in Chapter 2, Franco Ghilardi (quoted in Van der Hoorn 2012, p. 135) argues that "The idea that you build up a reputation, you do an amazing building and then people get to know you, is a bit outdated. There is a shift in speed: people coming right out of school are already famous, or even earlier." The effect of moving away from long-termism toward a 'short-term[ism],' as discussed by Zygmunt Bauman (2000, p. 147) in Chapter 4, underpins a change in mentality of (mostly) younger, but not exclusively so, go-getter, confident, and entrepreneurial architects. There is also the issue that more experienced architectural practitioners usually do not have the same level of digital prowess as Millennials and post-Millennials. In a stereotypical office, younger generations of architectural practitioners become the backbone of drawing production through their ability to produce digital drawing packages, renderings, visual animations, etc., while more experienced architects can often lean more towards management, client schmoozing and presentations, or design brand control. However. greater access to new digital technologies has created new opportunities for architects and their architectural practice.

In *Millennials in Architecture: Generations, Disruption, and the Legacy of a Profession*, architecture academic Darius Sollohub (2019, p. 5) argues that as 'digital natives' Millennial architects – for him born from the early 1980s up until the mid-2000s – are a "large wave of youth empowered with digital know-how." Due to "their digital inheritance," Millennials have the profound ability to "change industries, social structure, [and] politics…" (Sollohub 2019, p. xii) and this is beginning to occur in architecture. While architects have for many years been complaining about their loss of agency in architectural production, Sollohub (2019, p. xiii) sees that it is Millennial architects that have the potential to create positive change. He (Sollohub 2019, p. 14) explains that the most notable characteristic of the Millennial architect is "their role as the disruptors of economies, politics, and academia in a turbulent era." Using e-handbooks or YouTube videos on how to be a better architect-businessperson, the digitally savvy Millennial 'archipreneur' understands and exploits self-marketing and is more aggressive in creating their own opportunities. Digital Millennial disruptors in architecture can also impact through use of social media platforms to encourage systemic changes in architecture culture, including working conditions. Ideally, Sollohub sees that Millenial architectural disruptors might be able to offer other more sustainable models of architectural production and other models of balanced work life in architecture.

Digital tutorials, blogs, and e-books, etc., have emerged to support the growth in interest in 'archipreneurship.' Books and YouTube tutorials by Berlin-based architect, Tobias Maescher (2018; in Eerlings 2017), and American architects, Eric Reinholdt (2015a, 2015b) and James Petty (2018) exemplify how a new generation of mostly Western, Millennial, young, white, male architects encourage and support others online in ways to play the game of the business of architectural practice with greater freedom and less obligation to traditional modes of labour, with varying degrees of 'political positioning' (Zaero-Polo and Abascal 2016) or 'spatial agency.' (Awan, Schneider, and Till 2011) Here a new kind of 'archipreneur' seeks to capitalise on alternative, innovative money-streams, in association with or without the game of home life or family/household life and the potential to create more career choices.

According to Maescher (in Earlings 2017), an 'archipreneur' combines both the skills of an architect with that of an entrepreneur. Archipreneurship goes beyond the traditional service-centred business model used in architectural practice, where an architect gets a fee for the architectural services they provide to a client at stages in the conventionally-defined architectural production process. Since many architects are unable to control the quality of their design – which is dictated and paid for by their client, not them – or are unable to win commissions in an increasingly-competitive market of more and more architectural graduates, and like Howard Roark feel frustrated, undervalued, or are not adequately remunerated for their work, Maescher (in Eerlings 2017) proposes that architects use "their skill set in a creative and entrepreneurial way to create additional streams of income." Since younger architects increasingly want more autonomy, better work-life balance and pay, and are more inclined to use digital platforms like YouTube, etc., to guide them towards their own form of practice life as soon as possible, Maescher (in Eerling 2017) argues that a neoliberally-driven form of 'archipreneurship' is one way they can best build a portfolio of projects.

Reinholdt's *Architect and Entrepreneur: A Field Guide to Building, Branding, and Marketing You* (Volume 1) and *Architect and Entrepreneur: A How-to Guide for Innovating Practice: Tactics, Models, and Case Studies in Passive Income* (Volume 2), both published in 2015, emerged out of the sense that the material offered to architects by the American Institute of Architects (AIA) was 'uninspir[ing] and outdated.' (2015a, p. 6) Through the e-books and YouTube channel (30X40 Design Workshop) online, Reinholdt speaks to a vast international audience and subscribers to present and give helpful guidance about his experience of the process of making architecture as an emerging sole practitioner. Having a positive entrepreneurial mindset, defining a brand, marketing online or in traditional ways, getting commissions and being paid for them, as well as defining some essential Startup costs and then managing finances, are but some of the topics covered. Software essentials and a Startup Toolkit are shared with a community that might not yet have had access to this kind of information in their architectural education or practice experience. Turning to "online resources, blogs and forums" allows Reinholdt to find other young professionals who are grappling with the same problems as emerging sole practitioners.

Along similar lines to Reinholdt, Maescher (2018) argues in *The Archipreneur Concept* that young architects and students need to think 'outside the box' in terms of how they develop their architecture business and be fluid, influenced by all that surrounds them in these 'liquid times' (Baumann 2007) rather than be limited by the possibilities of the stereotypical models of practice. Maescher (2018) offers 32 architectural concepts for optimisation and economisation and argues that new generations of architects need to embrace the complexity and heterogeneity of society using new and emerging technologies. While others are listed, two common ways used by architects to create new work and a reputation is through, first, winning a high-profile competition and getting the design built and, second, morphing into a private architect-developer.

The *Grand Prix* architectural design competition was an essential element of the education of architects at the *Académie d'architecture* and École des Beaux Art (School of Fine Arts) in France in the late 18th century. (Lipstadt and Bergdoll eds. 1989; Andersson, Bloxham, and Rönn in Andersson, Bloxham, and Rönn eds. 2013, p. 9) The *charette method* – in which a student produced an esquisse drawing (or first sketch of a design) used to develop a set of detailed drawings – allowed teachers to quickly judge a student's ability to analyse a design problem. It has since been a hallmark of architectural studio work – which is usually not tied to a client, although this is changing as neoliberal universities become more centred on preparing students for employment post-university[5] – and can be used in architectural competitions in practice.

"Participating in architectural competitions is associated both with a playful learning process, delight, collaboration and with competition in dead earnest." (Andersson, Bloxham, and Rönn in Andersson, Bloxham, and Rönn eds. 2013, p. 9) While still working *for* a client but in a pre-formal appointment phase, the architect remains in an autonomous space of design play. Playing the game of design with less rules, Hélène Lipstadt (2009, p.18) defines a design competition as "the space in which architects can act as if, and believe themselves to be, full-fledged, relatively autonomous creators." In "Where design competitions matter," Paul Gottschling (2018) agrees that "...The design competition is a moment of architectural work in which architectural autonomy is uniquely pronounced, where the artistic statements of architects achieve a special efficacy." As such, many designers see the space of the competition typically as being freer and with fewer limitations than built projects with cost and time restrictions. Much like design projects are produced while in architectural education, the competition allows architects to operate in what might appear an entirely interior space of cultural production inside the profession, detached from mundane imperatives. Architectural competitions in practice are invited and closed or open, paid or unpaid, local, national, or international. Invited or closed competitions typically offer some fee for the payment of an initial phase of architectural work, while open competitions generally ask that the architect work for free knowing they are taking a risk of winning or losing the project commission game. However, because the prestige of the client and scale or prestige of the proposed project has the potential to create immediate reputational, social, and economic capital, emerging or unknown architects often see it as a risk worth taking. This is because winning a highly prestigious, open international competition over competitors can move them from architectural obscurity to world-renown. Winning a significant competition as a young practitioner is usually considered a lucky career break.

Hadid's winning of the Peak Leisure Club competition in Hong Kong, China, 1982–1983 in her 30s gave her instant notoriety. Renzo Piano and Richard Rogers with Gianfranco Franchini also rose to fame in their 30s when they won an open international design competition for the Pompidou Centre in 1971, chosen from 681 international entries. While entering competitions is not a long-term strategy for obtaining sustained work, the architectural design competition can supplement workflows in practice or allow an unknown architect the possibility of finding a wealthy client or patron to support their design ambitions and to get their work built if it is economically viable.

On the issue of design in relation to the budget of a project, Gottschling (2018) notes that "Scholars of design competitions have given us a picture of an architecture freed (at least illusorily) from economic imperatives, where what makes a difference are the designerly and philosophical positions of the architects...." However many competitions come with a project budget or other limitations that can prohibit a winning competition design being built.

Not being able to get a design built is a fundamental obstacle for many architectural practitioners, non-elite and elite alike, young or not. This is because it is through building up a portfolio of projects that architects build their reputational capital. Take the case of Hadid whose early career was plagued with fantastic competition-winning projects, like her Peak Project, which were often considered unbuildable but whose fate changed when she began to collaborate with the younger Patrik Schumacher, who she employed in 1988 as a student computer technician; Schumacher later became her business partner and successor.[6]

Between 1980 and 2013, Hadid went from "being the Architect Who Never Got Anything Built to someone who can't stop building." (Moore 2013) This is due, in part, to her shift from analogue to digital drawing which allowed the formerly-considered-unbuildable designs, because of their complex geometries, to be built.[7] Digital drawing, which will be discussed in detail in the following section, allowed the ZHA designs to become 'phantasmagorical' neoliberal commodities. (Spencer 2016, p. 73) This shift was also accompanied in part by a shift in Schumacher's 'political compass.'

While Schumacher and Hadid "were closer politically" when he joined the firm, Schumacher's politics moved more towards conservative, neoliberal positioning after the 2008 economic crisis. *Guardian* journalist, Oliver Wainwright (2016) explains that "Like a number of fellow rightwing [sic] libertarians, he [Schumacher] was a former Marxist who had become disillusioned. He was finally jolted out of his 'mainstream political slumber' by the financial crisis, when he discovered the writings of Ludwig von Mises and Friedrich Hayek, the godfathers of neoliberalism, along with Murray Rothbard's ideas of anarcho-capitalism." This shift in 'political compass' led Schumacher to propose a neoliberal vision of a privatised city of London in a public lecture that he later retracted.[8] During this post-economic crisis period, Schumacher fully embraced the neoliberalisation of the profession by looking more towards models in which the architect works for and can also become a private developer.

In 2013 Schumacher held the John Portman Chair in Architecture at Harvard's GSD (Graduate School of Design). Schumacher has an ongoing interest in Portman, who became world renowned for his success in the 1970s as an architect-developer, a notion that is becoming increasingly attractive to many Millennial architects who want ownership of the full architectural production process by being client, architect, and developer.

As already outlined in Chapter 2, British architectural theoretician, Andrew Saint (1983) identifies the architect-developer as a well-established image of the contemporary architect, most notably in the form of Portman.[9] Portman is recognised for his decadent and ambitiously designed hotels in Atlanta. (Figure 6.2) As luxury commodities in the property market, Portman represented the successful archipreneur-developer. Portman's 33-storey Westin Bonaventure Hotel in Los Angeles has been recognised as a symbol of 'the cultural logic of late capitalism.' (Jameson 1992) The postmodern political geographer and urban theorist, Edward Soja (1989, p. 243) describes the Westin Bonaventure Hotel as "a concentrated representation of the restructured spatiality of the late capitalist city." Like Hadid, Portman was a painter. He was also fascinated by complex architectural geometries and forms that were structurally ambitious, fluid, and decadent. However unlike Hadid he was a family man, a father of six children, and someone who worked six days a week. He grew his client base through his ability to produce dazzling corporate artefacts using his skills as property developer and designer and was able to generate, to a degree, his own work while still being driven by the need for "an architecture for people and not for things." (Portman and Barnett 1976, p. 57)

Of great influence on Portman was Frank Lloyd Wright, who was a visiting lecturer at Georgia Tech when Portman was a student there in the 1940s. (Barnett in Portman and Barnett 1976, p. 21) While Wright is an example of Saint's (1983, p. 12) heroic architect and genius, Wright also exemplifies the 'archipreneur' well before the phrase was coined. This is because Wright was an architect prepared to play the game of not working by the conventional rules (in his private life and) in professional practice creating inventive strategies to generate income and maintain his office. This occurred most notably through Wright's Taliesin studio. (Figure 6.1) Taliesin was the estate Wright built south of Spring Green Village in Wisconsin, U.S.A. as his home and studio after leaving his first wife, Catherine 'Kitty' Tobin Wright, and six children to live with his mistress and client, Mamah Borthwick. After two fires destroyed Taliesin, and after Borthwick's tragic murder, financial problems beset Wright and led to Taliesin being foreclosed by the Bank of Wisconsin in 1927. Through financial help from friends, Wright reacquired Taliesin in 1928 and quickly devised a new income stream known as the Taliesin Fellowship. The Taliesin Fellowship was "Originally founded in 1929 as a way for Wright to escape his creditors by selling shares in himself. Its main enterprise was the establishment of a 'School of Architecture' run on an apprenticeship basis at Wright's studio in Taliesin.... In practice they [students] carried out large amounts of domestic, farm and building work as well as acting as free architectural assistants, all the time having to pay substantial fees for the privilege." (Martin in Chance and Schmiedeknecht eds. 2001) Commissions such as Wright's infamous Fallingwater residence, 1936–1939, for Lilliane and Edgar J. Kaufmann, came to Wright through their son, Edgar Kaufmann Jr. who became an apprentice at Taliesin in 1934. Other famous projects followed so that Wright was able to reinvent his professional life through savvy entrepreneurialism.

Unlike during Portman and Wright's time, entrepreneurial books now exist on how to build a new architecture business quickly and profitably as architect-developer. In *Architect & Developer: A Guide to Self-Initiating Projects*, Petty (2018) advocates that architects have traditionally been passive in how they approach getting work and recommends that to take control over what is becoming a developer-led architectural marketplace in which architects bid for work, there are benefits in taking risks as an archi-developer. Petty explains on his book's Amazon page: "What developers do is not difficult; you need only have an appetite for risk. I sat down with over a dozen separate architects who are self-initiating their work. Some were doing this as a side hustle while holding down a nine-to-five job, some were small studios that were dipping their toes into the development game, and some were full-blown *Architects & Developers*."

As the game of a life in architectural practice is increasingly tied to creating new income streams of clients with money to sustain business, the production process has changed to suit neoliberal modes of drawing and building production. Computer drawing has been merged with building accounting software such as BIM (Building Information Modelling) to increase accuracy in building production and delivery. Design and construction team efficiency are central to how an architect can creatively compete in the game of architectural practice.

Digital Drawing, Productivity, Creativity, and Metric Architecture

People who dream of becoming architects often choose the profession because of the artistic, design aspect of the architect's work. However, the architectural design phase of any project is usually often only 5–10% of the entire architectural service. The design stage is often done by partners or select individuals in a practice who have design expertise. While less-experienced architects can be given opportunities to design parts or all of a project, it would be exceptional or virtually unheard of for a principal of a large corporate architectural practice to allow this to happen, simply because of a need to keep a level of architectural design brand identity and quality. The fact that most of any architect's work is not design, but instead mostly selling and marketing their designs and the production of technical reports, construction drawings and details, or being on site supervising a project's construction, can come as a shock to some newcomer architects. The range of building standards and contractual obligations that develop an understanding costings and time management, mean that project report writing is practical rather than creatively oriented. Under neoliberalism, a practicing architect nowadays can be far less able or willing to engage in design purism with a client, as Roark did, because practice is centred on service delivery and clients are often disinterested in or unaware of architecture's internal ideological design tribalism, instead only seeing a product. The process of producing architecture by human architectural workers of all architectural classes in any architect's office is tied to the use of new digital technologies and audit systems which are increasingly removing the hand, body, and mind of the architect from the architectural production process. Hand sketching and hand drawing on paper in most architectural practices is waning, unless it a nostalgic *esquisse* sketch coming straight from the most talented or famous architect's hand. Le Corbusier is famous for sketching his design as scribbles on serviettes and archiving them to reiterate their value. In *Sketches of Frank Gehry* (Pollack Dir. 2006), the Post-War Cohort of architects, born in 1929, returned architecture to its romantic hand-drawing *esquisse* phase, merging it with digital technologies for construction used in aviation design. The slick architectural render, 3D visualisation, or model, which is often defined as 'the money shot' that can win an architect a commission is nowadays mostly produced through computer drawing. The hand that draws on paper operates differently to the hand that draws on a computer screen/s and the bodily relationship the architect has with the object of design and its process of production can therefore change. Disembodiment and mechanisation of the architectural labourer can be heightened.

In *The Death of Drawing*, David Ross Scheer (2014, p. 2) argues that the world of the architecture is "being turned upside down as BIM and other digital technologies transform the professional landscape. Younger architects immerse themselves in virtual worlds and few learn to draw. Older architects struggle to understand how best to use these technologies and keep their firms competitive." What is important to Scheer (2014, p. 2) is how this affects the way an architect goes about their daily work. The methods are not "another pencil," (Scheer 2014, p. 2) but are instead "both evidence and agents of fundamental changes in the nature of [the practice of] architecture" which is increasingly being positioned within the building industry through building simulation. Simulations imitate designs in the real world, to reproduce reality. They focus solely on an operational understanding of building *performance* which includes "structural capacity, thermal comfort, energy consumption, cost, time to construct, functional efficiency, and conformity to building and other codes, among others. Once performance becomes the yardstick by which design is judged, every aspect of it can be viewed as a kind of performance that can be simulated and evaluated using the model." (Scheer 2014, p. 10) According to Scheer (2014, p. 11), the distinction between design and construction vanishes in the simulated digital model because the distance between representation and referent collapses. Issues of craft, standardisation, and material composition come to the fore. What these digital technologies do is turn design into '*computable*,' calculatable data that can be stored and transmitted virtually and rapidly 24/7 all over the world. (Scheer 2014, p. 11) Unlike CAD [Computer-Aided Drafting], BIM and computational design prioritise building procurement.

The rise in adopting BIM technology as a method of design production is in part due to "the powerful economic forces" which can eliminate or reduce "costly problems with faulty construction documents and project management, and the logistics of managing vast amounts of real estate" (Scheer 2014, p. 14) for major building owners. BIM is also a form of new and advanced technology that is seen to improve production. (Scheer 2014, p. 15) According to Scheer (2014, p. 103), BIM's 'forte' is the "problem [...] of information management." Scheer (2014, p. 106) explains that "The key to understanding BIM is that its fundamental purpose is to facilitate business process in the building industry by organizing [sic] information flows throughout the building lifecycle." The neoliberal focus on optimisation within the architectural production process can and often does override social or cultural agendas. As part of the BIM production team of professional experts, the architectural team can become, just as the academic does in the neoliberal university, a group of architectural, factory workers delivering increasingly-specialised services.

Prior to the pandemic crisis, architects were increasingly using new digital technologies to work locally, nationally, and globally no matter where the architect was in the world. Increasingly delivering buildings on time and on budget in in-person and online mixed teams of professionals can sometimes be of greater priority than the quality or ambition of an architect's design. In the global digital 24/7 marketplace, the business of architecture has become a primary focus and, as a consequence, the ethical consumption of resources and labour is becoming increasingly compromised by the *homo oeconomicus* architect.

In *The Future of Professions: How Technology will Transform the Work of Human Experts*, Professor of Internet Studies, Richard Susskind, and Daniel Susskind (2017) examine the decline of today's professions, which they perceive as antiquated, too costly, and prone to monopolisation, and argue new technologies will replace professional expertise. They claim that in a digitally- and technologically-advanced society, architects – along with most other professionals – will not work as they have previously worked. Instead of professional expertise, newly-formulated technologie, s from telepresence to AI (Artificial Intelligence), will be engaged at a lower cost or at no cost without requiring face-to-face interaction. Susskind and Susskind (2017) envisage that machines will potentially become more capable than humans and argue that a new generation of 'open-collared workers' (Susskind and Susskind 2017) will emerge in all professions in the 21st century. In the case of architects, it might be that what a life in architecture is at the time of writing this book or in the future is not what it was originally and that another type of work in the creative economy could better suit the life path of an architecture graduate who is (more or less) suited to working in a real or computational, simulated workspace.

I Don't Want to be an Architect Anymore

As freedom of choice widens for 'neoliberal subjects,' (Brown 2015, p. 33) architectural educators are teaching a growing number of mostly Generation Y'ers (or Millennials born between 1977 and 1994) and Generation Z'ers (born between 1995 and 2012) who, even after having studied multiple degrees to become an architect, can choose not to work in architectural practice. Many do not find architecture a good fit for a range of reasons. Some choose to purposely leave a life in architecture because of disillusionment and dissatisfaction with the nature of often repetitive and unimaginative work tasks given to recent graduates. Some choose to sidestep into other types of work which might or might not tangentially build upon their architectural knowledge or expertise. Some architecture students or graduates are drawn during their studies towards sectors that engage less with the 'real world' problems of building a building 'on time and on budget,' instead choosing to design architectures that are purposely only for the virtual realm. Others who are perturbed with architecture's lack of social engagement (if that is their experience) can move into areas in which policy writing, etc., may offer greater satisfaction. In addition, it is not uncommon for someone who has begun to study architecture to decide to move out of it, and then choose to return to it. In a neoliberal work climate in which career options and opportunities are limitless, to some job satisfaction arguably becomes more prone to being short-term. While there are many types of work that students who have partially or fully studied architecture can do, below are some areas that are emerging as being areas more commonly moved across into. They can include interior design, product design, computer and video game design, production design, visual effect for films, virtual reality, animation, photography, fine arts, graphic design, writing, city tour guide, policy writing, humanitarian (housing/planning) work, and working for not-for-profit housing associations to name but a few.

There are a range of reasons architects leave architectural practice. Some leave because the job is not as design-centred as they first envisaged. Others find the financial remuneration for working often long hours as an architect is not enough in comparison to other types of work. Then there is the serious responsibility of designing safe buildings. After many years of university study, an architecture graduate still needs to be licenced to practice independently and this comes with risks and the need for ongoing lifelong training. As architecture becomes more controlled by an audit culture and technocratic processes, it can lose appeal. Then there is the project pressure to deliver on time and on budget, the fact architects are increasingly losing project control to project managers, and on top of these, there remains gender, racial, and class inequality. While one might study architecture, it is often the case that graduates no longer work in traditional architectural practice because their skills in spatial representation can offer them other opportunities. As Quinn Levine (Unknown) notes, it is "a common misconception that designers have a significant amount of knowledge only applicable to building design and construction as there are clear parallels between real and virtual design processes."

Levine (Unknown) notes that architects and designers have skills that are transferable to video game design such as Assassins Creed II or LA Noire. As an authentic depiction of Los Angeles in the year 1947, La Noire composites "180,000 reference images, 1,000 newspapers, and 110,000 aerial photographs, along with historical publications such as *Architectural Digest* and *Home and Garden* to create the most accurate depiction of mid-century Los Angeles," but even so imagination is needed because some spaces are newly-designed. (Levine Unknown) The design process applied to a video game designs virtual space with the architect's involvement. "Training and working as a designer impart a unique set of skills in relation to spatial awareness, color [sic] and interior organization [sic] as well as architectural understanding and the importance of the creative process. Designing space with the purpose of habitability in a virtual world allows for a lot of creative headroom. The designs don't necessarily need to be constructible but should still hold true to the most important part of any video game: Gameplay." (Levine Unknown)

What differs is therefore not the process but the software tools. Revit is used by many architectural designers to create construction drawings and models. It can incorporate a high level of detail to instruct a contractor and subcontractors. "Virtual model creation for video games and other virtual reality spaces do not require that level of detail and thus use a different set of tools that focus on lighter models, texturing, and efficient rendering." (Levine Unknown) The 3D modelling software most commonly used in the gaming industry includes Maya, 3DS Max, and Blender. Noteworthy though is the fact that many architectural schools use these types of software. The difference is the precision and calculation of structures that do not collapse, or which are buildable in architecture. In game design there is a large tolerance for creative play which does not need to be structurally sound.

> Much like architecture, video gaming's power is in its ability to draw together countless other, well-established art forms; perfecting this amalgamation and its applications is where its own status as art lies. Instead of attempting to add sophistication to a game using architects and 'real-world' architecture, the focus should be on how games have borne bizarre, sophisticated and prescient architectures of their very own, and how this burgeoning medium can feed back into other professions and practice.
>
> *(Astbury 2014)*

Architects not only design across real and virtual environments, but they also work and live their everyday lives across those spaces. In the next section, we discuss the sites in which an architect undertakes their work, in person in the office or virtually through remote digital platforms. Using a neoliberal lens of increased opportunity the pros and cons of the various modes of flexible or remote work will be considered in relation to architects from different demographic groups.

Notes

1 The full quotation reads "I think we've been through a period where too many people have been given to understand that if they have a problem, it's the government's job to cope with it. 'I have a problem, I'll get a grant.' 'I'm homeless, the government must house me.' They're casting their problem on society. And, you know, there is no such thing as society. There are individual men and women, and there are families. And no government can do anything except through people, and people must look to themselves first. It's our duty to look after ourselves and then, also to look after our neighbour. People have got the entitlements too much in mind, without the obligations. There's no such thing as entitlement, unless someone has first met an obligation." Source: Prime minister Margaret Thatcher, talking to *Women's Own magazine*, October 3, 1987.
2 The ARB's 2017 12 standards of professional conduct and practice of the architect are: 1. Be honest and act with integrity; 2. Be competent; 3. Promote your services honestly and responsibly; 4. Manage your business competently; 5. Consider the wider impact of your work; 6. Carry out your work faithfully and conscientiously; 7. Be trustworthy and look after your clients' money properly; 8. Have appropriate insurance arrangements; 9. Maintain the reputation of architects; 10. Deal with disputes or complaints appropriately; 11. Co-operate with regulatory requirements and investigations; and 12. Have respect for others.
3 Dominant architectural styles and their most famous key players were first represented in Charles Jencks's diagram, "Evolutionary Tree of Twentieth Century Architecture," first published in 2000 and later elaborated in "Critique of 20th-Century Evolution" (Jencks in Garcia ed. 2010: 306). Inspired by *The Barr Chart* diagram for the *Cubism and Abstract Art* exhibition which opened at MOMA in March 1936 by Alfred H. Barr Jr., Jencks mapped select influential players and their styles over time, at the same time identifying opposing ideological architectural camps.
4 Italics have been added to highlight the seven architectural positions.
5 Live projects for real clients or community groups are an exception.

6 Hadid employed Schumacher as a student in 1988. He returned to work for Hadid in 1990 and became her long-term business partner. After Hadid's untimely death, Schumacher remains a principal board director of ZHA and heads the practice.

7 ZHA's architecture also followed suit, first in terms of its iconic 'phantasmagorical' (Spencer 2016, p. 73) brand image form making and second in terms of its production of 'ubiquitous workspace' (Spencer 2016, pp. 76–79) for client consumers.

8 Around eight months after Hadid's death, Schumacher delivered a keynote speech at Berlin's World Architecture festival where he advocated, through an Urban Policy Manifesto, the abolition of social housing and prescriptive planning regulations in favour of "the wholesale privatization of our streets, squared and parks." (Wainwright 2016) In his keynote address, Schumacher (in Wainwright 2016) welcomed overseas investment in London arguing that "even if these global entrepreneurs are only here for a few weeks, they throw some key parties and these are amazing multiplying events." Schumacher (in Wainwright 2016) argues that, in an effort to "loosen… the reins and roll… back the nanny state…we must unleash entrepreneurial creativity and individual empowerment for great prosperity and freedom for all." "Instead of calling for the state with every problem," he [Schumacher] (Wainwright 2016) asks, "why not see it as an entrepreneurial opportunity?" After public outcries about his speech, Schumacher claimed his vision of an idealistic neoliberal future city was a theoretical speculation.

9 Portman married Joan 'Jan' Newton and had six children. He died in 2017, aged 93.

References

Andersson E., Bloxham Zettersten, G., and Rönn, M. eds. 2013. *Architectural Competitions - Histories and Practice*. Stockholm: The Royal Institute of Technology and Rio Kulturkooperativ.

Astbury, J. 2014. Playing the Architect: Why Video Games and Architecture Need Each Other. *The Architectural Review*, June 25, 2014. https://www.architectural-review.com/essays/playing-the-architect-why-video-games-and-architecture-need-each-other, Accessed November 06, 2023.

Awan, N., Schneider, T., and Till, J. 2011. *Spatial Agency: Other Ways of Doing Architecture*. London: Routledge.

Banham, R. 1996. A Black Box: The Secret Profession of Architecture. In Banham R., *A Critic Writes: Essays by Reyner Banham*. Berkeley, Los Angeles; London: University of California Press, pp. 292–299. [Originally published in *New Statesman and Society*, 12 Oct. 1990, pp. 22–25.]

Bauman, Z. 2007. *Liquid Times: Living in an Age of Uncertainty*. Cambridge: Polity Press.

Bauman, Z. 2000. *Liquid Modernity*. Cambridge: Polity Press.

Benko, C. and Anderson, M. 2010. *The Corporate Lattice: Achieving High Performance in the Changing World of Work*. Brighton, Massachusetts: Harvard Business Review Press.

Bourdieu, P. 1996. *The Rules of Art: Genesis and Structure of the Literary Field*. Cambridge: Polity Press.

Bourdieu, P. 1993. *The Field of Cultural Production: Essays on Art and Literature*. Cambridge: Polity Press.

Brown, W. 2015. *Undoing the Demos: Neoliberalism's Stealth Revolution*. New York: Zone Books.

Castle, H. 2017. Find Your Inner Entrepreneur. *The RIBA Journal*, January 3, 2017, https://www.ribaj.com/intelligence/find-your-inner-entrepreneur, Accessed November 06, 2023.

Colomina, B. 1999a. Collaborations: The Private Life of Modern Architecture, *Journal of the Society of Architectural Historians*, 58 (3) (September 1999): 462–471.

Colomina, B. 1999b. Couplings, *Oase*, 51, 20–33.

Day, J. 2009. Genealogy as Diagram: Charting Past as Future, *Log*, No. 17: 121–126.

Davis, M. 2009. How Globalism Made Architecture's Professional Ethics Obsolete? In Owen, G. ed. *Architecture, Ethics, and Globalization*. London: Routledge, pp. 121–132.

De Graaf, R. 2017. *Four Walls and a Roof: The Complex Nature of a Simple Profession*. Cambridge, Massachusetts; London, England: Harvard University Press.

Dunleavy, P. 1981. *The Politics of Mass Housing in Britain, 1945–1975*. Oxford: Oxford University Press.

Eerlings, P. 2017. Three Alternative Ways for Architects to Earn (Big?) Money – with Tobias Maescher from Archipreneur, ArchiSnapper, April 12, 2017 https://blog.archisnapper.com /3-alternative-ways-for-architects-to-generate-revenue-with-tobias-from-archipreneur/, Accessed November 06, 2023.

Friedman, A. T. ed. 1998. *Women and the Making of the Modern House: A Social and Architectural History*. New York: Abrams.

Fulcher, M. 2013. The Thatcher Years: Architects on the Legacy of the Iron Lady, *Architects' Journal*, 237 (13): 12–13.

Glendinning, M., and Muthesius, S. 1994. *Tower Block: Modern Public Housing in England, Scotland, Wales and Norther Ireland*. New Haven; London: Yale University Press.

Gottschling, P. 2018. Where Design Competitions Matter: Architectural Artefacts and Discursive Events, *Journal of Material Culture*, 23 (2) (June 2018): 151–168.

Grenfell, M. and Hardy, C. 2007. *Art Rules: Pierre Bourdieu and the Visual Arts*. Oxford: Berg Publishers.

Grozdanic, L. (Unknown). How to Win Project and Make Money: 4 Business Moves for Architects. Accessed January 02, 2021.

Herbert, G. and Donchin, M. 2013. *The Collaborators: Interactions in the Architectural Design Process*. Farnham, Surrey: Ashgate.

Iloniemi, L. ed. 2019. *The Identity of the Architect: Culture and Communication* (Architectural Design), Hoboken, New Jersey: Wiley.

Jameson, F. 1992. *Postmodernism or, the Cultural Logic of Late Capitalism*. London: Verso Books.

Jencks, C. 2010. Architectural Evolution: The Pulsations of Time. In Garcia, M. ed. *The Diagrams of Architecture*. Chichester: John Wiley & Sons Ltd, pp. 288–309.

Klein, N. 2010. *No Logo: No Space, No Choice, No Jobs*. Great Britain: Flamingo.

Koolhaas, R. 1997. En%abling architecture. In Somol, R. E. ed. *Autonomy and Ideology: Positioning an Avant-garde in America*. New York: Monacelli Press, pp. 292–299.

Krauss, R. 1986. Sculpture in the Expanded Field. In *The Originality of the Avant-Garde and Other Modernist Myths*. Cambridge, Massachusetts: MIT Press, pp. 276–290.

Landau, R. 1992. (December) The End of CIAM and the role of the British, *Rassegna*, 14, 52 (4): 40–41

Lang, R. 2014. Architects Take Command: The LCC Architects' Department, *Volume* #41, October 24, 2014, http://volumeproject.org/architects-take-command-the-lcc-architects-department/, Accessed November 06, 2023.

Levine, Q. Unknown. The Role of Architects in VR, AR and Video Games, Unknown https://www.bergmeyer.com/trending/the-role-of-architects-in-vr-ar-and-video-games, Accessed November 06, 2023.

Lipstadt, H. 2009. Experimenting with The Experimental Tradition, 1989–2009: On Competitions and Architecture Research. In *Innhold* (NORDISK ARKITEKTURFOR-SKNING – Nordic Journal of Architectural Research) 21 (2): 9–22.

Lipstadt, H. and Bergdoll, B. 1989. *The Experimental Tradition: Essays on Competitions in Architecture*. Princeton: Princeton Architectural Press.

Maescher, T. 2018. *The Archipreneur Concept*. (175 page e-book), https://www.goodreads.com/book/show/31367943-the-archipreneur-concept, Accessed November 06, 2023.

Martin, I. 2015. The City That Privatised Itself to Death: 'London is now a set of improbable sex toys poking gormlessly into the air,' *The Guardian*, February 24, 2015, https://www.theguardian.com/politics/2015/feb/24/the-city-that-privatised-itself-to-death-london-is-now-a-set-of-improbable-sex-toys-poking-gormlessly-into-the-air, Accessed July 25, 2023.

Martin, H. 2001. The Greatest Architect Who Will Ever Lived. In Chance, J. and Schmiedeknecht, T. eds. *Fame and Architecture*, London: Academy, pp. 90–94.

Moore, R. 2013. Zaha Hadid: Queen of the Curve, *Guardian*, September 08, 2013. https://www.theguardian.com/artanddesign/2013/sep/08/zaha-hadid-serpentine-sackler-profile, Accessed July 26, 2023.

Owen, G. 2016. 'I Have No Power': Zaha Hadid and the Ethics of Globalized Practice, *Candide: Journal for Architectural Knowledge*, 10 (December): 41–64.

Owen, G. ed. 2009. *Architecture, Ethics, and Globalization*. London: Routledge.

Petty, J. 2018. *Architect & Developer: A Guide to Self-Initiating Projects*, South Carolina: CreateSpace Independent Publishing Platform.

Pollack, S. Dir. 2006 (May 12). *Sketches of Frank Gehry*. United States: Sony Pictures Classics (Distributor) (86 mins film)

Portman, J., and J. Barnett. 1976. *The Architect as Developer*. New York; St. Louis; etc.: McGraw-Hill Book Company.

Rand, A. 2007. *The Fountainhead*. London: Penguin. [First published in 1943.]

Reinholdt, E. 2015a. *Architect and Entrepreneur: A Field Guide to Building, Branding, and Marketing You* (Volume 1), CreateSpace Independent Publishing Platform. 1st edition released April 10, 2015.

Reinholdt, E. 2015b. (December 4) *Architect and Entrepreneur: A How-to Guide for Innovating Practice: Tactics, Models, and Case Studies in Passive Income* (Volume 2), CreateSpace Independent Publishing Platform.

Rodell, S. 2008 May. *The Influence of Robert Venturi on Louis Kahn*, Unpublished Master of Science in Architecture, Washington State University.

Roiphe, R. 2016. The Decline of Professionalism, *Georgetown Journal of Legal Ethics*, 29 (July 7, 2016): 649–681.

Saint, A. 1983. *The Image of the Architect*. New Haven; London: Yale University Press.

Scheer, D. R. 2014. *The Death of Drawing: Architecture in the Age of Simulation*. London; New York: Routledge.

Sollohub, D. 2019. *Millennials in Architecture: Generations, Disruption, and the Legacy of a Profession*. Austin: University of Texas Press.

Soja, E. W. 1989. *Postmodern Geographies: The Reassertion of Space in Critical Social Theory*. London: Verso.

Spector, T. 2001. *The Ethical Architect: The Dilemma of Contemporary Practice*. Princeton: Princeton Architectural Press.

Spencer, D. 2016. *The Architecture of Neoliberalism: How Contemporary Architecture Became an Instrument of Control and Compliance*. London: Bloomsbury Academic.

Standing, G. 2016. *The Precariat: The New Dangerous Class*. London: Bloomsbury Academic.

Stevens, G. 1998. *The Favored Circle: The Social Foundations of Architectural Distinction*. Cambridge, Massachusetts; London, England: The MIT Press.

Susskind, R. and Susskind, D. 2017. *The Future of Professions: How Technology Will Transform the Work of Human Experts*. Oxford: Oxford University Press.

Swartz, D. 1998. *Culture and Power: Sociology of Pierre Bourdieu*. Chicago; London: University of Chicago Press.

Thatcher, M. 1995. *The Path to Power*. London: Harper Press.

Theodorou, M. and A. Katsakou eds. 2019. *Competition Grid: Experimenting With and Within Architecture Competitions*. London: Routledge.

Till, J. 2009. *Architecture Depends.* Cambridge, Mass.; London, England: The MIT Press.

Troiani, I. 2010. An Architectural Genogram: Writing Architectural History Based on the Transfer of Social Capital, *The International Journal of Interdisciplinary Social Sciences*, 5: 1833–1882.

Troiani, I. 2005. *The Politics of Friends in Modern Architecture 1949–1987*, Unpublished Doctor of Philosophy, Queensland University of Technology, Brisbane, Australia.

Van der Hoorn, M. 2012. *Bricks and Balloons: Architecture in Comic-Strip Form*. Rotterdam: 010 Publishers.

Wainwright, O. 2016. Zaha Hadid's Successor: Scrap Art Schools, Privatise Cities and Bin Social Housing, *Guardian*, November 24, 2016, https://www.theguardian.com/artanddesign/2016/nov/24/zaha-hadid-successor-patrik-schumacher-art-schools-social-housing, Accessed November 06, 2023.

Wolff, J. 1993. *The Social Production of Art.* London: Palgrave Macmillan.

Zaero-Polo, A. and Abascal, G. F. 2016. Architecture's "Political Compass": A Taxonomy of Emerging Architecture in One Diagram, *ArchDaily*, December 16, 2016, https://www.archdaily.com/801641/architectures-political-compass-a-taxonomy-of-emerging-architecture-in-one-diagram, Accessed November 06, 2023.

PART III

Work-Life Balance in Architecture Beyond Neoliberalism

7

THE SITES OF NEOLIBERAL ARCHITECTURAL LABOUR

Work, Home, Everywhere

FIGURE 7.1   Ecole des Beaux-Arts à Paris. Photograph by Charles Ciccione/Gamma-Rapho via Getty Images. Image ID: 956766750, Object name: 5824501.jpg. Date created: 31 December 1899.

DOI: 10.4324/9781351199834-10

The Neoliberalisation of Architecture Workplaces

Neoliberalism has changed the patterns and spaces in which architects work today by focusing on flexibility. The flexible workplace has become a conduit for neoliberalism to optimise productivity. In *Non-Stop Inertia*, Ivor Southwood (2011, p. 35) contends that "The culture of flexibility and mobility paradoxically imposes an ever-tightening grip on the individual who is always accessible by mobile phone, email or laptop, while at the same time this culture is re-packaged as a gateway to leisure…." Southwood (2011, p. 33) claims that all workspace is prone to the "amnesic influence of the non-place, with its open-plan anonymity (no privacy, but no social structure either)…." The convenient portability of the digital workplace no longer restricts our relationship with time or space. (Southwood 2011, p. 34) According to Polish sociologist and philosopher, Zygmunt Bauman, with the transformation of work from its solid permanent state (one job, one company) to liquid fluid state (many jobs, many companies) comes work-life consequences. Bauman (2000, p. 147) notes in *Liquid Modernity* that "'Flexibility' is the slogan of the day, and when applied to the labour market it augurs an end to the 'job as we know it'"; the shift being to more zero-hour contracts, no contracts, or a culture of rapid job changing, so that an architect's labour can be enacted in a multitude of workplaces over their working lifetime, rather than in one corporate office, for instance. As such, as architectural work contracts become more flexible, so have the spaces in which architects work.

In *The Precariat: The New Dangerous Class*, Professor of Labour Economics and Market Flexibility, Guy Standing (2016, p. 139) explains that "The idea of doing a certain activity in a certain definable space of time is less and less applicable. The erosion of workplaces as the only place in which that work can be enacted and fixed workplaces is being accompanied by the erosion of the division of where different activities are done." Standing (2016, pp. 139–140) sees that things people previously only did at home like take a shower, are now being done in the office and things formerly only confined to the home, such as children or pets, are being brought to the office. As Douglas Spencer (2016, p. 77) elaborates "The separation between work and non-work is progressively dissolved so that a general condition of constant productivity prevails at all times, in all spaces." As such, the neoliberalisation of work life has direct ramifications on the production of architecture and the spaces in which architects work.

Neoliberalism has impacted on the spaces in which architectural education and architectural practice is practiced, in that flexibility becomes a mantra. In architectural practice, 'the rhetoric of flexibility' is commonly associated with modernity and "has very specific connotations…," literally suggesting the "immediate potential for movement and change" in and of space. (Schneider and Till 2007, p. 5) Architectural theoretician, Alan Colquhoun (1981) argues that the thinking that underpins the concept of flexibility is that modern life is complex and uncertain, implying that buildings should not be suited to any particular functional remit. In addition, flexibility makes economic sense because, theoretically, it reduces obsolescence of building stock. (Schneider and Till 2007, p. 43) Modernist housing was itself premised on the belief that open plan rooms liberated users, creating greater freedom to adapt and change space over time. Designing spaces that were "indeterminate of use" challenged notions of bourgeois dwelling. (Schneider and Till 2007, p. 18) The Swiss-French architect, Charles-Édouard Jeanneret (known as Le Corbusier) and Max Du Bois's *maison domino* or Domino house frame of 1914, a system which builds into the concrete grid frame flexible design possibilities, was described as the "'rationionalization [sic] of building production' based upon the scientific efficiency principles of Taylorism." (Emmons 2012, p. 132) As a consequence, the *maison domino* frame has subsequently been co-opted – because of its economy of construction – for rapid industrialised neoliberal development of high-rise housing blocks to corporate office towers, which architects both design and occupy.

In *The Architecture of Neoliberalism*, Spencer (2016, p. 4) claims that "As neoliberalism presents itself as a series of propositions in the pursuit of liberty" ... "the function of architecture [...] is that of producing endlessly flexible environments for infinitely adaptable subjects." The flexibility toll is not only on the workforce – younger generations bearing, arguably, the greater brunt of being asked to be more flexible – but it also affects the spaces we occupy. The portable networked computer/phone emerges as the most flexible site of work in 'liquid modernity,' with the office taking secondary position to 'knowledge cafes,' (Kane 2004, p. 259) and 'junkspace.' (Koolhaas 2002)

According to the Dutch starchitect, Rem Koolhaas (2002, p. 184) junkspace is the exemplification of corporate power tying architecture to entertainment and leisure rather than any other meaningful purpose; "Junkspace happens spontaneously through natural corporate exuberance – the unfettered play of the market...." The material consequences of junkspace come about because of optimisation for competitive market advantage. Koolhaas (2002, pp. 175–176) describes architecture as having transformed into "the product of an encounter between escalator and air-conditioning, conceived in an incubator of Sheetrock...; it deploys the infrastructure of seamlessness...; and is always interior... sealed, held together not by structure but by skin, like a bubble" – four walls (or a curvaceous tube) and a roof. (De Graaf 2017) The spaces in which architects design signature architecture to junkspace and beyond are not only the office and the home, as will be discussed later, but can happen anywhere, even while in motion, in flight. In *The Global Architect*, urban design academic, Donald McNeill (2009, p. 154) refers to how the 'kerosene architecture' produced by starchitects including Koolhaas, Richard Meier, I. M. Pei, Arata Isozaki, Norman Foster, and Zaha Hadid is/was sometimes "seemingly designed in-flight as the chief partner dashes from city to city, airport to airport." Architects, though, are shaped and shape the design of workspaces.

Literature on workplaces that gives advice is directed at designers outlining how best to design optimal workplaces today or in the future (Usher 2018) or is directed at business managers. (Becker 2004; Becker and Steele 1995) That literature focuses on how to offer diverse workplace options to accommodate diverse types of workers. Others showcase exemplary examples at their time (Myerson and Ross 2006; Myerson and Ross 2003; Littlefield 2009) and are detached from much deep criticality about the relationship between workplaces and wellbeing at work. A lot of literature is already compromised – convinced that neoliberal arguments for ways to make efficiencies in business can use workspace as a key avenue to economise; after all as Becker and Steele (1995) note, workspace is the second most costly aspect for any business, after labour costs. Throughout the existing literature there is little questioning of the positives for heightening flexibility in the design of spaces. In architecture schools and architectural practices, the design of workspaces mirrors this sentiment.

Traditionally, architects are trained to design site-specific and, increasingly so, flexible workspaces for themselves and others. English architectural theoretician, Robert Kronenburg (2007, p. 7) lists the benefits of flexible architectural design as considerable: "it remains in use longer; fits its purpose better; accommodates user's experience and intervention; takes advantage of technical innovation more readily; and is economically and ecologically more viable." The economic benefits of flexible workplace design are attractive for many organisations, and as such are increasingly seen more as necessity rather than choice. This changes the role of the architect to "a sort of facilitator for the building user to create their own place that they can change as frequently as they wish…. Architecture still provides settings for the theatre of human existence, but these settings may now, if it is desired, be as variable as the occupants' moods or alternatively a fixed element in the changing pattern of living and working." (Kronenburg 2007, p. 109) Whatever the functional use, flexible architecture offers users vast opportunities and choices for working and living. A fluid work-life for any worker, including architects, emerges as an unobstructed 'workspace' which allows the worker more freedom to literally move their work and living to wherever and however they want.

Over the duration of their working life, architectural practitioners learn their craft through working in a range of different spaces, which are themselves flexible in use. Traditionally, an architect's education begins as a student on the university campus, working in person in the design studio, attending lectures in lecture halls, going on field trips – all of which architectural educators and practitioners also occupy as their places of work. Architectural practitioners traditionally worked in the office or on the construction site. Work on the construction site, such as site measurement or building construction, is one of the few remaining places in which an architect is required to be in-person. However, changes in mass education have required universities and offices to become more flexible open-plan, factory-style workplaces. As architectural production shifts from being manually-produced to digitally-produced with computers, remote work has escalated. Post-pandemic, architectural labour in the university and the office is, out of necessity, increasingly being enacted more online and in our homes. The places outside of work in which architects work remotely on computers and hours of work are increasing in parallel. Architectural work is becoming more dependent on a stable, strong internet connection to work online and having a spare or quiet room away from others in the home to work in. While remote work can mean that architectural labour may be optimised, this shift means that Michel Foucault's (2008) concept of *homo oeconomicus*, Pierre Bourdieu's (2019) *homo academicus*, or Wendy Brown's (2015) *femina domestica* – previously understood as distinct categories of types of workers – are no longer associated with simple gendered divisions of labour enacted in specific places. Reputational capital accumulation in architecture and the ability to progress one's career is equally possible to achieve working from home or anywhere, rather than the university or the office.

This chapter sets out first, the sites in which contemporary architectural education and practice emerged beginning in the late 17th century at the Académie d'Architecture (and later the École des Beaux-Arts). It describes the kinds of site-specific locations and slow work with long hours culture from the École des Beaux-Arts that has set the disciplinary limits of an architect's work life in which architects still (roughly) work today. It fast-forwards to contemporary university design which has become more open plan, or which favours the creation of iconic university architecture (for marketing purposes), and which hybridises home life with traditional university life. Second, it discusses the way in the architect's office has shifted to sites of more 'fluid' and flexible work for architects since the late 20th century after the invention of computers and then further post-pandemic. It does so to examine how capitalism and neoliberalism employ new digital technologies to increase production in architectural education and practice in the global marketplace. Third, it discusses how the increased choice of different sites of architectural labour can be liberating or not for architects of different demographics. There are pros and cons of the recent dismantling of the traditional model of work for the work-life balance of architectural workers of different gender, race/ethnicity, class, and age. Being able to flexibly work some days in person at the neoliberal university on campus, office, or on site and other days at home or elsewhere has challenged some stereotypes of the enactment of architectural work in architectural education and practice and the architectural educator and practitioner. Conversely, working everywhere and anywhere can mean there are no limits to work hours; such that sometimes before we even get up in the morning, we have already begun to work by reading our emails on our phones in bed. Just as private property becomes the most valuable commodity in a neoliberal marketplace, the private university and private corporate architectural practice – which occupies an iconic architectural statement building – become increasingly valuable commodities, both physically and virtually, for social, cultural, and economic capital accumulation during an architect's lifetime. Importantly, one need not work in person on campus or in the office nowadays to obtain reputational capital. Instead, you need only be associated with the elite university or elite architectural office as a brand. The capital contained within the university we attend, and the offices for which we work is carried in architectural workers to later offer varying degrees of enablement.

The Flexible Spaces of Architectural Education

Schools of architecture have progressively shifted from sites of slow, mostly in-person manual labour within the university to faster modes of digital production delivered as mass education through the neoliberal university. Accompanying the shift in the way architectural education is taught and learned and the way an architecture curriculum is framed are the spaces in which it takes place. Here, a survey of the spatial transformation and transition of architectural schools from the École des Beaux-Arts to the virtual neoliberal architecture school is set out to showcase the effect that 'academic capitalism' and neoliberal frameworks of production have had on the pace of work life and places of work of architectural students and educators. Sites of solely slow hand drawing in studio drawing rooms such as in the Académie d'Architecture, later École des Beaux-Arts (Figure 7.1), have shifted to fast, hybrid, in-person, and online/virtual education that takes place in the modern university, as well as everywhere and anywhere, to optimise productivity.

As already discussed in Chapter 5, the Académie d'Architecture (or the Académie Royale d'Architecture was founded by Louis XIV in 1671 to create architects who would decorate his royal apartments at Versailles. It was housed mostly in the Louvre in Paris. Its director, the engineer Jacques-François Blondel (1756), describes that its members met weekly in ground floor lecture halls for public talks on mathematics and architecture. A large room was devoted to the display of architectural models and there was a space for the society's secretary. Short-lived, it was transformed into the Académie des Beaux-Arts, or the Academy of Fine Arts, and moved to the site of a former monastery (of the Petits Augustine monks built between 1608 and 1619) which was later converted into the Musee des Monuments (between 1791 and 1816). The Musee des Monuments housed tombs, sculptures, and architectural fragments from other notable buildings. (Van Zanten 1978, p. 161)

In redeveloping the monastery for the École des Beaux-Arts, campus architect, Félix Duban designed the main building, The Palais des Études,' or Palace of Studies, in 1830. The Palace of Studies – Duban's architecture school in the École des Beaux-Arts – was inspired by the Renaissance Palazzo della Cancelleria (or the Palace of the Chancellery) by Donato Bramante and represented architectural values at the time. Originally in an open courtyard that was covered later, the Palais des Études was designed as a gallery of objects in an artist's studio space to showcase and allow students to study through hand drawing, copies of antiques, architectural patterns, etc. However, the contemplative space of architectural education in the École has now become a distant idyllic memory of artistic-architectural scholarship. In the U.K., rooms in which to paint and draw by hand and slowly look and study architecture have vanished, replaced by open plan studios in mostly modular buildings or, more recently, iconic university buildings.

In the U.K., universities expanded most dramatically post-World War 2 in order to increase access to H.E. With the passing of The Further and Higher Education Act 1992, the divide between 'old' universities and 'new' modern universities – the former polytechnics (technical colleges that focused more on vocational studies) – was abolished. The inclusion of the 'new' modern universities instantly doubled the number of universities in the U.K.

In *The Postwar University: Utopianist Campus and College*, Stefan Muthesius (2000, p. 59) explains that "compared with other major countries, the world of the English university was small," often referred to as 'conservative' and 'elite' and characterised by a college quod. With the advent of the formation of new universities came a change in the planning and a name change to 'campus,' and just as the architecture absorbed the ambitious modernist style of planning, the architectures of the new universities celebrated prototyping, standardisation, and mass-production in their use of materials (bricks, curtain walls, concrete panels, etc.), but also in their tectonic form-making. Seen at the time as being visionary, the 'new' universities aimed to breathe new life into the higher education sector in the United Kingdom through image making centred on being modern.

By expanding their 1950s and 1960s prefabricated university buildings and campuses, 'new' modern U.K. universities became a conduit through which to also optimise 'academic capitalism.' (Slaughter and Leslie 1997) As "the sense of place helps universities market themselves to potential students," (Edwards 2000, p. 5) the design of the campus and buildings in mostly 'new' modern universities has become complicit in the promotion of mass university education for everyone to make more of themselves, climb the ladder, and contribute to the national economy rather than drain it.

Since then, to take on more students, the most recent iteration of the 'new' modern university, the neoliberal university, has been forced to become a more productive 'edufactory' (Aureli in Deamer 2015, pp. 1235–1259); the university being compared to a factory for education. Like any large factory plant, universities have rapidly expanded physically – acquiring more land for campus expansion and more university buildings locally, sometimes nationally and internationally – as well as non-physically through virtual teaching platforms, as discussed later in this chapter. Many U.K. universities have embarked on grand large-scale expansion plans (Coulsen, Roberts, and Taylor 2015, p. 10) and marketing strategies to invigorate buildings and campuses that were in decline. (Troiani and Carless 2021)

In the book *Deciphering Advertising, Art and Architecture: New Persuasion Techniques for Sophisticated Consumers*, Graham Cairns (2010, p. 1) argues that the persuasion techniques used by advertisers and architects (and clients) are vastly different to those used in former times, the relationship having "developed on the basis of converting buildings into promotional devices." To promote themselves, universities deploy a range of marketing techniques of their architectures in order to engage a more discerning prospective student consumer market.

University marketing exploits the landmark university buildings, the town or city in which a university is located, and the landmarks in that town or city as a 'brandscape' (Klingmann 2007) for H.E. tourism. The tie of place to prestige is because historically "the idea of university education … [has been] inviolably associated with the idea of place." (Coulson, Roberts, and Taylor 2015, p. 10)

Unlike placemaking, placemarking incorporates the physical features that give a campus a unique local, national, and global visual presence (Dober 1992, p. 5), and so the 'unibrandscape' relies on marketing its landmark university architectures and garden or urban estates because all university "landmarks are cultural currency." (Dober 1992, p. 5) Selling the image of the university and its on-site experience is important to gain market advantage. This is because of the sense that university life on campus is a rite of passage. As such, the design of university estates or campuses and their buildings, and the towns and cities they are in, play a major part in where prospective students and educators choose to study and work.

In the competitive H.E. global marketplace, 'old' and 'new' U.K. universities alike have had to modernise existing architecture and build new buildings for greater home and international market capture. Old universities have transformed their identity, appearance, and size, thereby changing the 'bodies' of their estates to improve their university brand in relation to the onsite experience they offer their staff and students. For instance, The University of Oxford's £1.8bn development push over 10 years began in 2014 in order to compete with its international rivals. Arguably, the most dramatic U.K. campus building upgrades required to serve neoliberal agendas have taken place in the former polytechnic set of post-1960s prefabricated post-war universities. In this instance, often-tired, modular, quickly-built, prefabricated concrete panel buildings have undergone façade facelifts being reclad in more contemporary colourful panels that erase their Brutalist concrete past.

Aside from the refurbishing of existing buildings, many U.K. universities have taken on debt or spent capital reserves to construct new buildings: either modern versions of gridded 'edufactory' buildings or something more architecturally unique. In sometimes vastly ambitious buildings programmes, many U.K. universities have built 'state-of-the-art' lecture halls, (often sterile) 24-hour accessible, open plan architectural studios filled with computer workstations, 24-hour accessible libraries, 24-hour accessible open plan offices, and standardised student accommodation, all of which are replicating a corporate language of globalised professionalism and 'excellence' within academia. However the most marketable neoliberal contemporary university architecture typology manifests most extremely in its unique form as "'phantasmagorical' form." (Spencer 2016, p. 73) Phantasmagorical university architecture aims to revitalise a university's estate or campus 'brandscape' and is used as a persuasive marketing technique.

University clients increasingly appoint a fashionable, elite signature architect – foreign or national – to enhance their campus (brand) status. Some of the most renowned modern and contemporary starchitects in the world have won university commissions and built landmark university buildings in 'old' and 'new' modern universities with varying degrees of client and user satisfaction. In the U.K., the Investcorp Building for the Middle East Centre at St. Anthony's College, University of Oxford, built between 2013 and 2015, was designed by Pritzer and RIBA prize winner, Zaha Hadid Architects (ZHA). It is an example of the spectacle of Spencer's "'phantasmagorical' form" in a 'uni-brandscape.'

So, just as a city uses architectural landmarks to define its cityscape as 'brandscape,' the image of a 'uni-brandscape' visually defines the university's brand image. Landmark buildings in the traditional old university estate project a different image to signature buildings in 'old' or 'new' modern university campuses. The architectural style in which a university campus is predominantly built – whether Gothic, Georgian, or Brutalist for example – conveys meaning about a university's uniqueness and exclusivity, which enables the transfer of reputational capital (or not) through both the quality of education on offer and the buildings in which one studies in-person.

However, it is not only the exterior image of university architecture that carries reputational value, so does the interior. Interior university image-making is key to the neoliberal marketising of tiers of H.E. Many refurbished or new buildings at U.K. universities centre on the production of what Spencer (2016, p. 76) describes as 'ubiquitous workspace' which dismantles the boundary between work and life or leisure. So, while the neoliberalisation of U.K. university buildings has spatial consequences in urban planning and at the level of architectural design, their interior design impacts on how, in this case, architecture students and staff, work in them. To make university work seem less like work and more like leisure requires blurring the boundaries between university workplace and home through a strategy centred on flexible use. Many university campuses don't just provide spaces for teaching and learning, they provide showers, gyms, kitchenettes, and can include shops, thereby commercialising architectural education for maximum economic return. Just like the bodies of architectural students are required under neoliberalism to be flexible and resilient to constant change, every new space in the university needs to be designed to be spatially changeable or be so generic that it can be altered for an alternative use at no or minimal cost.

Many teaching and learning spaces in U.K. universities have been converted into, or are designed into, versions of casual, corporate hubs for 'lounge space' learning with vast volumes of circulation space, devoid of specific teaching or learning functions to support flexible working by a 'Nonstop Society.' (Austin and Sharr in Troiani ed. 2021, pp. 69–97) Many universities have been modelled on open plan, flexible, Silicon Valley-style company headquarters with soda machines and communal lunch areas using lounge-style furniture that aim to make the university workplace feel less like work and more like home, or more likely, to make the two indistinguishable. (Troiani with Dutson 2021) Take, for example, The Hub at Coventry University, built in 2011 and designed by Hawkins Brown, which contains a series of booths: "Playing on the idea of a 'home from home,' the booths are house shaped, the nests contain super-sized 'fatboy' bean bags and domestic fittings including sofas, low slung chairs, rugs, wallpaper and lampshades." (Unknown, 2011)

The architectural design studio – which has shifted from the decadent Beaux-Arts spaces of hand-drawing and painting – have in most schools been transformed and economised into banks of computers, in others, into rows of studio desks, often used for hot-desking for efficiency of use.

In addition, the neoliberalisation of the architectural education through the vertical unit model, which emerged in the U.K. in the 1970s, has only heightened the relationship between an unhealthy work hour culture in the architectural studio that remains the 'elephant in the room.' (Troiani 2021, pp. 9–33) Many architecture schools rent their studios from their university and so there are limitations to floor space. The making of physical models or prototypes happens mostly in digital fabrication laboratories, wood, or metal workshops, etc., under strict supervision and training, so that creative practice abides by booking slots and Healthy and Safety regulations and policies. Outside of teaching time, digital fabrication facilities can be outsourced to industry in order to optimise revenue streams. It is not only the conventional spaces of architectural education in the university that have modified for 'academic capitalism,' however, so has student accommodation.

Student accommodation is also changing to meet the needs of a more discerning student market of Generation Z 'kids,' or the PlayStation generation. This generation have grown up in more affluent times than their parents and are recognised for having a heightened sense of consumerism and luxury. They are attuned to and dependent on highly sophisticated media and computer environments, both in their online learning and in their playing of video games, etc., when not working.

One of the main reasons for going to university was, and still is, to experience university life away from home in order to become independent. However, learning to be independent does not correlate with austere living conditions. No longer is student accommodation dormitory-like. In the race for universities to compete for students, many U.K. universities have had to expand or upgrade their halls of residence.

Halls of residence have transformed because of the neoliberalisation of U.K. universities. To increase their competitive edge, many university estates and campuses have undertaken ambitious building redevelopment by grabbing available land to build new expensively-priced student housing. Providing student accommodation in existing buildings they own outside the main campus or in purpose-built halls of residence on campus was emerging for many U.K. universities, until the pandemic, as a secondary but vital revenue stream beyond student fees to sustain their business. Still, student housing standards and expectations of standards have altered as students become more discerning customers. University students who have grown up as a 'neoliberal subject' (Brown 2015, p. 33) are increasingly more accustomed to more luxurious standards of living. To meet the neoliberal student's expectations, halls can look more like serviced apartments or hotels. Every "student 'hotel'" room has their own ensuite, and kitchens are often designed like those in the shared-houses of young professionals, luring students into independent living in accommodation that can sometimes exceed their own home.

In the book, *Future Campus: Design Quality in University Buildings*, Ian Taylor (in Taylor ed. 2016, p. 70) argues that building "student 'Hotels'" is one key rebranding tactic to transform university-owned heritage. U.K. universities have developed sophisticated on site and digital marketing strategies to advertise their newly-fashioned campuses and the various types of "student 'hotel'" experience. The creation of the image of luxury student accommodation and the glossy animations of figures walking through a virtual simulation of student rooms is invaluable marketing material for any university wanting to be competitive in a neoliberal marketplace, even before being built.

Just as spaces within the university shift to become more like home, "home becomes work," (Hochschild 2001) particularly post-pandemic. Through the need to shift to online teaching platforms in which lecture courses and studio have been run, the bedroom, living room, etc., of the student in student accommodation or at home has had to transform into the lecture theatre or design studio, making all hours of work at university work hours at home. Architectural education is increasingly moving online, saving on costly teaching and learning, and accommodation buildings. In a swirl of confusing and exciting potential, architecture students and their educators grapple and juggle with in-person lecture and design studio teaching in generic university lecture and studio spaces alongside digital online teaching platforms. Where an international student is being taught online in an architecture programme in the U.K., architectural education is made more efficient in its delivery in that scheduled teaching and tutorial time slots do not slip beyond the scheduled period. In this highly-efficient delivery of architectural education, the absence of ancillary and tangential conversations in which an educator can better understand a student's interests and level of skill can be reduced. The space for casual conversation for learning can be sacrificed and students graduate able to meet criteria but can be disembodied both from building networks and the potential for building reputational capital with their peers, and the physical act of making their architectural propositions, even in model form.

In summary, having access to study architecture at an elite university and to live in an expensive city like London versus studying in a less costly city in the U.K. or studying modules online depends on access to personal economic, social, and reputational capital. The university at which one chooses to and can study architecture has both the capacity to facilitate 'cumulative advantage' (Rank et al. 2014, p. 107) or not and can contribute to architectural social stratification through providing more or less opportunities later in professional life. Attending a more 'prestigious' U.K. architecture school whose reputation and building brand has been established over a longer period of time such at the University of Cambridge, or are a newer elite brand such as the Architectural Association (AA) in London, and which simultaneously has buildings which are older, built-in styles that are pre-modern, and are generally hand-crafted, more decorative, robust, solid, and better built, can add instant value to an architect's later career. This is because the design of the architecture school and the city in which that university is located carry symbolic, cultural, and economic capital which is carried to the student who attends it.

What has become increasingly universal is the commercialisation and commodification of both the physical experience of university campus buildings for teaching and learning and of student accommodation. University workspaces are increasingly morphing aspects of previously domestic space into H.E. workspace. The dissolution of working at the university as a relaxing home environment can condition a worker into longer work hours so that 'work becomes home and home becomes work'. (Hochschild 2001) The problem of working in the physical university or at home for long hours while an architecture student can be carried into professional work life after university.

The Flexible Open Plan Architectural Office

The architect's office has evolved in much the same way that the university has changed to best enable flexible work. Its original form followed the École des Beaux-Arts open studio model in which architects painted, sketched, and hand-drew their designs. Over time, the architect's office became industrialised so that the office studio transformed to an open space, much like a classroom, with rows of architects working in disciplined lines at their individual drafting or drawing boards. (Figure 7.2) Until the emergence of digital technologies, there was a distinct split between the architect's office as a place of work (where they produced architectural plans) and their home where they either rested, painted, or drew. Work and home life were separated spatially and in terms of work hours. The industrialisation of architecture as building under mid-20th century modernism, epitomised by the corporate office or tower impacted on the architect's body working in it.

Since the post-war period, architects have been designing rational open plan office spaces and towers and working in them themselves in the mode of what the American sociologist, William H. Whyte Jr.'s (1956, p. 44) termed *The Organization Man.* Whyte Jr.'s "organisation man" is "the ideal subject of "human relations" who identified with his corporation as though it were his family." (Martin, 2003, p.121) American architectural historian, Reinhold Martin notes that Whyte's figure "had internalized the logic of organization itself. Conformist yet adaptable and resourceful, he '[does] not question the system' (Whyte 1956, p. 68) but rather seeks out integration at the office and at home, in the new suburbs that hold the alter ego to his corporate family in near-perfect symmetry."

The corporate office tower, in its efficient, open plan became the site and the symbol of the corporate organisation and the corporate worker. Not only does the tall office building exert spatial control on the worker who works in them to work openly and fluidly, as Italian theoretician, Manfredo Tafuri (1979, p. 419) notes in *The Disenchanted Mountain, The American City*, it is also "an element capable of exercising a formal control over the urban complex as a whole." The design of the efficient office reaffirms internally and externally neoliberal strategies of scientific management, accountability, and the neoliberal state. (Parker and Jeacle 2019)

While the architect who is the "organisation man" working in the corporate office tower remains a worker-type today, the increase in digital media and online work has morphed their workplace into what Martin (2003, pp. 3–4) calls "the organizational complex," i.e., "the aesthetic and technological extension of what has been known since the early 1960s as the "military-industrial complex.""

FIGURE 7.2 Lord Norman Foster overlooking the studio of Foster + Partners, Riverside, 22 Hester Road, Battersea London SW11 4AN. Photograph by Martin Goodwin. Date created: c. 2017.

Since then, the types of architects and the on-site spaces in which they work includes the while male architect-in-a-suit working long hours in-person in an open plan office tower while someone else undertakes any care responsibilities outside work for him, but has also diversified to include the white and non-white male and female architect-in-a-suit or not-in-a-suit working in a multitude of places including and excluding the conventional architect's office who juggles care responsibilities with their 'office' work load.

It makes sense that the changing work patterns and lives of knowledge workers, including architects, require new types of office workplace design. In the research on U.K. interior office design by Jeremy Myerson et al. (Turner and Myerson 1998; Myerson and Ross 1999; 2003; 2006; Myerson and Privett 2014; Myerson, Bichard, and Alma 2010), a clear trajectory is mapped in which office design adapts to the needs of a changing workforce. The key trends in new office design captured and expanded are four 21st century concepts: narrative, nodal, neighbourly, and nomadic for flexibility of labour enactment through one-on-one human interaction and new digital technologies. The way the office workforce has changed and is changing due to 'Generation X' graduates, the increase in diversity of the workforce, the emergence of the 'non-territorial workplace,' and its relationship to 'real lives' and how workers work (in real and digital domains) is a theme that carries from early research. (Turner and Myerson 1998)

English interior design theoretician, David Littlefield (2009) explains in *Good Office Design* – a book that focuses on award-winning British offices produced between 2002 and 2008 – that 15 to 20 years ago, the open plan 'organizational complex' now incorporates both formal and informal work spaces. Littlefield (2009, p. 2) explains that "[....] clients appear to have seized the potential of wireless working to allow staff to work flexibly anywhere [in the office], and a wide range of spaces are provided, from conventional desks, to cafes, cellular rooms, 'breakout' areas, light-filled atria and courtyards." He sees that 'plug-in-and-work' and hot-desking are becoming commonplace so that office workplace design has "a certain informality, based on the idea that it is a person's knowledge, capability and attitude that is important rather than where they sit." (Littlefield 2009, p. 2) Littlefield (2009, pp. 2, 3) also argues that allowing staff the flexibility to work where they want and how they want, with additional facilities such as "a gym, showers, coffee bar, roof terrace, retail outlets, restaurants and libraries" is also a way to "attract (and retain) high-quality staff...." Here, formulaic, efficient office planning based on the Taylorism-inspired, American workstation module – where the average operational density is 12 m^2 and average light levels is 400 lux" (Littlefield 2009, p. 2) – is hybridised to offer spaces which allow the worker to work freely in a controlled and uncontrolled office space, monitored not through being seen to be at their workstation but instead by output productivity.

In "Office Design, Neoliberal Governmentality and Professional Service Firms," Canadian Professor of Accounting, Claire-France Picard et al. (2021) argue that neoliberal governmentality is optimally promoted though office design technologies used by professional service firms (PSFs). As already highlighted previously, architectural firms, as PSFs, are knowledge-intensive companies that provide professional expert service to clients. Their primary asset is their expert architectural knowledge, experience, and reputation which are all intangible products being offered to the architectural marketplace. Architecture firms rely on customer-centric business and so in-person relations are important at the client/patron–architect/director level but, arguably, are less important at other tiers of the architectural workforce. For this reason, foyers or showrooms and meeting room spaces in showcase buildings/ office towers and the restaurants, sports/golf clubs, etc., in which the management class of architects socialise with clients are essential workplaces for obtaining and sustaining architectural commissions. Unlike the architectural management class and architectural workers producing drawing packages, site or project architects occupy alternative spaces of architectural production.

However, while the construction site remains unchanged, visiting it has become less available to all classes of architectural worker and in some instances is entirely avoided if photographs and building and site data is available digitally. The opportunity to work during work hours in the office, at home, or anywhere else rather than in the office depends on the architectural class in which one works and often aligns to particular stages in the worker's life.

Following the Standing-inspired architectural class structure set out in Chapter 6, different architectural classes have different access to sites and types of architectural workplace. In the traditional architect's office, those working on the shop floor producing architectural drawing packages and specifications, i.e., the architectural precariat class of drafting technicians, ungraciously but commonly referred to as CAD monkeys, often occupy more open plan spaces that resemble studios. They can now work in front of one to multiple computer screens. Architects in the managerial class work mostly in more traditional private office spaces within the office, meeting in private meeting rooms, or simply working elsewhere. Directors of signature architecture firms have always worked flexibly between the workhome and office when they weren't globetrotting around the world for teaching, lectures, or visiting clients and commissions. Work is increasingly enacted in live-work spaces. (Holliss 2015)

Here the home and office of Iraqi-born, Dame Zaha (Mohammad) Hadid (1950– 2016) are described to showcase an example of the sites in which a starchitect works in relation to their lifestyle. It describes her penthouse where she lived and worked from 2006 to 2009; and her London office on 10 Bowling Green Lane which was occupied by ZHA (Zaha Hadid Architects) from 1983 to 2021. The London ZHA office was located next door to her penthouse. Due to her excessive global travel associated with her international teaching and commissions, Hadid's penthouse became more of an office showroom than home during its existence but eventually became obsolete.

For two-and-a-half years, Zaha Hadid lived in a penthouse apartment in Clerkenwell. Hadid purchased the top-floor open warehouse of a five-story loft building and refurbished it internally to convert it into her penthouse through an uncompromising vision of whiteness. Journalist Simon Hatterstone (2010) describes the space as "The whitest whiteness everywhere—white floors, white wall, white ceilings, white fibreglass sculptures that double up a white sofas" – even "the Astro Turf that carpeted her roof terrace" was white. (Holub 2016) The two-level penthouse for spinster Hadid included a main dining/living room/studio space, another small room, her bedroom, and bathroom.

The main living room or studio space in Hadid's penthouse was an unconventional, blindingly white room, often used as a gallery stage to showcase Hadid's designs and her personal collections of designer objects. Acting more as a clutter-free showroom for photo-shoots of her, her paintings, furniture designs, or clothing collection, "light plays an important role, courtesy of an enormous skylight that permeates the central seating area, and a wall of windows leading to the back terrace." (Woodward 2013) Decorated by Kazimir Malevich-inspired ZHA digital drawings, and with her Aqua table taking centre stage (sometimes photographed with or without the Rifatta Bella chairs designed by William Sawaya around it), the 'studio' was undomesticated in its appearance, operating more as an office foyer. As Dagmar Holub (2016) noted; "There were no books, no CDs and perilously little sign of human occupation"; another small room in the penthouse was devoted to showing her "collection of Murano glass, vases, plates [...] consisting of different forms and colours." Designer furniture, the Marshmallow sofa by George Nelson, and Tongue Chair by Pierre Paulin, were positioned around the Murano glass as a perfectly staged scene of designer home life.

On another floor was Hadid's bedroom, also starkly white, with white blinds and an adjoining bathroom. Unlike the other hard surfaced rooms which show "perilously little sign of human occupation," Hadid's bedroom contained a large double bed with cushions and cover (which she designed for the Hotel Puerta de America, 2003–2005), a flat screened television, and a "white dressing table with dozens of perfume bottles shaped into their own skyline." (Hattenstone 2010) It also included a small black and red work desk. Located near her bed, this allowed her to continue to work in her bedroom.

Noteworthy is that the penthouse was without a kitchen. This follows the penthouse typology for a bachelor who has a minimal or no kitchen because they do not want or need to cook. The penthouse, as an apartment type, has mostly been analysed in architectural literature from the standpoint of masculinity and bachelorhood as a space of play for the unmarried, "family-free" man. For instance, "Playboy's penthouse apartment," an article first published in *Playboy* magazine and republished in *Stud: Architectures of Masculinity* (Sanders 1996) sets out how the penthouse, with its extraordinary views and its planning focused on a large seating area, bedroom, and bathroom, allowed the playboy to accentuate his independence, masculinity, and sexual performativity. Playboy's penthouse was marketed as a lair to court and bed women. Domestic labors such as cooking were devalued through the inclusion of a bare-minimum kitchen with only a microwave oven. The penthouse has evolved since but remains a space for singles or "family-free" couples that are metropolitan wealthy (to afford the views). The penthouse had an existing kitchen, but Hadid (in Hattenstone 2010) chose to have it removed because, "it was 'ugly'." When the penthouse did have a kitchen, Hadid (in Hattenstone 2010) had "someone to cook" for her, but because she went "out all the time" with clients or work colleagues, a kitchen became an unnecessary feature.

For 38 years, Hadid's architectural office was in the classroom accommodation of the grade II listed Victorian former school at 10 Bowling Green Lane. (Hopkirk 2021) Holub (2016) notes that, "Hadid never had her own office [in ZHA]; she would sit right in the middle of her studio for many years. Arriving late in the morning, she would sketch for an hour or so, and then begin asking to see projects, and her employees would feed her plans and renderings."

As Hadid's practice grew, her business partner, Patrick Schumacher increasingly managed the Clerkenwell office. She would then work or have meetings at her home, which was within walking distance. Hadid's penthouse was a 'workhome' (Holliss 2015, pp. 1–2 of Introduction) which operated outside the space of the ZHA office. As ZHA grew, Hadid's penthouse became a place for working, publicity, exhibition, sleeping, and bathing, when she was not travelling overseas for work. As her business grew, and with it travel increased, her workhome became obsolete but ZHA expanded its offices and showrooms, locally and internationally. In 2013, ZHA set up a showroom in 101 Goswell Road in London to market her architectural products to prospective clients and to build her reputational capital. ZHA had already occupied seven floors of Goswell Road since 2012. New offices were established overseas too. On the 7th of November 2016, the ZHA Middle East Office was opened in the Design District of Dubai, "established in response to the solid growth demand from new and existing clients across the region; providing even greater levels of assistance, coordination and communication with our increasing client base throughout the Middle East." (Unknown ZHA website 2016) However, following the 2020–2021 COVID-19 pandemic, in July 2021, ZHA "quit [their] 'inflexible' Bowling Green Lane Headquarters" (Jessel 2021, unpaginated) because it was "not adaptable to post-Covid work requirements" (Hopkirk 2021, unpaginated) and relocated to 101 Goswell Road London. Unlike the classroom layout of their Bowling Green Lane office, Goswell Road, as a former garment factory has large open plan floor space that ZHA reconfigured "to create flexible work environments that are healthier and more supportive." (Unknown, ZHA website 2021) ZHA argue that this shift allows the office to offer "our teams more options in how they work, maintaining the primary role of our studio as a place for meaningful collaboration and interaction." (Unknown, ZHA website 2021) Like other corporate offices, remote work allows architects to work nomadically from home for work that is not required to be in person.

Architect Nomads, the Workhome, and Remote Work

While remote workers were, 30 years ago, more typically well-educated, predominantly white-collar professionals, equally male or female, very likely married in their 30s and 40s (Romei 1992 in Becker and Steele 1995, p. 105), todays remote workers (formerly referred to as teleworkers) have expanded in their demographic. Pandemic restrictions created a workplace culture shift that returned architects to working from home. While dwellings continue to support the functions of private life – including cooking, eating, bathing, sleeping, etc. – homes have increasingly been transformed into the workplaces of architectural students, educators, and architects due to access to, and demand for, remote work. Unlike formerly working only in-person in the neoliberal university or office, dwellings have progressively become the sites where people live *and* work, or what British academic Frances Holliss (2015, pp. 1–2 of Introduction) describes in *Beyond Live/Work: The Architecture of Home-based Work* as the 'workhome.' While the workhome has existed for thousands of years, Holliss (2015, pp. 2, 3 of Chapter 1) claims there was no distinct differentiation between dwelling and work for lower-class craft workers in medieval England, a model that sustained itself until the Industrial Age split the location of work and homelife. While Industrial capitalism and mass production in factories and workhouses relied on the separation between place of work and dwelling, there has always been a long tradition of home-based work by architects since the late 19th century known as the 'studio-house.' Take for instance, American architect, Frank Lloyd Wright's home studio on 951 Chicago Avenue, Oak Park, Chicago, built in 1889, where he lived with his wife, Catharine Lee Tobin and six children and in which he produced "more than a third of his life's work" (Unknown, Oak Park Home & Studio, unpaginated); or Sarah Wigglesworth's workhome-office, the Straw Bale House on Stock Orchard Street, Islington, London, 2004; or Atelier Bow-Wow's workhome in Tokyo, Japan, 2005. Then there is the converse in which the office becomes the workhome. In this instance, Holliss (2015, Chapter 1) notes that German architect, Walter Gropius's 1926 art and architecture school, 'The Bauhaus' in Dessau, was where "…The Bauhaus students and staff lived together as well as work[ed] together. This was central to the way the school ran […]." Teaching staff were given more room, living further away from students. Students and junior staff "slept in individual studios at the heart of the teaching complex, seven to a floor sharing a single WC. Communal bathrooms, laundry and gymnasium were in the basement; on the ground floor were a centralized [sic] kitchen and a collective refectory whose environment and furniture were expressly designed for discomfort, as a way of encouraging students to get back to work." (Holliss 2015, Chapter 1) Another example is Wright's Taliesin studio or Taliesin East, south of Spring Green in Wisconsin, built in 1911, in which Wright initially lived with his mistress, Mamah Borthwick, but which also housed a design community who lived, studied, and built live projects on site as a form of architectural pedagogy.

The digital age has reinvigorated the workhome model of architectural work, however. The increase in global, digital economies and remote work has meant that 'telecommuting' nullifies the geographical location of work and has, instead, often for knowledge workers like architects, brought the two spheres back together. (Holliss 2015, p. 3) "Telecommuting" – the "flexible work practices" that "mean zero commute or work-at-home" (Holliss 2015, Note 6 in Introduction) allow a worker to complete work from outside the traditional workplace by using telecommunications tools such as video conferencing apps, email, phone, etc. Changes to the way that architectural students, educators, and practitioners worked during the pandemic fast-tracked a return to working from home. At the time, Zoom and Teams allowed architectural education, including the design studio, to move entirely online in order to not stop the flow of students progressing through their courses. In practice, this allowed architects to continue producing digital drawings and written documentation of projects unabated. The university became an efficient online teaching factory supporting 'academic capitalism' and the architectural office become an online drawing/documentation factory producing planning applications, drawing work packages, etc., in order to not slow down the construction industry. While telecommuting happened beforehand mostly from home, since the pandemic it has expanded to everywhere and anywhere and become increasingly more pervasive in the fluid spaces in which architectural education and practice exist. As the ways in which the architectural curriculum, neoliberal university, and work home or remote sites of work are still in flux, changing in new ways that we are yet to uncover, the benefits of telecommuting to architectural students, educators, and workers who do not fit the one-size-fits-all model (Troiani 2024) of a white male architect who "works long hours"… focusing solely "on his career, often to the exclusion of family and personal life" (Martin in Berkeley and McQuaid eds. 1989, p. 232) remains unclear.

Since literature on remote work originally surfaced in the Information Technology (IT) industry – not architecture – reference will be made here to the writing of theorists working in that industry, namely Jason Fried and David Heinmeier Hansson, founders of the software company, 37Signals (later Basecamp). At the time of writing their book in 2013, Fried and Hansson had a remote workforce that was scattered globally. In architecture, the newly-emerging online platforms and software programmes, that have increased in number and which are affecting how architectural work is enacted in the early 2020s, are not solely about the mode of design drawing representation. Instead, as Fried and Hansson (2013) note, new digital technologies address how to work remotely and collaboratively together while being away from each other. They thereby dismantle the model of work created in the Industrial Revolution that required working under one roof of a factory into a remote digital production factory. This new feature of work needs to consider generational differences in computational thinking and working, as discussed in Chapter 3. Arguably, architectural 'digital natives' or the architectural "N-[for Net]-gen or D-[for digital]-gen" Millennials – who have grown up within high digital technology environments – are better able to engage in remote work because they are "all 'native speakers'" of the digital language of computers, video games, and the Internet" (Prensky 2001, p. 1), unlike older generations of 'digital immigrants' who did not grow up with these digital technologies. Consequently, remote work or telecommuting has benefits and challenges for architectural workers of differing ages and other demographics.

Before the lessons of pandemic working, Fried and Hansson (2013, p. 8/151) wrote of the generic benefits of remote work, arguing that it offers the possibility of "access to the best talent, freedom from soul-crushing commutes, and increased productivity outside the traditional office…" because of the autonomy to manage one's own work time, reduce workplace interruptions, and not be tied to living in cities. Some of the 'excuses' they list against remote work include "that innovation only happens face-to-face, that people can't be trusted to be productive at home, that company culture would wither away." (Fried and Hansson 2013, p. 8/151) Talent can also be lost because of a distance/lack of connection to an architectural organisation or practice but this depends on what architectural class of work is being enacted. Overall, however, in the opinion of Fried and Hansson (2013, p. 8/151), remote work is more positive than negative for workers to undertake because it "has opened the door to a new era of freedom and luxury" that has increased "quality of work and job satisfaction." The problem is that the nostalgia tied to working in the old ways is an obstacle to remote working. (Fried and Hansson 2013, p. 12/151) Still, advantages abound.

Remote work enables 'the best talent' to be sourced beyond the physical site of the university or office. In the virtual university, 'talent' can be international and national speakers who are not able to attend the campus in person but who deliver lectures/talks or teach online, or architectural students, educators, or university managers who do not live nearby the physical site of the university but who can undertake all or some of the work they need to do remotely rather than in person. In the case of architectural practice, 'talent' can refer to architects with expert knowledge that they can transfer to a practice remotely but can also refer to cheaper outsourced workers who offer their 'talent' by undertaking work elsewhere, sometimes in another country. These workers can produce visualisations, drawing packages, etc., at a lower cost to the business than if it were done in the country in which the main office is located. While the remote architectural workers with 'talent' can take a multitude of forms, the benefits of working remotely relate to any extra time made available to them to undertake a particular form of work because they are not commuting and have reduced workplace interruptions.

While work hasn't solely happened *in* The Office or during Office hours, not having to commute to work is a fundamental argument for remote work because not commuting wastes less work time. (Fried and Hansson 2013, p. 10–12/151) As a consequence, remote work has the capacity to increase productivity by reducing stresses and can help "a company's bottomline," (Fried and Hansson 2013, p. 24/151) Unlike office work time, remote work time can escape the 9 to 5 routine of traditional office hours. This is because worktime is not "disciplined by the clock" (Thompson 1967) but can be determined, to a greater extent, by the remote worker. For Fried and Hansson (2013, p. 15/151), "The beauty of relaxing workday hours is that the policy accommodates everyone – from the early birds to the night owls to the family folks with kids who need to be picked up in the middle of the day. … We try to keep a roughly forty-hour workweek, but how our employees distribute those hours across the clock and days just isn't important." Work can, in principle, happen night or day depending on how a worker wants to organise when they need to get their work done. Complications arise, however, when a worker needs to "collaborate[…] with people in multiple time zones." (Fried and Hansson 2013, p. 15/151)

Working in a global virtual office enables workers to escape the problem of in-person offices becoming "interruption factories," (Fried and Hansson 2013, p. 10/151) thereby better enabling "meaningful work, creative work, thoughtful work, important work." Being able to focus and work alone to gather one's own thoughts are arguably more possible when working away from the office through enabling an alternative form of relaxed productivity. This does not mean that remote work from home or elsewhere cannot have their own distractions, but people have the capacity to control them either by limiting doing other domestic duties or moving to another site that is less distracting. (Fried and Hansson 2013, p. 10/151) This applies not only to the building in which one works but also whether to work remotely in the city or the country regardless of where the head office is located.

By releasing oneself from the 9 to 5 work routine and mentality and not being required to work *in* the office means that workers diminish the draw of finding work in higher density cities, which are generally more costly to live in. Being able to work for a practice in London, for instance, and live the countryside at the edges of the city or in, is an increasing trend. Remote working has "made remote culture and living much more desirable" (Fried and Hansson 2013, p. 17/151) because advances in technology have allowed not only access to work but also to wider cultural experiences with "… access to every movie ever made, every book ever written, every album ever recorded, and nearly every sports game live." (Fried and Hansson 2013, p. 17/151) Being able to leave the city or suburb to live wherever one wants relies on the right technology (software and hardware) to facilitate all the communication and work modes that happened previously in person. It is also taken up more-or-less positively by different generations, those "bred on the idea that good work happens from 9am to 5pm, in offices and cubicles in tall buildings around the city" versus those "raised on Facebook and texting" who are unable to "be sentimental about the old days of all-hands-on-deck, Monday morning meetings…." (Fried and Hansson 2013, p. 12/151)

In the case of architecture, remote and flexible working has been offered in architecture schools and offices for some time but has increased recently. Casual work contracts offer flexible work across industry and the university but are still tied to traditional 9 to 5 hours of work. What remote work offers, however, is a deep cultural shift that can make life easier for people with a life outside architectural work and who love other things equally or more than work, most notably family caregivers.

In the case of architectural workers who are family caregivers, remote work can allow more freedom to manage work time since zero-commuting allows more time to balance domestic homelife commitments with work life. The ability to work from home while caring for a child/ren or other family dependents or pets allows architectural workers of different gender and age the potential to better balance work and home life, depending on their ability to ring-fence time to ensure they do not work longer hours. While the architect and artist studio has always blurred the two zones by generally not differentiating between work and domestic life, there is also the problem that "combining workspace with a family home raises issues about physical, emotional and psychological boundaries." (Holliss 2015, p. 3 of Chapter 3) While working from home removes hours for commuting, balancing working online while caring or teaching small children, for instance, can increase, rather than decrease, the pressure on architect parents. For a sole practitioner whose office is in their home, chosen to reduce overheads, home base work can suffer from either being what Holliss (2015, Footnote 11 in Chapter 3) describes as "all 'work dominated' [or] 'home dominated'" so that achieving 'equal-status' between the two can be difficult to achieve. This depends on whether there is 'no, some or total spatial separation' (a latter example being the studio shed in the back garden) and how much space is required. (Holiss 2015) However, working from home can also be disadvantageous if one is living alone as it can increase feelings of isolation, since social contact with work colleagues is reduced through physical distancing. Conversely, Franklin Becker and Fritz Steele (1995, p. 114) note how Howard Rheingold (1993) sees benefits in *The Virtual Community* who he "describes [as] people who have never seen each other becoming fast friends; helping each other out and rallying around to provide social support, advice, and a good ear in times of personal crisis." Remote work can be healthy or unhealthy for the bodies of different types of architectural workers depending on their degree of ability to nurture social work networks remotely or balance work associated with the roles of *homo oeconomicus* and *femina domestica*. However, there is no question that remote work has benefits for the environment.

Home-based work can reduce greenhouse gas emissions to support an environmentally-sustainable workplace. Occupied for more time than when work is split between the office and home, "home-based work can reduce carbon emissions by helping us to travel less, heat less, and make less, [all economic advantages] while simultaneously improving people's quality of life." (Holliss 2015, Chapter 6) This economisation of work time in one workplace has economic advantages when work can be done remotely. As noted in *Remote: Office Not Required*, this requires that employers understand that work productivity by "the virtual workforce" (David Allen quoted in Fried and Hansson 2013, p. 2) is not dependent on the need for an employee to be seen with their bottom on their seat in the office. Where work cannot be delivered solely at home through remote work, as in the case of on site or the construction site, most architecture schools and practices offering a hybrid work model in which some days' work is done in the office, and other days are worked from home.

Importantly, the class of an architectural workers dictates the degree to which remote work can be enacted and dictated. If we take the architectural precariat class, whose work takes place for many through their computer rather than on site, they can more easily morph into a virtual workforce. However, where architectural educators, office managers, and site architects rely on social interaction with students, clients, contractors, sub-contractors, consultants, etc., to build their social capital, then the hybrid model or solely-working-in-the-office model are required. The division of labour in architectural work dictates that those involved in social networking are at a greater advantage than those unable to obtain those experiences. The potential of an "an office-less future" is therefore not "better for all." (Adam L. Penenberg quoted in Fried and Hansson 2013, p. 2) Neoliberal subjects or architectural educators and practitioners who aren't as high up on the career ladder can be disadvantaged by not being able to build and consolidate their social capital for future career progression.

Key is that "embracing remote work doesn't mean you *can't* have an office, just that it's not required. It doesn't mean that all your employees *can't* live in the same city, just that they don't have to. Remote work is about setting your team free to be the best it can be, where that might be" (Fried and Hansson 2013, p. 25/151) and at whatever stage of their working life they are at. The benefit, for those who don't miss working in the office, is that remote work doesn't require holding off on doing the things in one's life that one might want to do at any life stage, rather than following a more traditional mindset that one would wait to do them after retirement. "Your life no longer needs to be divided into arbitrary phases of work and retirement. You can blend the two for fun and profit—design a better lifestyle that makes work enjoyable because it's not the *only* thing on the menu." (Fried and Hansson 2013, p. 19/151) So while the office loses its relevance as *the* primary site of architectural production which can have advantages for some types of workers, there are ramifications for the work architects do in designing commercial offices. As work changes so does the design of workspace such that renting a handful of desks to hot desk is more economical for a practice rather than rent whole tenancy floors or buildings at greater expense. The purpose of the office also changes, responding to neoliberal branding.

The image of the office building is arguably more important for clients of architects or architects themselves than employees. "For… companies where the trappings of success are an important part of the image—for example, advertising agencies or law firms or G-level recruiting outfits [or corporate architects]—having a showy office may make sense. Acknowledging that the office is there to impress clients sets an owner or manager free to make it the best theatre experience it can be—and employees can remain free to work from home when they're not needed as extras on the scene." (Fried and Hansson 2013, p. 26/151) The trade-offs of working remotely – 'freedom, time, money' and "not seeing your coworkers [sic] in person every day… (if you are an introvert)" (Fried and Hansson 2013, p. 27/151) – are the lack of in-person contact and conversation with colleagues and the "loss of imposed structure and regimen" which can be highly problematic for anyone who has a tendency to procrastinate." (Fried and Hansson 2013, p. 27/151) For women or men working from home, it can be difficult to set boundaries.

Home working and remote working, full-time or part-time, as an architectural student, educator, or practitioner has advantages and/or disadvantages depending on one's gender, race/ethnicity, class, and age, as well as other variables. Unconventional work schedules can provide opportunities for extra time for family or hobbies or to work around patterns where people want to start earlier and finish earlier or start later and finish later. (Fried and Hansson 2013, p. 55/151) As discussed in Chapter 4, freedom of choice, in this instance of when and where to work, is a key attribute of contemporary architectural life and can increase job satisfaction for groups of differing demographics depending on if it is more convenient for them considering their home life. However, the change in an architectural worker's flexible work lifestyle can also result in an arguably false belief that you can *Design your Life* (Nash 2021) and be in control to do so. Here it is less so, but still of influence, what one's gender, race/ethnicity, social class, or age are, and more so in what architectural class of worker one is. This is because flexible work is one way in which neoliberalism blends home life into work life to unconsciously increase productivity. As Robert Kronenburg (2007, p. 12) notes "The requirement for flexibility stems not just from desire and possibility, but also from economy and necessity."

Remote work in architecture may diminish relationships and reduce peer-to-peer mentorship and learning support at university or industry between mentees and mentors, putting more pressure on wellbeing support systems in the institutions. Loyalty to architectural organisations may also diminish due to lack of social connectivity to co-workers leading to talent being lost. As noted, "All of these employee populations coexist in the modern virtual corporation. The result is a level of chaos and mixed loyalties unimaginable in the traditional corporate organization [sic] chart. Replacing the standard hierarchical organization [sic] will be something resembling a bull's-eye: concentric rings of real and pseudo-employees emanating out from the small core of full-time—often lifetime—employees who hold the key knowledge of the organization [sic], maintain its philosophy, pass on its myths, and will be the cultivators of long-term relationships with employees and partners." (Edvinsson and Malone 1997, p. 130) Due to the 'phenomenal' pace at which organisations are changing (Becker and Steele 1995, p. 1 of Preface) and the generational differences in expectations and outcomes of work in the real and virtual workspaces of architectural labour, it is not yet possible to determine how shifting to home-based and remote work will transform work (Susskind and Susskind 2017) will affect the work-life balance of architectural workers. At the time of writing this book, the demands on universities and architectural practices was to optimise productivity by distributing work off site, in order to remain competitive so as survive in the marketplace. However the quality of whichever workspace can affect performance.

"Good facilities will not guarantee success, nor will poorly designed ones guarantee failure. The same can be said for management, employees, and equipment. By themselves, none of these elements of a business is enough to ensure success. They are part of an integrated system, and to function effectively all the parts have to be in harmony." (Becker and Steele 1995, p. 7) As Becker and Steele (1995, p. 14) note, the 'the total workplace' which is "not simply one's desk, office, or work station in the office building [but] also the cafeteria, the conference and break rooms, the project room, corridors with water fountains, the fitness center [sic] […] *All the places* in which one works" is about a 'process' in relation to 'product.' Discussing "One Size Doesn't Fit All," Becker (2004, p. xxi) writes:

> Diversity in workstyles and workplaces, from workstation to building portfolio, strengthens a company's competitive advantage by giving it a more multifaceted set of solutions for dealing with a highly predictable business environment. This kind of ecodiversity goes against the grain of standardization [sic] and universal planning which is the bedrock for workplace design strategies in most large organizations [sic] today. It reflects, however, current thinking in biology about the value of biodiversity. The greatest threat to a species over time, and to the ecology system, is the absence of a rich and diverse gene pool.

Becker (2004, pp. 104–106) argues that different stages of a working life often require different types of workplaces that are suitable and that is why flexible architecture can better support workers. Creating physically healthy environments requires combining high quality air flow, temperature, ambient sound conditions, lighting, physical body positions, and green building design (Becker and Steele 1995, pp. 86–99) with patterns of work that nurture rather than replete the energy of architectural workers.

References

Aureli, P. V. 2015. Form and Labor: Toward a History of Abstraction in Architecture. In Deamer, P. ed. *The Architect as Worker: Immaterial Labor, the Creative Class and the Politics of Design.* London: Bloomsbury Academic, pp. 103–117.

Austin, S. and Sharr, A. 2021. The University of Nonstop Society: Campus Planning, Lounge Space, and Incessant Productivity, *Architecture and Culture*, ed. Troiani, I. 9 (1): 69–97.

Bauman, Z. 2000. *Liquid Modernity*. Cambridge: Polity Press.

Becker, F. 2004. *Offices at Work: Uncommon Workplace Strategies that add Value and Improve Performance*. San Francisco: John Wiley & Sons, Inc.

Becker, F. and Steele, F. 1995. *Workplace by Design: Mapping the High-Performance Workscape*. San Francisco: Jossey-Bass Publishers.

Blondel, J.-F. 1756. *Architecture Françoise*, Vol. 4, Book 6, Paris: Charles-Antoine Jombert.

Bourdieu, P. 2019. *Homo Academicus*. Stanford: Stanford University Press. [Trans. by Collier, P. First published in 1988.]

Brown, W. 2015. *Undoing the Demos: Neoliberalism's Stealth Revolution.* New York: Zone Books.

Cairns, G. 2010. *Deciphering Advertising, Art and Architecture: New Persuasion Techniques for Sophisticated Consumers.* Farringdon, Oxfordshire: Libri Publishing.

Colquhoun, A. 1981. Plateau Beaubourg, In *Essays in Architectural Criticism*, Cambridge, Mass.: The MIT Press, pp. 81–89.

Coulson, J., Roberts, P. and Taylor, I. 2015. *University Trends: Contemporary Campus Design.* London: Routledge.

De Graaf, R. 2017. *Four Walls and a Roof: The Complex Nature of a Simple Profession.* Cambridge, Mass.: Harvard University Press.

Dober, R. P. 1992. *Campus Design.* New York; Chichester: John Wiley and Sons, Inc.

Edvinsson, L. and Malone, M. S. 1997. *Intellectual Capital: The Proven Way to Establish your Company's Real Value by Measuring its Hidden Brainpower.* London: Piatkus.

Edwards, B. 2000. *University Architecture.* New York: Spon Press.

Emmons, P. 2012. The Play of Plans: Le Corbusier's Serious Game of Dominoes. In *The Cultural Role of Architecture: Contemporary and Historical Perspectives.* eds. Emmons, P., Lomholt, J., and Hendrix, J. London: Routledge, pp. 132–140.

Foucault, M., Davidson, A. I. ed., Burchell, G. (Trans). 2008. *The Birth of Biopolitics: Lectures of the Collège de France, 1978–1979.* Houndmills, Basingstoke, Hampshire [England]; New York: Palgrave Macmillan.

Fried, J. and Hansson, D. H. 2013. *Remote: Office Not Required.* Ebury Digital (Kindle version).

Hatterstone, S. 2010. Zaha Hadid: I'm Happy to Be on the Outside. *Guardian,* October 9, https://www.theguardian.com/artanddesign/2010/oct/09/zaha-hadid, Accessed November 06, 2023.

Hochschild, A. R. 2001. *The Time Bind: When Work Becomes Home and Home Becomes Work.* United States: Owl Books.

Holliss, F. 2015. *Beyond Live/Work: The Architecture of Home-based Work.* London; New York: Routledge.

Holub, D. 2016. Zaha Hadid's World of Fluid Freedom, May 31. www.designersatelier.co.uk/dagmars-articles/zaha-hadid-s-world-of-fluid-freedom/, Accessed November 06, 2023.

Hopkirk, E. 2021. Pandemic Blamed as Zaha Hadid Calls Time on Historic Bowling Green Lane Home, *Building,* July 15. https://www.building.co.uk/news/pandemic-blamed-as-zaha-hadid-calls-time-on-historic-bowling-green-lane-home/5112793.article, Accessed November 06, 2023.

Jessel, E. 2021. Covid Crisis Leads ZHA to Quit 'Inflexible' Bowling Green Lane HQ, *Architects' Journal,* July 14, https://www.architectsjournal.co.uk/news/covid-crisis-leads-zha-to-quit-inflexible-bowling-green-lane-hq, Accessed November 06, 2023.

Kane, P. 2004. *The Play Ethic: A Manifesto for a Different Way of Living.* Oxford: Macmillan.

Klingmann, A. 2007. *Brandscapes: Architecture in the Experience Economy.* Cambridge, Mass.: MIT Press.

Koolhaas, R. 2002 Spring. Junkspace, *October,* 100: 175–190. https://doi.org/10.1162/016228702320218457

Kronenburg, R. 2007. *Flexible: Architecture that Responds to Change.* London: Laurence King Publishing.

Littlefield, D. 2009. *Good Office Design.* London: RIBA Publishing.

Martin, R. 2003. *The Organizational Complex: Architecture, Media, and Corporate Space.* Cambridge, Mass.; London: MIT Press.

Martin, R. 1989. Out of Marginality: Toward a New Kind of Professional. In Berkeley, E. P. and McQuaid, M. eds. 1989. *Architecture: A Place for Women.* Washington, DC: Smithsonian Institution Press, pp. 229–236.

McNeill, D. 2009. *The Global Architect: Firms, Fame and Urban Form*. New York; London: Routledge, pp. 153–155.

Muthesius, S. 2000. *The Postwar University: Utopianist Campus and College*. New Haven; London: Yale University Press.

Myerson, J., Bichard, J., and Erlich, A. 2010. *New Demographics, New Workspace: Office Design for the Changing Workforce*. Farnham: Gower.

Myerson, J. and Privett, I. 2014. *Life of Work: What Office Design Can Learn from the World Around Us*. London: Black Dog Publishing.

Myerson, J. and Ross, P. 2006. *Space to Work: New Office Design*. London: Laurence King Publishing Ltd.

Myerson, J. and Ross, P. 2003. *The 21st Century Office*. London: Laurence King Publishing Ltd.

Myerson, J. and Ross, P. 1999. *The Creative Office*. London: Laurence King Publishing Ltd.

Nash, C. 2021. *Design your Life: An Architect's Guide to Achieving a Work/Life Balance*. London: RIBA Publishing.

Parker, L. D. and Jeacle, I. 2019 Fall. The Construction of the Efficient Office: Scientific Management, and the Neo-Liberal State, *CAR* (*Contemporary Accounting Research*), 36 (3): 1883–1926.

Picard, C.-F., Durocher, S., Gendron, Y., de Vaujany, F-X., Leclercq-Vandelannoitte, A., Munro, I., Nama, Y., and Holt, R. 2021. Office Design, Neoliberal Governmentality and Professional Service Firms, *Organization Studies*, 42 (5): 739–759.

Prensky, M. 2001. Digital Natives, Digital Immigrants, *On the Horizon*, 9 (5): 1–6.

Rank, M. R., Hirschl, T. A., and Foster, K. A. 2014. *Chasing the American Dream: Understanding what Shapes our Fortunes*. Oxford: Oxford University Press.

Rheingold, H. 1993. *The Virtual Community: Homesteading on the Electronic Frontier*. Reading, Mass.: Addison-Wesley.

Romei, L. K. 1992 May. "Telecommuting: A Workstyle Revolution?" *Modern Office Technology*, 37 (5): 38–40.

Sanders, J. 1996. *Stud: Architectures of Masculinity*. Princeton: Princeton Architectural.

Schneider, T. and Till, J. 2007. *Flexible Housing*. Amsterdam; Boston; London: Elsevier.

Slaughter, S. and Leslie, L. L. 1997. *Academic Capitalism: Politics, Policies and the Entrepreneurial University*. Baltimore; London: John Hopkins University Press.

Southwood, I. 2011. *Non-Stop Inertia*. Winchester, U.K.; Washington, U.S.A.: Zero Books.

Spencer, D. 2016. *The Architecture of Neoliberalism: How Contemporary Architecture Became an Instrument of Control and Compliance*. London: Bloomsbury Academic.

Standing, G. 2016. *The Precariat: The New Dangerous Class*. London: Bloomsbury Academic.

Susskind, D. and Susskind, R. 2017. *The Future of the Professions; How Technology Will Transform the Work of Human Experts*. Oxford: Oxford University Press.

Tafuri, M. 1979. *The Disenchanted Mountain, The American City*. Cambridge, Mass.: The MIT Press.

Taylor, I. ed. 2016. *Future Campus: Design Quality in University Buildings*. London: RIBA Publishing.

Thompson, E. P. 1967 December. Time, Work-Discipline, and Industrial Capitalism. In *Past & Present*, 38: 56–97.

Troiani, I. 2024. Not A One-Size-Fits-All Architectural Education. In Choi, G. and Durham, H. eds. *Inclusion Emergency: Diversity in Architecture*. London: RIBA Publishing.

Troiani, I. 2021 December. The Elephant in the Room: How Neoliberal Architecture Education Undermines Wellbeing, *Charrette*, Themed issue, 'Practice, architecture education and wellbeing,' eds. Rice, L., Meraz, F., Drozynski, C., and Marco, E., 7(2) Autumn: 9–33.

Troiani, I., and Carless, T. 2021. The Death and Life of UK Universities and the Cultural Spaces They Consume, *Architecture_MPS*, 19(1): 12 pages.

Troiani. I with Dutson, C. 2021 March. The Neoliberal University as a Space to Learn/ Think/Work in Higher Education. In Troiani, I. ed. *Architecture and Culture*, 9 (1): 5–23.

Turner, G., and Myerson, J. 1998. *New Workplace New Culture: Office Design as a Catalyst for Change*. Aldershot: Gower.

Unknown, *Oak Park Home & Studio*. date unknown, https://franklloydwright.org/site/oak-park-home-studio/, Accessed November 06, 2023.

Unknown, ZHA website. 2021. ZHA Relocates Head Office to our 101 Goswell Road Site in London, July 13, https://www.zaha-hadid.com/2021/07/13/zha-relocates-head-office-to-our-101-goswell-road-site-in-london/, Accessed November 06, 2023.

Unknown, ZHA website. 2016. 13 July 2021. Zaha Hadid Architects Opens Middle East Office, November 7, https://www.zaha-hadid.com/2016/11/07/zaha-hadid-architects-opens-middle-east-office/ Accessed November 06, 2023.

Unknown. 2011, Hawkins Brown, The Hub, Coventry University, 2011. https://www.hawkinsbrown.com/news-and-events/press/mix-magazine, Accessed December 21, 2021.

Usher, N. 2018. *The Elemental Workplace: The 12 Elements for Creating a Fantastic.* London: LID Publishing.

Van Zanten, D. 1978 October. Félix Duban and the Buildings of the Ecole des Beaux-Arts, 1832–1840, *Journal of the Society of Architectural Historians*, 37 (3): 161–174.

Woodward, D. 2013. Top 10 Architects' Homes. *AnOther*, June 22. http://www.anothermag.com/art-photography/2809/top-10-architects-homes Accessed November 06, 2023.

Whyte, W. H. Jr. 1956 *The Organization Man.* New York: Simon and Schuster.

8

24/7 ARCHITECTURAL CAPITALISM, NO TIME, NO SLEEP

FIGURE 8.1   Harold Lloyd finds himself in a precarious situation dangling from a clock in a scene from the film *Safety Last*. Photograph: Evening Standard/ Stringer/Getty Images). Editorial #: 2642648. Collection: Moviepix. Date created 01 January 1923. Barcode HH6907; Object name: dave22/cat3/ min/038.

DOI: 10.4324/9781351199834-11

The Limits of Work Time and the Continuous Global Marketplace Clock

This chapter focuses on how our sense of time has changed under industrialisation and neoliberalism, looking at work time in relation to architectural production. It examines the shift in how we perceived worktime in the agrarian era, the industrialised era in modern times (Figure 8.1), and then in contemporary *Liquid Times* (Bauman 2007) in order to understand the effect over work and under work can have on the physical, mental, and psychological wellbeing of architectural workers. It looks at the consequences of what Jonathan Crary (2014) defines as a 24/7 work life to sustain continuous economic production and consumption in a global market society. On the way, it recognises how this has been made possible by shifting to digital technologies – rather than analogue/handmade or site-specific modes of architectural production – changing how and where we work. The length of the working day (eight-hour day, six-hour day, more or less), work-discipline associated with efficient time management, debt, and responsibilities at home and at work are discussed. The stress of too much work or lack of work (a consequence of architecture's close relationship with boom-bust cycles of consumption and production) and the happiness or unhappiness experienced from working excessively or not working has a significant effect on the bodies of architectural labourers.

Work-life balance in architecture is often considered in terms of potential alternative patterns of daily labour other than those enacted in neoliberally-oriented architecture schools or offices. Relevant here are the hours of work demanded of some managers (including educators, university managers, and architectural practice managers) in relation to the number of hours worked daily, the number of days worked in a week, personal wellbeing, and the wellbeing of the households, family, and friends of the architectural student, educator, or practitioner. The demands that neoliberalism makes on the body of its workers is discussed through a selection of writings by Michel Foucault including his theory of 'biopolitics.' The consumption and depletion of 'human capital' as a resource in architecture due to the demands for marketisation, globalisation, and productivity and the ethics associated with those conditions are central to the study of time and labour in architectural economies. Fundamental too is the value of doing other non-work-related activities to recharge including free time to think and inspire thinking for no productive purpose whatsoever – not solely to regain energy to keep working.

In the chapter entitled "Labour, Work and the Time Squeeze," Guy Standing (2016, p. pp. 135–154) argues that our sense of time has dramatically changed because of the global market. In an agrarian system of production, people worked according to seasonal rhythms and variable weather condition. They would never have imagined working "a regular 10- or 8-hour working day" because they needed to work around these natural times. It was industrialization [sic] that brought in 'time regimentation.'" (Standing 2016, p. 135) It was the historian, E. P. Thompson (1967) who eloquently chronicled in "Time, Work-Discipline, and Industrial Capitalism" that "the nascent proletariat was disciplined by the clock" and the calendar.

In the shift from an agrarian to an industrial life to a "global market system geared to services, two changes in time occurred. The first was the growing disrespect for the 24-hour body clock" (Standing 2016, p. 135) through the standardisation of time in countries that resulted in international time zones. For example, Mao Zedong standardised the entire People's Republic of China to use Beijing time as a nation-building project. At the time of writing this book, there were 24 international time zones in which the global economy operates with workday time varying depending on the kind of (architectural) labour class in which a labourer works. As some architectural classes work longer or shorter hours in one or more time zones, their natural body clock can be compromised.

A time zone mostly operates around how the body is conditioned to work during daytime in that place. Body rhythms of work, sleep, and relaxation were previously aligned with daytime and nighttime. Standing (2016, p. 136) astutely notes however that: "…the global economy has no respect for human physiology" because the global marketplace functions much like a machine that has no rest, running on a 24/7 clock, night and day, disregarding when countries have daylight or darkness. Overall neoliberal, free market economies seek to eliminate any distractions that create 'barriers to trading' and which are counter to "the totem of the age, competitiveness, and contrary to the dictate of flexibility. If a country, firm or individual does not adapt to the 24/7 time culture, there will be a price to pay. It is no longer a case of 'the early bird catches the worm'; it is the sleepless bird that does so." (Standing 2016, p. 136) For this reason, global academic and architectural capitalism values the person who can sleep less and work more in continuum.

According to Standing (2016, p. 136), the second change that emerged in industrial society is how time became divided into blocks, with blocks of work or non-work time being assigned to specific workplaces and homeplaces respectively. Under industrial labour laws, workers rose in the morning, worked 10- to 12-hour days in factories, mines, shipyards, etc., under no or very loose contractual arrangements and then went home. They were given holidays (originally holy days to celebrate special religious days, later becoming special days to rest or relax from work) although these diminished during the industrial period and were replaced by short holiday periods which were numerated and taken mostly in blocks. "Work, labour and play were distinct activities, in terms of when they were undertaken and where the boundaries of each began and ended." (Standing 2016, p. 136) In contrast, in liquid modern times, neoliberalism asks for increased flexibility and productivity which demands that work be enacted "in continuum everywhere," (Standing 2016, p. 138) thereby crumbling the former models and spaces of industrial proletariat and salariat labour. As "'hours at work' are not the same as 'hours of work'," (Standing 2016, p. 152) additional time pressures can be put on those with demanding work life and home life responsibilities.

In the book, *The Time Bind: When Work Becomes Home and Home Becomes Work* Arlie Russell Hochschild (1997) uses the 1936 comedy film, *Modern Times*

(Chaplin 1936), to contemplate the problem of work time in contemporary life. Hochschild (1997, p. 225) notes that the speedup of labour in modern life is no longer confined to work and now "extends to the home." Neoliberalism has contributed to the breaking down of the limits of the industrial model of productive time previously adopted in factories and office blocks. It has simultaneously increased the monitoring of productivity driven by optimization [sic] using an ever-increasing number of time management audit systems. This has left workers "without a stable time structure" (Standing 2016, p. 139) and thereby puts pressure on the work-life balance mostly of the architectural precariat class who are "at the risk of being in a permanent spin, forced to juggle the demands on limited time" and the stresses that accompany their inability to control and manage their time. This is often because even though they are working longer hours, they are often required to take on more work in a cycle of work which many accept they can *never* fulfil. Extra free work done by choice by or required of architectural workers that is not factored into the paid work equation exploits the unpaid labour that needs to be done to deliver the output. Any form of service or creative labour, including architectural labour, involves a considerable amount of free and 'immaterial labour,' which is difficult to quantify or 'outside measure' (Hardt and Negri 2000) and therefore is prone to potential exploitation of the mind and body, in this case that of the architect.

A 24/7 Architectural Work Culture at University and in the Office

Architecture, both in the university and the office, has arguably always been a profession premised on an 100% commitment to work and so a 24/7 globally-oriented work culture only exacerbates an already work-only centred profession. However, a 24/7 architectural work culture intensifies work life further in a neoliberal, global free marketplace in two ways. The first is by demanding more and more of the body of the architectural worker (student, educator, or practitioner) and second by employing digital machine technologies to enhance and facilitate more efficient productivity 24/7. Work sites, as places which previously were sites for a specific function, have changed to support 'fluid' and flexible digital architectural production. No longer is the architect's home for domestic functions and the university or office for architectural labour. Using machine technologies (mobile phones, computers, etc.), architectural labour under neoliberalism facilitates longer working hours so that, as Hochschild (1997) notes, 'work becomes home and home becomes work.' This can create an issue in relation to the limits of work time resulting in a culture of over work.

It is problematic that over work is often deemed by select notable architects to be either an essential rite-of-passage of the profession or – perhaps more curiously and arguably sadomasochistic – invigorating. For instance, Rem Koolhaas claims to delight in the excesses of over work and has argued that having limited time to produce vast projects should be approached 'with vigor [sic]' by architects. When discussing OMA's frenetic production of architectural proposals in China in the 1990s, Koolhaas (in Owen ed. 2009, p. 1) writes that "It seems clear that somehow we [architects] should be able, when given the impossibly difficult problem of designing in two weeks a city for three million people, to respond with vigor [sic] and skill." The established culture of being invigorated by being pushed to the limits of architectural production in practice in pressured timeframes is linked to the nurturing of a conditioning towards a 'curious masochism' in architectural education. (Stead 2003, p. 50) The unhealthy and imbalanced long work hours culture of the 24/7 architectural design studio that emerged at the École has only been exacerbated under neoliberalism and post-pandemic through online or hybrid teaching. As a recognised cause in the decline of student and staff wellbeing, the pattern of work acculturated in the neoliberal vertical unit studio remains 'the elephant in the room' of architectural education. (Troiani 2021, p. 9)

In the global higher education market, in order to increase productivity many universities, and with them their schools of architecture, have shifted to 24/7 opening hours for architectural studio spaces and libraries to support, enable, and encourage work at all times of the day and night. Building in part upon the model of the Beaux-Arts architect working tirelessly and happily in their arts studio, many architectural courses encourage students to work continuously 'without breaks' and some demand almost immediate email responses from their educators 24/7. Global architectural practice – where a firm creates architecture 24/7 across multiple time zones in multiple countries so that a job never stops being worked on – is mostly not questioned under neoliberalism because it is deeply tied to how private practice can better profit. In fact, many solely money-driven practitioners see this as the sign of a successful, 'healthy' practice, as is exemplified by the comment by Koolhaas (in Owen ed. 2009, p. 1) and prioritise the production of designs and buildings over the wellbeing of the workforce that procures them. Some practices have an endless supply of employees interested in working for them and so staff turnover – whether because of workplace unhappiness, over work, or a resistance to do so – does not detrimentally affect production.

The over work culture, working day and night, is enculturated in architectural education in three ways. First, it typically starts in the first year of architectural education as a conditioning to 'work load shock'; second, through the valuing of 'a never leave the studio culture'; and third, the valuing of competition, 'commitment, and endurance' which drive high energy levels for the production of work without complaint or objection.

In *Architect? A Candid Guide to the Profession*, Roger Lewis (1998, p. 61) discusses the experience of an architecture education focusing on the first year of study. Lewis analyses in detail the effect of 'the work load shock' that typically occurs in the first year and notes the emergence of Stead's (2003, p. 50) 'curious masochism' in architectural education. Lewis (1998, p. 62) explains: "The work load shock, like any assault on the mind and body, produces both positive and negative responses. Negatively, it is tiring, enervating, and numbing. Much of the studio work is labor [sic] intensive rather than intellect intensive. [...] If you can tolerate it all, it will toughen you." As a result, Lewis (1998, p. 62) recommends that the best approach to first-year workload in an architectural education is to adopt "a positive, have fun, on-to-victory one. *Illegitimus non carborundum*, interpreted liberally to mean 'Don't let the bastards grind you down!'" (Lewis 1998, p. 62)

Essential to coping with the 'work load shock' is 'time management.' (Lewis 1998, p. 62) The vast amount of mostly manual-skilled work architecture students do in their first year of study both conditions them to a life without work time boundaries and can nurture the illusion of the necessity to stay at work in the studio to meet demanding deadlines. This can develop a never leave work mentality that can encourage some students to "practically live in the studio in what can best be described as camping-out conditions." (Lewis 1998, p. 62)

However this is changing nowadays due to the increased use of digital drawing technologies, so that students can continue studio work on their laptops at home or elsewhere, in order for them to become disciplined to working "in continuum everywhere." (Standing 2016, p. 138) Becoming acculturated to working everywhere and for longer tests the body's normal rhythms. The 'all-nighter' is made possible and is normalised in architectural education because, as already stated, many neoliberal schools of architecture provide 24-hour access to studios and computer facilities. The 'all-nighter' is symbolic in that it shows commitment to a life fully devoted to work and shows competitive spirit.

'Commitment and endurance' is in part tested in architectural education through how students cope with time pressures that are placed on them by their university educators. Neoliberalism encourages efficient and productive use of time by the student for optimum productivity of the highest quality. An architectural education in the best schools of architecture in the world conditions students to work in this manner, although there is still 'wasted' creative time (under a capitalist mindset) in student university labour. What is important in this cycle of working day and night is that it can, depending on the employer, set expectations by the employee and employer for a long work hour culture. It also means a student has, in the past, found "little sympathy" among staff to "air complaints about the amount of work [… being asked to do], the overlapping deadlines and exams, the pressures, and the state of [a student's] mental and physical health," (Lewis 1998, p. 63) although this has changed post-pandemic. Some educators, including Peggy Deamer, challenge a long-work day studio culture by asking her students to sign work hour contracts with their design tutors that limit studio work hours for wellbeing. Deamer's criticality of the exploitation of labour in the architecture studio in the university aims to empower the minds and bodies of emerging architects in order to challenge such a lifestyle, since they may likely be required to work 24/7 in the global marketplace in their career as a practicing architect.

Here I discuss an example of how a 24/7 architectural practice work life culture is enacted to the extreme, referring to the work life of Iraqi-born Dame Zaha Hadid (1950–2016). Focus here is on how Hadid devoted every hour of her day and night entirely to her career and how she epitomised the entrepreneurial, global architect pushed to their limits. Tangential architectural comparison is made to Koolhaas – Hadid's tutor at the Architectural Association (AA) – and to Baroness Margaret Thatcher, the latter both a proponent of and exemplary model of a neoliberal work life and who was invigorated by a culture of over work. The way in which a 24/7 architectural practice life affected the body of Hadid and Koolhaas showcases issues the profession has with expectations of excellence and how it can affect work-life balance and wellbeing. The artistic, chaotic nature of architects can put some starchitects at higher health risk.

By the time Thatcher became Prime Minister she was already married with twin 26-year-old children. After graduating from university, she devoted herself fully to her political working life and practiced the long work hours, with minimal sleep, work life that enables maximum productivity. Thatcher's chief press secretary from 1979 to 1990, Sir Bernard Ingham (in De Castella 2013) claims Thatcher only slept four hours per night during weekdays but could have slept more on the weekend. Less than the minimum requirement of sleep allowed Thatcher to put into practice her belief that disciplined long hours of hard work with little rest was the path to personal and economic success. While Thatcher's work ethic might have been regarded once as exceptional, as Aronowitz, Esposito, DiFazio, and Yard (in Aronowitz and Cutler eds. 1998, p. 64) note, "the 'workaholic' model, once regarded as an individual pathology, has become the enforced, ethically approved standard…."

In Hadid's case, not having a partner, children, or care commitments allowed her to devote herself entirely to her work. This led to her being labelled by Stuart Jeffries (2004) as a "workaholic and single… destined to have only one longtime companion—galloping influenza" as the price of her global travels and success. Jeffries claims that at the time of his interview with a flu-ridden Hadid in 2004, after she had won the Pritzker Prize, being unwell did not stop her travelling. The pattern of pushing herself to her limits of travel for work was sustained by Hadid from (at least) the age of 53 for a 12-year period. Jeffries (2004) writes:

> She's just back from Vienna, where she teaches, and will be jetting off again soon to oversee her many projects. To Rome, perhaps, where her extraordinary National Centre of Contemporary Arts […] is under construction. Or to Leipzig, where her offices and technical spaces for BMW's HQ will mingle white and blue collars in a hearteningly egalitarian manner. Or to Wolfsburg, also in Germany, where she's building a science centre. Or to Italy, where her Salerno ferry terminal is being thrown up.

Continuous work and ill-health became a recurring theme in interviews with Hadid. Hadid (in Jeffries 2004) claimed her ill-health was due to all the flying she did, Hadid explaining "I don't know what they put in the air on those planes, but it is really affecting my health." In an interview in *The Guardian*, Hattenstone writes that when he asked Hadid what she did to relax, Hadid seemed to have "not quite understood the question. [Hadid replying,] 'Relax? Nothing.' But with buildings on site in France and Britain and Milan and Azerbaijan and Spain and China, there's not much time for relaxing." (Hadid in Hattenstone 2010) Hadid (in Hattenstone 2010) explained the problem with women working in the contemporary workforce was that: "now they're liberated; they look after the home, they look after the children, they look after the work and with architecture I think it's important to have continuity. It's not like nine to five, you can't just switch on and off."

While Hadid designed some healthcare architecture, namely the Maggie Centres in Kirkcaldy, Scotland (2006), around the ideal of calmness for wellbeing, she demanded many of her staff, female and male (and as most large starchitect and commercial firms do), work long hours. The work-life pattern at architecture school develops further in corporate practices into working (not always) in the office well beyond the hours of nine to five, sometimes (or often as) seven days a week, or with years of work without vacation. This can lead to staff being rarely at home or being able to only have limited sleep. While this pattern of work has changed post-pandemic, there remains in many large corporate practices the long work hours culture where sleep is given up for work in the hope of later career success and esteem.

Rather than be a site of sanctuary and rest, Hadid's bedroom doubled as a place for work thereby contributing to the imbalance between her work and sleep. (Troiani 2018) Like other people, Hadid admitted that she would often lie awake in her white-painted apartment in Clerkenwell, London. However, what was going through her head wasn't the usual insomniac's litany of anxiety and regrets. "No, no, I lie awake thinking about buildings. I dream about buildings quite often and I've even trained myself to work out plans in my head, not just on paper, on a computer screen." (Hadid in Holub 2016) Just like Thatcher, a life with limited or no sleep, and for Hadid where even sleep time was work time, allowed Hadid to achieve optimal architectural productivity to acquire maximum reputational capital.

While the reasons why women leave architecture are multifarious, as Despina Stratigakos (2016) explains, women (and men) architects who stick with an architectural career and who, it is contended here, are made in the extreme image of *homo oeconomicus*, can be so driven by neoliberal and corporate values of careerism that they push their body to or beyond its limit. After contracting and being treated for bronchitis at a Miami hospital at the age of 65, Hadid died of a heart attack. (Davies 2016) In *Reflections on Zaha Hadid* (Hadid 2017) Patrik Schumacher eulogised "Zaha lived an intense, physically draining life that took its toll, but she coped gracefully and bravely with this, never complaining, just focussing on her missions large and small, soldiering on, in good humour."

After 11 years as PM, Thatcher resigned on the 28th of November 1990. Suffering from dementia, struggling with her memory "as far back of 2000," and with her health declining, Thatcher stepped out of the limelight, initially withdrawing to live in her home in London, then the Ritz Hotel in London, which was paid for by it's owners,

Barclay brothers. (Hill and Adams 2013) In 2013, three years before Hadid's passing, Thatcher, then aged 87, died in the Ritz of a stroke. While Thatcher's will shows "she left a £4.7 million estate to be shared among family members," commentators revealed she "may have avoided millions in inheritance tax by keeping a chunk of her fortune offshore" (Sommerlad 2013) since her £12 million home in London was owned by an anonymous trust registered in the British Virgin Islands.

Survived by her brother Haytham (whom she left £500,000), Hadid's total fortune worth £67,249,458 was bequeathed (but later contested) to Schumacher (£500,000), her four nieces and nephews (£1.7 million), "past, current and future employees and office holders of the companies," (Booth 2017) and the Zaha Hadid Foundation, which was set up to promote architectural education and exhibitions of Hadid's work and other charities. Her architecture practice, ZHA, of which she was sole owner, was left in trust. "In the [fiscal year ending] April 2015, Zaha Hadid Ltd turned over £48m and employed 372 people." (Booth 2017) ZHA continues as a global enterprise and brand after her death.

Like Hadid, Koolhaas's wellbeing suffered too from the jet-setting lifestyle of flying around the world for architectural commissions. Unlike Hadid, however, Koolhaas's work life was interwoven with a more complex personal life. Koolhaas lived between two 'families' – one based in London with his partner and original OMA founder, the painter Madelon Vriesendorp with whom he has two children, the other life in Amsterdam with his lover, the interior and garden designer, Petra Blaisse. When Koolhaas was not moving between England and the Netherlands, he lived in hotels. However his urge to travel to market and expand his practice had a potentially life changing effect on Koolhaas's physical wellbeing. In 1999, Lubow (2000) notes that Koolhaas "was forced to 'do completely nothing' after he underwent 15 vaccinations in preparation for a visit to Lagos; 'The 14th injection went wrong and I developed meningitis and almost died,' he says." After a period of eight months of restful recovery in which Koolhaas (in Lubow 2000) claims to have become "a peaceful observer with a contemplation of architecture" … "the end result of this meditative respite… [was that Koolhaas] grew ''very invigorated but very intolerant of any delay," he says. … In short, he worked even harder." (Lubow 2000)

In the case of these two starchitects, a neoliberal, 24/7 work-life has proved to be professionally advantageous while physiologically detrimental – Hadid literally working herself to death; Koolhaas surviving to only heighten his total commitment to work. These examples of frenetic architectural labour by prominent practitioners who devote their entire lives to work reiterates Carl Cederström and Peter Fleming's (2012, p. 43) argument that "work is no longer something we only *do*, but is also something we resolutely *are* …." The architect's body works on a continuous 'factory (in its *virtual form*)' (Deleuze 1992) shift. In 'Postscript on the Societies of Control,' Gilles Deleuze (1992) argues "It was a factory – not an actual factory, but the factory in its *virtual form*, as a way of life, a gaseous ethos – that has infected our biosphere." (Cederström and Fleming 2012, p. 13) Most notable is how the body of the architect is conditioned gradually through governmental rationality from a docile to productive state for capital accumulation.

Capital Accumulation and the Docile Architect's Body in the Digital Workplace

In *Discipline & Punish*, Michel Foucault (1995, p. 136) distinguishes between the docile body and the manipulated body. Foucault (1995, p. 136) argues that "A body is docile that may be subjected, used, transformed and improved" and it is through the exertion of disciplinary power on the docile body (here, of the architect worker at university or in practice) that it suffers through being disciplined and punished. In the architecture academy and in architectural practice, the body of the worker is the vessel in which 'capital' is contained and as Foucault (1995, p. 221) notes under our current economic system "the two processes – the accumulation of men and the accumulation of capital – cannot be separated"; they are co-existent. For Donna Haraway (1995, p. 510), "the body is an accumulation strategy in the deepest sense." Cederström and Fleming (2012, p. 14) explain:

> The traditional line-in-the-sand between capital and labor no longer makes sense to anyone. Today, the real struggle is between capital and *life* (bios), although the struggle is not played out under especially unfair rules, given that we can hardly tell what life is anymore. We should consider here what Foucault and his followers called bio-power. If work was once primarily regulated by bureaucracy through depersonalization [sic] then today we witness the emergence of a new regime of control which we call *biocracy*, in which life itself is an essential "human resource" to be exploited.

Neoliberalism conditions the body of the architect differently to the architect's body working under industrial capitalism. While Harvey (1982, p. 157) argues that "Capital circulates … through the body of the laborer as variable capital and thereby turns the laborer into a mere appendage of the circulation of capital itself," neoliberalism goes further than capitalism to pretend to empower the architectural worker into thinking they are freely choosing to do so and are in control of their body.

The way in which the body of a worker has been conditioned to work under neoliberalism is deeply linked to global production. Under eight- to ten-hour workday industrial capitalism, the body of the labourer operates as another site of production, to be capitalised upon if it can work faster – like Chaplin's (1936) character in *Modern Times*. Instead under 24/7 global capitalism, a worker is never able to clock in and clock out of work. Time zones in the globally-operational marketplace mesh so that the duration of a working day in any one country is no longer finite since a worker can be required to shift to work the hours of another country. Under neoliberalism, the 'globalised body' (Barajas in Lee and Baumeister

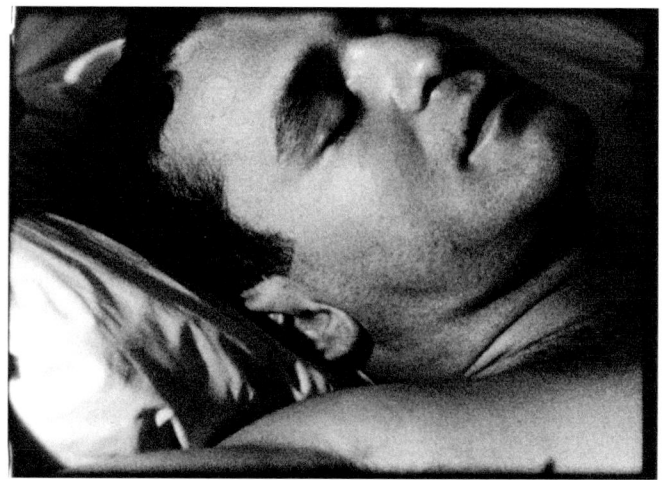

FIGURE 8.2 Screen shot from *Sleep* (Warhol Dir. 1963). Copyright: The Andy Warhol Gallery, Pittsburgh.

eds. 2007, p. 243) of the labourer is pushed further, physically, mentally, and emotionally and required to work in continuum.

In the book, *24/7: Late Capitalism and the Ends of Sleep*, Jonathan Crary (2014, pp. 9–10) claims that to work a 24/7 work life global capitalism "renders plausible, even normal, the idea of working without pause, without limits. It is aligned with what is inanimate, inert, or unageing." Working almost like machines the worker whose body can work more efficiently at a faster rate and with less pauses becomes more valued. 24/7 markets require and promote "continuous work and consumption" (Crary 2014, p. 3) blurring the boundaries between the human body and the machine, such that workers never need to pause, rest, or sleep.

If the body of the architect who works 24/7 has family or care responsibilities beyond university or the office, their time is hurried and their bodies are demanded more of, than the *architect homo oeconomicus* who is 'family-free.' Strong work demands for high job performance can create family life pressures. As work is no longer about working more time at work, it is the "displacement of non-work into the office … in which *we are always at work*" (Cederström and Fleming 2012, p. 17) that can create additional work time and stresses. Referring to Andrew Ross's study of workers in the IT firm Razorfish, Cederström and Fleming (2012, pp. 17–18) note that "ideas and creativity were just as likely to surface at home or in other locations, and so employees were encouraged to work elsewhere... the goal was to extract value from every waking moment of an employee's day" and in the case of architect parents or carers, this can put pressure on their domestic and care work at home. The architecture student, educator, or practitioner with family or care commitments is hurried and stretched in their university or office workplace.

Being able to manage time in an architectural university life or in the life of an architect in practice is a fundamental attribute when playing the game of architecture. Management of one's time can be less compromised if the architect is able to be a more flexible worker, not tied down by having to contribute time to supporting the lives of others. Being able to have the time to always be logged into project work everywhere and through their proficiency in using digital technologies can also advantage some workers.

According to Standing (2016, p. 21) "The digitised world has no respect for contemplation or reflection…." It creates a certain kind of thinking mind which he defines as 'the precariatised mind.' (Standing 2016, p. 21) Standing sees that the electronic gadgetry that pervades all our lives is profoundly affecting how, and for how long, we can think in a focused way for lengthy periods of time. By nurturing a precariat class, neoliberalism can promote short-termism in every aspect of a working life and the inability to think long-term has a profound impact on the ability to progress personally or build a long-term career. (Standing 2016, p. 21)

Short-termism allows the neoliberal subject to be fluid in order to adapt to changes beyond their control but also can also lead to some being less able to develop or fix thoughts and plans for their long-term future. While digital technologies allow the architectural student, educator, or practitioner to work longer and therefore be potentially more able to engage in digital architectural capitalism, it can demand that the body is perpetually active so as to discourage rest.

Conversely, being able to work flexibly using digital technologies at times that are not the conventionally set 'normal' work hours can be liberating for many women and men with care responsibilities because it allows them to juggle their domestic life with their work life. However, while the body of the architect who has care responsibilities is enabled to work for longer, and therefore can be stretched physically and mentally, it is also tested emotionally through working longer online at home and at work. In the late 1980s, Rochelle Martin argued in *Architecture: A Place for Women* (in Perry Berkeley ed. and McQuaid assoc. ed. 1989, p. 232) that "A woman with a family is usually not free to follow this pattern [of long work hour commitment] and she suffers by seeing herself, as well as by being seen, as not quite a "real" architect." However, with the increase in the use of digital technologies since then, women and men architects alike with a family can similarly see themselves as an arguably more exhausted version of 'not quite a "real" architect.'

Energies, Exhaustion, and Architectural Economies of Production

> The bottom is falling out and with it our sense of wellbeing.
> *The Post-Work Manifesto by Aronowitz,*
> *Esposito, DiFazio, and Yard in Aronowitz and Cutler eds. 1998, p. 31*

It is unquestionable that working as an architectural student, educator, or practitioner can be invigorating, and because of such can lead to taking on more and more work to show dedication and commitment. Still, there is a line between when work shifts from being balanced to unbalanced, manageable to unmanageable, rewarding to unrewarding, and energising to exhausting.

In the book, *Exhaustion: A History*, Anna Schaffner (2016, p. 5, 7) explains that "'to exhaust' means to draw off or out, to consume or empty something in its entirety, to account for or utilize the entire quantity of something"; "… Exhaustion generally suggests the vampiric depletion or harmful consumption of a limited (and usually nonrenewable [sic]) resource, which leaves an originally well-functioning person, object, system, or terrain in a weakened or dysfunctional state." She argues that exhaustion is "a specifically modern affliction, irrevocably bound up with the rise of capitalism and new technologies." (Schaffner 2016, p. 8) "… The ubiquity of new information and communication technologies (Machines brought in by managers that allow us to work for longer) and … which no longer allow us … to [properly] disconnect and to relax, blur the boundaries between work and life…." (Schaffner 2016, p. 9) A non-stop architecture university or architectural practice work culture can conflict with the rhythms of people's bodies that naturally seek out rest. "Sleep, Jonathan Crary (2014) argues, has become the true enemy of capitalism, as the capitalist economy envisages a machine-like, willingly surveillable citizen who is always productive and perpetually engaged in the circulation and consumption of goods." (Schaffner 2016, pp. 147–148)

Like Chaplin's character in *Modern Times* who is increasingly hurried in his work on factory shop floor and who eventually has a collapse because of it, an increasing number of architecture students, academics, and architectural practitioners have and are suffering physical and mental illness, burnout, or exhaustion on the Deleuzian (1992) 'virtual' factory shop floor. In a work-oriented paradox, rather than reduce excessive workloads, most architecture schools, limited by the requirements of funding bodies, have created additional work for students and staff through an ever-growing audit culture, for 'adminstrivia' or mundane labour associated with running an organisation. Universities and architecture schools employ elaborate bureaucratic monitoring systems. 'Administrivia' in the university workplace includes the monitoring of student attendance, engagement and interaction, performance and wellbeing, future employment, etc. Large Human Resource departments of universities and offices are now devoted to providing medical and psychological advice and support for staff and students. Some architecture schools or practices provide for external companies to run wellbeing classes and courses to be taken by their employees and students, often outside set work hours, so as to rectify work overloads created within their own workplaces.

Many argue that capitalism requires the exhaustion and exploitation of resources – natural, material, human, or other. Referring to Rosa Luxemburg's (1961, p. 387, 416) *The Accumulation of Capital*, Bauman sums up the unsustainability of capitalism's logic of 'energy' consumption, which drains resources to accumulate capital and states that; "The inborn paradox of capitalism, in the long run is its doom: capitalism is like a snake that feeds on its own tail…" drawing 'life-giving energy' through 'asset stripping.' (Bauman 2007, p. 27) '… Luxemburg envisaged a capitalism dying for lack of food: starving to death because it had eaten up the last meadow of 'otherness' on which it grazed." (Bauman 2007, p. 28)

The body, mind, and creativity of the architecture educator and practitioner who is paid minimum or low wage and on a precariat contract – which often demands more hours of work than have been assigned for a task – can become exhausted because of neoliberal profit making. Those able to survive the long hours work culture for low pay tend to be younger workers who often have more energy. Select workers thrive in high-pressure work environments to work their way from the bottom up are rewarded for their ability to be tirelessly productive for the university or practice's success. The shaping of, and capacity of the architect whose body and mind is pushed by internal and external forces and who can cope, not be drained, and in fact flourish, will have a greater probability of winning the game of an architectural life. How the ethics of workplace exploitation of human resources is nurtured in the academy and can continue in the architectural office and site is drawing more critical reflection because of its adverse effects on the working architectural polis and its link to neoliberal de-regulation. (Owen ed. 2009)

Commentators like Teresa Brennan (2003, pp. 19–22) have "coined the term 'bioderegulation' to describe the brutal discrepancies between the temporal operation of deregulated markets and the intrinsic physical limitations of the humans required to conform to these dynamics." (Crary 2014, p. 15) As work hours grow, the time to rest decreases. This imbalance has detrimental effects on health (mental and physical) and wellbeing as noted in *Dead Man Working* (Cederström and Fleming 2012). Architects in practice can die of exhaustion, their bodies being depleted as a resource from over working in a competitive, limitless work hour space (Hadid, James Stirling, Louis Kahn to name a few).

In architectural practice "the process of architecture can be commodified as the services of architects and designers as measured in hours and productivity. Designers become labor-commodities in the building process as their services are measured for the exchange-value they contribute to a project." (Mangold in Flowers ed. 2014, p. 17) Under liquid modernity, stresses from time pressures relating to building procurement, i.e., problems with projects, cost overruns, construction time overruns, etc., or from precariat contracts are in stark contrast to a lifestyle of creativity and contemplation.

"…The university …[as] a protected space for unhurried scholarly contemplation" has vanished. (Anderson 2006, p. 578) The studio – at university or in professional practice – is no longer a protected site for creative exploration and experimentation, with time imperatives driving the technical and practical side of architectural procurement. Architects are having to become more managerial, managing and monitoring themselves, their workers, and the time of project production in relation to budgets. All the while, many architectural classes are suffering strain from operating in a neoliberal competitive space of liquidity, which can, arguably, lead more easily to varying degrees of disillusionment, dissatisfaction, exhaustion, fatigue, stress, and burnout. The rise of a burnout culture, in physical and mental wellbeing in the architectural academy and in private practice is linked to the consumption and exhaustion of the labour workforce as a resource and so it is essential to rethink the hours of work in the future.

In *Not Working: Why we have to Stop*, Josh Cohen (2020, p. 48) refers to Andy Warhol's 1963 four-hour film, *Sleep* in which Warhol films his naked lover, John Giorno, who sleeps soundly. (Figure 8.2) Normally recognised as one of the only human activities that does not have the capacity to generate income, sleep is concerned with replenishing both physical and mental energy. In times when architectural commissions are not attainable, architects have traditionally refreshed and replenished their energy, some having to downsize on the way. However, in times of busyness, we need to consider a responsible trajectory for how to maintain a balance in the mind and body of architectural labourers, in order to reconsider how to play the game of architecture in the future and by future generations being critical of, not subservient to, the systemic modes of production that underpin neoliberalism. In the final chapter of this book, a series of reflections are set out for a less consumptive approach to an architectural life. It is argued that one fundamental change needs to relate to how architectural workers deal with time and purposefulness. That involves "… a much deeper process of reform – a politics not just of time, but also of resource and autonomy… Time spent away from work should not just be an occasion for more leisure, or even more care, but for a rethinking of human purposefulness" (Kane 2004, p. 181) and not a purposefulness that is simply about accumulation but rather about the desire for collective betterment. That betterment can be offered by a multitude of strategies such as the unionisation of architectural labour as "a shorter workday and a shorter workweek." (Cutler and Aronowitz in Aronowitz and Cutler eds. 1998, p. 17) Overall, however, it is important that the individual working in architecture take control of their work life to dictate their pathway rather than follow an architecture culture which has failed to support the wellbeing of a diverse range of people at the expense of ego and reputational capital.

References

Anderson, G. 2006. Carving out Time and Space in the Managerial University, *Journal of Organizational Change Management*, 19 (5): 578–592.

Aronowitz, S., Esposito, D., DiFazio, W., and Yard, M. 1998. The Post-Work Manifesto. In Aronowitz, S. and Cutler, J. eds. *Post-Work: The Wages of Cybernation.* New York; London: Routledge, pp. 31–80.

Barajas, D. 2007. Globalised Bodies. In Lee, S. and Baumeister, R. eds. *The Domestic and the Foreign in Architecture.* Rotterdam: 010 Publishers, pp. 243–260.

Bauman, Z. 2007. *Liquid Times: Living in an Age of Uncertainty.* Cambridge: Polity Press.

Booth, R. 2017. Zaha Hadid Leaves £67m Fortune, Architect's Will Reveals. *Guardian*, January 16, 2017, www.theguardian.com/artanddesign/2017/jan/16/zaha-hadid-leaves-67m-fortune-architects-will-reveals, Accessed November 06, 2023.

Brennan, T. 2003. *Globalization and Its Terrors: Daily Life in the West.* London: Routledge.

Cederström, C. and Fleming, P. 2012. *Dead Man Working.* Alresford, Hants: Zero.

Chaplin, C. Dir. 1936. *Modern Times.* United States: United Artists. (89 mins)

Cohen, J. 2020. *Not Working: Why We Have to Stop.* London: Granta.

Crary, J. 2014. *24/7: Late Capitalism and the Ends of Sleep.* London; New York: Verso Books.

Cutler, J., and Aronowitz, S. 1998. Quitting Time. In Aronowitz, S. and Cutler, J. eds. *Post-Work: The Wages of Cybernation.* New York; London: Routledge, pp. 1–30.

Davies, C. 2016. Zaha Hadid, 'Queen of the Curve' Zaha Hadid Dies age 65 from Heart Attack. *The Guardian*, March 31, https://www.theguardian.com/artanddesign/2016/mar/31/star-architect-zaha-hadid-dies-aged-65 Accessed November 06, 2023.

De Castella, T. Thatcher: Can People Get by on Four Hours' Sleep? *BBC News Magazine*, April 10, 2013. https://www.bbc.co.uk/news/magazine-22084671 Accessed November 06, 2023.

Deleuze, G. 1992. Postscript on the Societies of Control, *October*, 59: 3–7.

Foucault, M. 1995. *Discipline & Punish: The Birth of the Modern Prison.* New York: Vintage Books.

Hadid, Z. 2017. *Reflections on Zaha Hadid (1950–2016).* London.

Haraway, D. 1995. Nature, Politics and Possibilities: A Debate and Discussion with David Harvey and Donna Haraway, *Society and Space* 13 (October): 507–527.

Hardt, M. and Negri, A. 2000. *Empire.* Cambridge, MA.: Harvard University Press.

Harvey, David. 1982. *The Limits of Capital.* Oxford: Blackwell.

Hattenstone, S. 2010. Zaha Hadid: I'm Happy to Be on the Outside, *The Guardian*, October 9, 2010. https://www.theguardian.com/artanddesign/2010/oct/09/zaha-hadid, Accessed November 06, 2023.

Hill, A. and Adams, R. 2013. Margaret Thatcher Spent Final Years out of Limelight, *The Guardian*, April 08, 2013, https://www.theguardian.com/politics/2013/apr/08/margaret-thatcher-final-years, Accessed November 06, 2023.

Hochschild, A. R. 1997. *The Time Bind: When Work Becomes Home and Home Becomes Work.* New York: Metropolitan Books.

Holub, D. 2016. Zaha Hadid's World of Fluid Freedom. May 31. www.designersatelier.co.uk/dagmars-articles/zaha-hadid-s-world-of-fluid-freedom/, Accessed July 31, 2023.

Jeffries, S. 2004. Maybe They're Scared of Me. April 26, 2004, www.theguardian.com/artanddesign/2004/apr/26/architecture/, Accessed November 06, 2023.

Kane, P. 2004. *The Play Ethic: A Manifesto for a Different Way of Living.* Oxford: Macmillan.

Lewis, R. K. 1998. *Architect? A Candid Guide to the Profession.* Cambridge, Mass.; London, England: The MIT Press. [First published 1985.]

Lubow, A. 2000. Rem Koolhaas Builds. *The New York Times Magazine*, July 9. www.nytimes.com/2000/07/09/magazine/rem-koolhaas-builds.html, Accessed November 06, 2023.

Luxemburg, R. 1961. *The Accumulation of Capital.* London: Routledge & Kegan Paul Ltd.

Mangold, W. 2014. Architecture and the Vicissitudes of Capitalism. In Flowers, B. ed. *Architecture in an Age of Uncertainty.* Farnham, Surrey: Ashgate, pp. 15–24.

Martin, R. 1989.Out of Marginality: Toward a New Kind of Professional. In Berkeley, E. P. ed. and McQuaid, M. Assoc. ed., *Architecture: A Place for Women.* Washington, DC: Smithsonian Institution Press, pp. 229–236.

Owen, G. ed. 2009. *Architecture, Ethics and Globalization: Ethics, Efficacy and Architecture in the Globalized Economy.* London: Routledge.

Schaffner, A. K. 2016. *Exhaustion: A History.* New York: Columbia University Press.

Sommerlad, N. 2013. Margaret Thatcher Tax Shock: £12 Mansion Where She Saw Out Her Days Registered in TAX HAVEN, *The Mirror*, November 30, 2023. https://www.mirror.co.uk/news/uk-news/margaret-thatcher-tax-shock-12m-2866929, Accessed November 06, 2023.

Standing, G. 2016. *The Precariat: The New Dangerous Class.* London: Bloomsbury Academic. [Originally published 2011.]

Stead, N. 2003. Three Complaints about Architectural Criticism, *Architecture Australia* 92 (6): 50, 52.

Stratigakos, D. 2016. *Where are the Women Architects?* Princeton: Princeton Architectural Press.

Thompson, E. P. (1967 December) Time, Work-Discipline, and Industrial Capitalism, *Past & Present*, 38: 56–97.

Troiani, I. (2021 December) The Elephant in the Room: How Neoliberal Architecture Education Undermines Wellbeing, *Charrette*, Themed issue, 'Practice, Architecture Education and Wellbeing', eds. Rice, L., Meraz, F., Drozynski, C., and Marco, E., 7(2) Autumn: 9–33.

Troiani, I. 2018. Zaha Hadid's Penthouse: Gender, Creativity and 'Biopolitics' in the Neoliberal Workplace. In Staub, A. ed. *The Routledge Companion to Modernity, Space and Gender in Section: Liberal and Neo-liberal Values*. New York: Routledge, pp. 131–149.

Warhol, A. Dir. 1963. *Sleep.* United States. (321 mins)

9

PLAYING *THE GAME OF LIFE* IN ARCHITECTURE BEYOND NEOLIBERAL CAPITALISM

FIGURE 9.1 The inventor Reuben Klamer, left, with the television host Art Linkletter in an undated photo. Mr. Linkletter's endorsement helped draw attention to *The Game of Life*, which Mr. Klamer created, when it was introduced in 1960. Credit: Reuben Klamer Toylab Photo Archive.

DOI: 10.4324/9781351199834-12

Reflection on a Traditional Architect's Game of Life

Since Reuben Klamer invented the board game, *The Game of Life* (Figure 9.1) in 1959 it has evolved into various versions including *The Game of Life: Twists and Turns*. This makeover is described by Judith La Brasca (in Unknown 2007) from MB & Parker Games as a game that offers "the players options and dilemmas, surprises good and bad – just like in real life. We have tried to emulate the current issues such as the environment and our obsession with celebrity to engage with players and make it relevant to all ages. The game is unique and, although there is an element of luck associated to how quickly players can move around the board, winners need to be tactical and make the right decisions to live the most fulfilling life."

Using *The Game of Life* framework of choice-making, this book has analysed the challenges facing diverse architects in managing work-life balance in real life. Part 1 has shown how the neoliberal conditions of production and consumption, in which most architectural workers operate, have exacerbated problems with wellbeing while simultaneously presenting a front of offering people greater freedom. The consequences of living a life in architecture under neoliberalism's 'flexible capitalism' (Sennett 1998, p. 9) shows how economics has reframed architectural education and professional practice stretching the demands on, and bodies of, architectural workers.

Since the 1970s, neoliberalism, as a particular kind of *laisse-faire* global capitalism, has grown in its virulence in all aspects of everyday life in many countries. As neoliberal society was nurtured under Thatcherism and Reaganomics and as private property ownership creates greater social, economic, and housing inequality, learning how to become a heightened competitor becomes more vital. Knowing how to competitively 'play the [economic] game' impacts on the potential to live a fulfilling and satisfying architectural life, although it does not guarantee success or satisfaction. Conversely, not knowing how to be a competitive game player can lead to work dissatisfaction and a decline in wellbeing. A life in architecture is not necessarily as glamorous or easy as it can appear to the wider public. Nor is the pathway of work under an individual's total control to dictate, regardless of what the American dream leads us to believe.

Neoliberal thinking has globalised the American dream, so that it manifests in a roughly equivalent form in every country in the world. Arguably, the belief that entrepreneurialism in life is the key route to social mobility for everyone is universally shared. In the creative economy, architectural entrepreneurism takes a particular form in relation to commodifying aspects of a prominent architect's life. Architectural innovation is used to heighten the celebrity status of the most elite architectural class, the starchitect, who frequently travels in person as a globe-trotting *Yes Man [or Woman]*. To win a job, so that someone else doesn't get it, architects corroborate within the global capitalist marketplace to get their 'phantasmagorical' (Spencer 2016, p. 73) commissions built. The production of this exceptional architecture can often be produced while neglecting or exploiting social, cultural, or environmental capital. However, as Nobel economist, Joseph Stiglitz (2009, p. xxxix) notes, Adam Smith's "invisible hand theorem" – articulated in the 1776 *Wealth of Nations* and the foundation for neoliberalism in which individual and company self-interest is the main driver – eventually leads "to *Pareto efficiency*, in other words, no one can be made better off without making someone else worse off." As Stiglitz (2009, p. xlvi) explains "… Smith's invisible hand only said that markets would lead to an efficient allocation of resources; no one, in defending the market economy, ever claimed that it would lead to a distribution of income consistent with principles of social justice." It is not only human capital that produces architecture that is exploited and capitalised upon, but so is the image of the architect as an autonomous creative who works tirelessly for their art in non-fiction and fiction in the media. The bodies of many renowned architects, their architecture, and images of both are used to increase an architect's reputational and economic capital. Acquiring one form of capital – social, economic, and cultural (Bourdieu 1986 in Richardson 1986, pp. 241–258) can better enable an architect to accrue other forms of personal and professional capital. Not all types of architectural identities have the chance to accumulate the various forms of capital equally however.

This book has sought to understand the identity formation of the traditional white-male architectural persona that is exemplified in Michel Foucault's non-gendered neoliberal *homo oeconomicus* – the economic wo/man – and second, the hybridisation of *homo oeconomicus* with *feminina domestica* – the domestic wo/man – due to the entry of women architects into the profession and men architects' increase in domestic labour. The lives of these types of architects present harder or easier career pathways because of the challenges presented by the different lifestyles.

The typical professional architectural career life path involves graduating from architecture school, working as a junior architectural graduate, then gaining architectural registration to open a practice or work one's way up to the corporate architecture practice ladder. Sometimes people complete or partially complete architecture degrees but for various reasons return to become educators in university. A professional architectural educator career path normally involves moving from zero-hour contract labour while completing a PhD or not, to moving up the university ladder to a position of management in an architecture school or university senior management team. The traditional stages in the personal life of an architect include finding a partner, marrying, having children, then buying private property to ideally then build a property portfolio. However, the opportunities and obstacles for architects to move through professional and personal career stages can be accentuated by demographic differences from birth.

Part 2 of the book, entitled 'Gameplay Moves: Become an Architect (or Not)' followed the normal stages in an architect's life starting from birth or early to late childhood. Harvey's view that "neoliberalism … [is] a class-based political project …[used] to create new means of capital accumulation" (Newman 2012, p. 157) was expanded so as to consider how a prospective architecture student's upbringing from birth and economic class can create a fertile environment, or not, from which to accumulate capital over their lifetime.

The life choices parents make as to where to live, send their child to school, or who they socialise with can influence where a prospective student of architecture chooses to study architecture, who they are taught by or work for – whether a global corporate practice or a small architectural practice –, marry or partner, where they buy a house, or whether they have children or not, etc. All contribute to the evolution of a certain kind of professional architectural narrative. Outside schooling, the role that fathers, mothers, friends, and relatives have in constructing a level of life ambition and aspiration are determining factors in the possibility of acquiring 'distinction.' (Bourdieu 1996) Family or independent wealth can be a major contributing factor in continuing into secondary or tertiary education for people of different demographics. For instance, the importance of wealth, understood as "total assets and debts, not income" is a primary influence on the economic success of whites and blacks. (Oliver and Shapiro 2006) The thesis presented by Oliver and Shapiro is "that wealth brings advantage – in housing, education, health care, and generally in a sense of security." (Kaplan 2006, p. 11) Whether parents or family members are already architects or know architects can be another determining factor that can create privilege or educational inequality. Prospective architects without support at home or school need to navigate the pathway to an architectural life more independently and as such must work harder to get the same outcome.

The lack of a "level playing field" in the way "the economic race... [is] run" (Rank et al. 2014, p. 107) means that there are unequal possibilities for progression in an architect's life. The knock-on effect of these variable demographic differences results in an uneven 'landscape of opportunity' (Rank et al. 2014, pp. 67–83) because not everyone has the same starting point at university. Rank, Hirschl, and Foster (2014, p. 107) observe that any life journey is marked by "cumulative inequality, or cumulative advantage or disadvantage" where early advantages or disadvantages due to demographic discrimination can result in further advantage or disadvantage that multiplies over a lifetime.

Making careful life choices to study a long course like architecture or not is compounded by what Zygmunt Bauman (2007, p. 1), inspired by Sennett (1998), sees as "the collapse of long-term thinking." Living in liquid times "stimulates 'lateral' rather than 'vertical' orientations" (Bauman 2007, p. 1) in which choice-making becomes pivotal. The class of a university one can study architecture at – ranked according to university league tables in the U.K. – can parallel its wealth and prestige, and subsequent ability to draw in more wealth for those who study or work there. However university education does not always guarantee social advancement or fulfilment. As Richard Sennett and Jonathan Cobb (1977) note, the game of 'achievement' can be injurious or harmful to different socio-economic classes. First generation children of working-class background who graduate from university can "fulfil" the desires of their father or mother "for upward mobility" while sometimes rejecting the ways of a parent/s. (Sennett 1998, p. 18)

Physical and mental resilience, competitive drive, and entrepreneurialism also play a significant role in surviving architecture education because of its long work hours. Architecture education often encourages, rather than discourages, a culture of over-work for innovation and an imbalanced work-life pre-graduation. Long work hours in the design studio, often inherited from design tutors, can have a detrimental effect on some. (Troiani 2021) As neoliberal universities increase the quantitative performance of their workers, they have simultaneously increased the audit cultures that staff use to monitor students, and university managers use to monitor architectural educators which all take up more work time. The optimally-performing architecture student or educator manages these challenging conditions so they don't need additional care to continue into practice.

Private practice or enterprise in architecture is the predominant model of office a graduate architect works in in the U.K. since the Thatcher government's free-market capitalism diminished the opportunities for architects to work for government in the social welfare sector. Deregulation of the financial markets, and then professions, and government funding cuts in 1980s Britain followed by the 1990 recession 'finished off' the number of local authority architects. (Martin 2015) While the removal of mandatory architecture fee scales for architects was originally seen to disempower architectural 'cartels' and improve quality (Addy in Fulcher 2013), others contend it only led to architectural services being pushed down due to architects undercutting their fees to obtain commissions in order to survive a competitive marketplace. Larger corporate and entrepreneurial practices which exhibited a "deep commitment to marketing and the financial side of the business" (Terry Farrell in Castle 2017) embraced private practice and developed a new approach to the structure of their internal organisation, marketing, and publicity. The architect from the creative class that was nurtured in an elite school of architecture who is typically a founding director or partner, who is adaptable, flexible, business savvy, with an unquenchable thirst and limitless time for architecture to accept its over-work culture, is often able to better build their and their practice's reputational capital.

Arguably, the *homo oeconomicus* architect is better placed to succeed than the worker who is a hybrid of *homo oeconomicus* and *femina domestica* (in their female and male forms) because they are less time compromised. Intersectional inequalities including gender/sexuality, race/ethnicity, class, age/generation, etc., can influence traditional career progression presenting obstacles to the professional diversification of workers and types of architectural practices. Technology is transforming the work of architects of different generations both positively or negatively. If they don't excel in practice, some architectural graduates use their digital skills learned in their architectural training to sidestep into other careers including interior design, product design, computer and video game design, production design, visual effects for films, virtual reality, animation, photography, fine art, graphic design, city tour guiding, writing, policy writing, humanitarian (housing/planning) work, not-for-profit housing associations, etc. The choice to leave architecture, made by more women than men architects, can be made to undertake more artistic labour, be better paid, or offer a more balanced work life.

To consider avenues of potential change in work-life balance in architecture, Part 3 of this book examined the two aspects of architectural work under neoliberal capitalism which contribute to affecting an architect's wellbeing: space and time. The flexible workplace is the main conduit through which neoliberalism optimises productivity. This affects both the spaces in which architectural work is undertaken and the architecture that architects are increasingly tasked to produce. All workspace is now more susceptible to needing to be open plan and the convenient portability of the digital workplace through our mobile phones, portable computers, networked computers, etc., is no longer a restriction on where architectural work takes place. This means that a traditional nine to five work-life pattern is a fading reality. Increasingly work is done less in the traditional office because it is not "the only place in which that work can be enacted." (Standing 2016, p. 139) During *Liquid Times* (Bauman 2007) in which 'flexible capitalism' (Sennett 1998, p. 9) is central to how work is driven, the flexible workspace has flourished because of the "immediate potential for movement and change." (Schneider and Till 2007, p. 5) Models of cost-efficient architecture exhibit the capacity to be easily adaptable and the architect's open studio becomes the site for fluid architectural labour and interactions.

While the open plan studio space is common in universities, elite architects increasingly design open plan style office buildings of "phantasmagorical form" (Spencer 2016, p. 73) to promote unique university campuses or estates. Architecture schools sometimes occupy spaces of new phantasmagorical architecture which is used to rebrand tired 'uni-brandscapes' or improve university estates. Whether architectural education takes place in a Gothic, Georgian, Brutalist, or building of "phantasmagorical form" displays a pedagogical approach to future work. New phantasmagorical university architecture often follows the style of flexible, Silicon Valley-style workspaces that present the university as a 'home from home,' furnished with "bean bags and domestic fittings including sofas, low slung chairs, rugs, wallpaper and lampshades." (Unknown 2011) Both the open plan studio and 'home from home' spaces in a university support digital learning anywhere on the university campus, which carries into practice.

The architect's office has evolved in much the same way the university has evolved to best enable flexible work. While work and home were once separated, industrialisation enacted in 20th century modernism became epitomised in corporate office towers which supported what William H. Whyte Jr. (1956, p. 44) termed *The Organisation Man*; the worker "who identified with his corporation as though it was his family." (Martin 2003, p. 121) Martin's observation that Whyte's figure "had internalized the logic of organization itself. [Being] conformist yet adaptable and resourceful" is a character that can carries into all walks of life including architecture. This character was once personified as the traditional white, male corporate worker who travelled to the office and returned home to his family in the suburbs. Nowadays, architects of all architectural classes commonly use live-work spaces in which home-based work is enacted. (Holliss 2015)

The ability to work across the office and home and everywhere and anywhere else, regardless of care commitments or responsibilities in one's personal life, is the ultimate victory of flexible neoliberal work. Remote work has benefits and disadvantages for architects of different classes and generations. Post-pandemic remote work has meant that architectural workers might not have to work in cities if they are not compelled to physically come into the office. While there are environmental benefits in remote work, it presents many challenges for people with different intersectional characteristics for whom it may increase rather than decrease stresses. One feature it does enable to benefit enhanced neoliberal productivity is the end of clearly delineated work hours.

The way in which work time affects work-life balance is fundamental to consider because of how it creates a 'time squeeze.' (Standing 2016, pp. 135–154) What Taylorism-inspired office work does is discipline the body of the worker to productively deliver what Sennett describes as "lumps of labor, [sic] pieces of work, over the course of a lifetime." Working remotely or in person in a global marketplace either in architecture schools or in an architect's office has meant that architectural work happens 24/7 since there are no barriers to economic trade. By changing the body's pattern of work from "hours at work" to "hours of work" (Standing 2016, p. 152) can impact the bodies of different types of architectural workers.

The management of time in architecture, a discipline which traditionally did not value units of time for artistic, creative practice has now become seminal to business sustainability and the work-life balance of the workforce. The relationship between the way in which the bodies of architectural workers can accumulate and circulate capital (Harvey 1982, p. 157), which can be built upon to create more capital, is one factor that determines whether survival and flourishing in a long work hours architecture culture. The way in which human, non-human, and environmental resources are exhausted is notably a "modern affliction, irrevocably bound up with the rise of capitalism and new technologies." (Schaffner 2016, p. 8) If we are to improve work-life balance in the profession we need to change the culture in which architectural workers are pushed to work tirelessly like machines for maximum productivity. One way to achieve this is to counter the neoliberal drive through strategies of degrowth, or no growth; to go beyond constant neoliberal growth.

No Growth, Degrowth, and Beyond Economic

In *The Theory of Economic Growth*, the industrial economist W. Arthur Lewis (2003, p. 420) asks the question, "Is Economic Growth Desirable?" Lewis sees that economic growth comes at a cost. While it offers advantages like increased freedom and choice, economic growth has 'real disadvantages,' (Lewis 2003) including the favouring of first, individualism; second, of economies of scale; third, of reason which seeks to improve technology; fourth, the devaluation of stable institutions; and fifth, increased stresses that affect happiness and wellbeing.

The capitalist focus on individualism where "individuals attend primarily to their own interests and those of their more immediate relations than if they are bound by a much wider net of social obligations" (Lewis 2003, p. 426) that underpins economic growth is regarded by some as a major disadvantage. People who are not materialistic or "dislike the economizing [sic] spirit" (Lewis 2003, p. 425) object to prioritising economic growth. The valuing of private institutions, corporate businesses, or monopolies that exploit human, non-human, and environmental resources rather than support stable, societal institutions is problematic. The need for economic growth which specialises and divides labour and increased use of machinery undermines traditional handicrafts and increases the size of administrative units. It poses challenges because 'in the process, men [and women] are ... proletarianized [sic]." (Lewis 2003, p. 427) Large scale organisations bring with them problems in terms of hierarchical lines of leadership whereby "a few command [,] while the majority obey." (Lewis 2033, p. 428) The imposing of discipline and routine work "reduces human beings to the mechanical role of cogs in some vast wheel" (Lewis 2003, p. 428) in a machine dependent on inequality of income. Economic growth is derived from its association with 'reason' which "depends on improving technology" leading to favouring those with "a reasoning attitude." (Lewis 2003, p. 426) When the rate of economic growth becomes excessive it can have detrimental effects on "the health of society." (Lewis 2003, p. 429) When economic growth becomes excessive, there can be social and spiritual costs and sometimes excessive losses.

Fast forward to neoliberal capitalism, which is the nightmarish, sped up reality that Lewis describes. David Harvey (2007), Wendy Brown (2015), and others (Stiglitz 2013) agree that neoliberalism comes at a price. The free-market orthodoxy has accentuated inequality, undermined democracy, and depleted and deteriorated everyday life and the physical world in which we live. There has been debate on whether the neoliberal era is officially over or not pre-pandemic and post-pandemic with its obituaries being written by some commentators. In contrast, Harvey (2019) considers that while it had already begun to lose legitimacy, neoliberal practices remain alive and kicking. Regardless of the type of economic crises society is encountering, most neoliberal governments remain committed to it because of its ability to drive the economy regardless of the damage it does to humans, non-humans, and the environment. While some neoliberal governments are committed to improving the environment, often commodifying sustainability to drive further economic growth, there are pockets of research being done to join the dots between economic growth and environmental exploitation and deterioration. To re-balance human, non-human, and environmental health and wellbeing, resistances to economic growth including no growth (Jackson 2009), degrowth

(D'Alisa, Demaria, and Kallis eds. 2015), and beyond growth (Stiglitz, Fitoussi, and Durand 2018) have emerged.

The British ecological economist, Tim Jackson's (2009) *Prosperity without Growth? The Transition to a Sustainable Economy* is a report by the Sustainable Development Commission, commissioned two years early by the U.K. Government. At the core of Jackson's review is the search for sustainable prosperity that is not dependent on economic growth. Jackson's research examines whether a broader vision of prosperity – longer lasting and a shared rather than singular vision that goes beyond the theory that more is always better – is possible in a world that has limits put on its consumption of social and environmental resources. At its core is Jackson's (2009, p. 5) contention that society "clings to … a myth of economic growth," driving many towards the ongoing ramping up of global marketplace activity which takes the "default assumption … that – financial crises aside – growth will continue indefinitely." Jackson (2009, p. 5) sees that society's 'collective blindness' in the belief that resources, and our consumption of them, is pervasive, tied to the belief that "the modern economy is structurally reliant on economic growth for its stability." Changing this mindset in government policymaking in relation to labour economics is a core area of change explored since the environmental movement of the 1970s.

In 1972, André Gorz coined the word décroissance or degrowth and defined it as "a rejection of the illusion of growth and a call to repoliticize [sic] the public debate colonized [sic] by the idiom of economism." (D'Alisa, Demaria, and Kallis eds. 2015, p. 3) Like *The Limits to Growth* (Meadows 1972), Gorz's theory of degrowth endorses shrinking industrial production and consumption to improve social justice and environmental sustainability. During the 1970s, much of the work in the environmental movement was being done in a space of cross-disciplinary exchange. For instance, the mathematical economist, Nicholas Georgescu-Roegen (1971) reflected on economics in relation to entropy, which in physics is understood as a measurement of energy available in a system but which is not available to do work. Inspired mostly by the work of Gorz, and in response to ongoing and rising social, health, and environmental crises, the Degrowth Movement began in Paris with its first conference held in 2008. Subsequent conferences have been held biannually in Spain, Canada, Italy, Germany, Hungary, Sweden, Mexico, Belgium, etc., where social scientists, environmental scientists, and other experts come together to focus on the interconnected relationship between economics, social justice, and sustainable long-term living. Degrowth campaigners, Croatian sociologist, Branko Ančić and political ecologist, Mladen Domazet (2015, p. 456) argue that "Avoiding a whole-scale collapse of the civilisation-supporting ecosystems within this [and the next] century will require a change in the social metabolism, as well as expectations, aspirations, behaviours and attitudes of the majority of the global population …." Since architects play a key role in contributing to environmental consumption and production and are increasingly affected corporeally by the economic growth paradigm, it is essential that limits to growth be considered for a sustainable earth and architectural work life future. The book *Degrowth*, that has come out of this body of environmental and social research, is important to review when considering future trajectories of change.

In their "Introduction: Degrowth futures and democracy" in the *Degrowth: A Vocabulary for a New Era*, the political ecologist and ecological economists, Giacomo D'Alisa and Giorgos Kallis and the environmental scientist, Federico Demaria (2015, p. 515) suggest that Meadow et al.'s predictions in *The Limits of Growth* have all been forgotten, regardless of them being right in foreseeing crises in peak-oil supplies, climate change, and accelerating ecosystem decline, alongside socio-economic and biophysical crises. The fact that economic growth and sustainability are fundamentally incompatible fails to be recognised. They propose a solution of 'degrowth transition,' (D'Alisa, Demaria, and Kallis 2015, p. 515) which disentangles economic proposals and the economic idiom of 'economicism' – tied to the 'ideology of development' – to change 'the collective imaginary.' Referring to the research by ecological economist, Mauro Bonaiuti (2014), D'Alisa, Demaria, and Kallis (2015, p. 515) consider what "the right to a good life [might go] … beyond the desire for growth in material affluence." They argue for Barbara Muraca's (2013) focus on moral and ethical considerations rather than economic considerations. Expanding theories in *The Quality of Life* by Amartya Sen and Martha Nussbaum (1993), Muraca concludes "that a critical challenge for democracy and degrowth to achieve a good life is to decide who …has a saying in determining what a good life is." (D'Alisa et al. in D'Alisa, Demaria, and Kallis eds. 2015, p. 518) In order to facilitate the 'degrowth transition' D'Alisa, Demaria, and Kallis (eds. 2015, p. 519) suggest a radical break from 'business as usual.' The neoliberal model of 'business as usual' which prioritises GDP (Gross Domestic Product) measures the size of an economy and how it is performing in order to determine the general health of an economy and its peoples. An economy that is increasing its GDP is generally regarded as performing well. To challenge 'business as usual,' some economists challenge using GDP to measure the health of a nation state's economy.

In collaboration with Jean-Paul Fitoussi and Martine Durand, the Nobel economist, Joseph E. Stiglitz (2018, p. 116) seeks alternative ways to revise "the narrow view of the economic system as separate from the social and natural environment where it operates, … and where the only policy concern is that of maximising economic efficiency, i.e., 'doing more with less.'" In *Beyond GDP: Measuring what Counts for Economic and Social Performance*, Stiglitz, Fitoussi, and Durand (2018, p. 116) explain the beyond GDP philosophy is not 'anti-growth,' but rather a model of "growth that is equitable and sustainable." They explain: "What we are arguing is that growth that increases a GDP number but does not reflect an increase in the well-being [sic] of most citizens, does not reflect the degradation of the environment and the depletion of natural resources, makes the economy and its citizens more insecure, erodes trust in our institutions and society, opens up conflicts because of disparate treatment of those of different ethnic or racial groups, is not 'real' growth." (Stiglitz, Fitoussi, and Durand 2018, p. 116)

FIGURE 9.2 Denise Scott Brown and Robert Venturi. The architectural 'coupling' had a long career in practice, fighting for recognition for women architects. They raised a family while running an internationally-recognised practice which dramatically changed architectural theory and practice today. Photographer: J.T. Miller. Date: September 3, 1987.

And while philosophers like Henri Lefebvre (1991; 2002; 2014) and Felix Guattari (1989; 2014)[1] offer theoretical frameworks for understanding the entanglement of the production of space with everyday life, societal, mental, and environmental justice and balance there is much that governments can, and need to, practically implement through policy changes to challenge the disconnect between a healthy economy and a healthy workforce. In the case of the production and consumption of architecture and the architectural workforce who collaborate to produce it to build nation state capital, no growth, degrowth, and beyond growth philosophies offer opportunities for deeply systemic mental and societal changes to better the flawed neoliberal model of work which architects currently operate within in architectural education and practice.

By examining alternative economic paradigms, new opportunities for better work-life harmony and wellbeing in architecture could emerge at every or any stage of an architect's life. Re-thinking the economic growth paradigm incorporates revising current biopolitical, social, and environmental concerns in the understanding that human existence in the world is part of a much more complex system than simply a financially driven one. If a positive relationship between the city and soul (of the architect and city users) is to be revived, the machinations behind architectural production need revisiting to reinvigorate social equilibrium. As Guattari (1989, p. 144) notes, "The time has come to take serious account of other value systems: of 'profitability' in the social and aesthetic sense, of the values of desire, etc... We have reached a point where new social associations should be drawn upon...." This will likely involve the decline of a *homo economicus* mindset which Peter Fleming (2017) recognises is already showing signs of collapse. Challenging the belief in infinite growth in the architectural marketplace, with theories of no growth, (Jackson 2009) degrowth, (D'Alisa, Demaria, and Kallis eds. 2015) or slow growth are routes to sustainability of all aspects of ecology including human geography. Further research to improve work-life balance requires formulating a response to the question: What non-economically-growth-driven models of sustainable production and consumption in architecture are required to rebalance work-life in architecture? What needs to change in architecture culture to provide a satisfying 'good life' in architecture for diverse people? Which architects are role models for a long and balanced life in architecture?

Wellbeing, Eudaimonia, and a Balanced life in Architecture

Wellbeing, as the state of being well or absent of disease, conveys the positive attributes of health experienced by avoiding sickness, exhaustion, or burnout. Through the analysis of work-life balance in architecture, this book has centred on how the wellbeing of architectural workers of differing gender, race/ethnicity, class, and age can be understood at different career stages and over an architectural worker's full work life. It has focused on how workers in architecture operating in a neoliberal culture are able to make or not make opportunistic career choices which cumulatively affect their short-term and long-term health and wellbeing for the better or the worse. It has contextualised work within dominant economic models to show that major systemic changes are required to enhance the age-old notion of wellbeing.

Not a modern concept, wellbeing was the subject of study of Plato, Socrates, Epicurus, and Aristotle, who defined two schools of thought about wellbeing: hedonistic and eudaimonistic. "The hedonistic view argues that the good life consists of a life with more positive than negative pleasures. On the other hand, eudaimonism argues that the good life consists of a life that is worth seeking or living." (Scaria, Brandt, Kim, and Lindeman in Kim and Lindeman eds. 2020, p. 4) Of the later, Aristotle claims the ultimate purpose of human existence or life is the pursuit of 'eudaimonia' or happiness. In *The Nicomachean Ethics*, Aristotle (2004) sees that 'eudaimonia' is not about short-term pleasurable sensations including the accumulation of material pleasures, but is the possible outcome of the totality of one's life; how we participate in life in full across the private and public domains. Aristotle (2004) contends that love, friendship, and political commitment are fundamental to a fulfilling life. D'Alisa et al. (in D'Alisa, Demaria, and Kallis eds. 2015, p. 92) write that those three 'spheres of life':

> … can only be enjoyed through reciprocity. This characteristic renders them particularly fragile – a fragility that is put to a tough test by the profit logic of the market. For example, love, as such, exists only when it is mutual; when buying sex, you can only enjoy a surrogate of physical, psychological and emotional support, but certainly not love. Taking care of your own children implies an enormous amount of hours; paying a babysitter to assist, on the other hand, is a surrogate of parenting.

Referring to Easterlin's paradox, D'Alisa et al. (2015, p. 92) note that the demand for economic growth which promises the potential for increased income does not necessarily increase happiness in the short or long term. Wealth and happiness do not necessarily correlate. The rich aren't always happier than the poor and as people make more money, they aren't automatically happier. Lewis (2003, p. 420) explains that "Happiness results from the way one looks at life, taking it as it comes, dwelling on the pleasant rather than unpleasant, and living without fear of what the future may bring." If wealth increased resources but not wants, it has the possibility of increasing happiness, but there is no evidence to support this. Importantly Lewis (2003, p. 420) explains that "Wealth decreases happiness if in the acquisition of wealth one ceases to take life as it comes, and worries more about resources and the future." As nowadays "production and the market constantly expand, occupying spaces of care, social life and reciprocity, [they have] lead […] inevitably to the disintegration of relationships and engendering negative consequences on well-being." (D'Alisa et al. in D'Alisa, Demaria, and Kallis eds. 2015, p. 92). Fear of being behind others in private or professional life or not achieving success, and the outsourcing and commodification of care, broadly as a service for all, is having a damaging effect on society. The former is negatively affecting identity formation and the latter means that not having time to care and therefore be with family, friends, others, or look after one's health can decrease wellbeing.

If we return to the reading of a hedonistic life, for an architect, being able to build one's own architectural designs, gain notoriety for one's architectural practice and writings or research from colleagues and the wider public, being able to make money to buy private property or go on vacation, be loved by others, or enjoy good food or wine may all be simple life pleasures which centre on valuing materialism. Negative experiences can include; being discriminated against – consciously or unconsciously – such that one's career progression in architectural education or practice is hindered or stilted; being overworked and underpaid or undervalued or unrecognised for contribution to an architectural project or team; not being renumerated adequately to sustain a quality of living or to build a property portfolio; or be given the time to take vacations; to not find love; or not be able to afford to enjoy good food or wine. "However, if the positive pleasures outweigh the negative pleasures, then the hedonistic approach to wellbeing is sustainable." (Scaria, Brandt, Kim, and Lindeman in Kim and Lindeman eds. 2020, p. 4) Conversely, the eudemonistic view of a good life for an architect encompasses and values other aspects of life beyond the materialistic.

Eudemonistic harmony can emerge in how architectural workers define their relationship to work and home life and what they produce, care for, or nurture including buildings, partnerships, children, etc. *over their lifetime.* Unlike the penchant of neoliberalism to metricise, quantify, and commodify every aspect of life and prioritise short-termism and economic growth, eudemonia is not measurable during one's lifetime. Importantly, it centres on our ability to reach higher moral and phycological goals. However, Aristotle recognises that when individuals encounter hardships during any period of their life, they have greater difficulty in achieving a state of eudaimonia. Bauman (2007, p. 94) rightly notes that, "The lives of even the happiest people among us (or …, the luckiest) are anything but trouble-free." In architecture education and professional life it is not always understood why architectural students, educators, or practitioners leave their place of work. This space of professional silence can overlap with the space of gatekeepers who, until recently, can marginalise, exclude, and obstruct the career progression others. Those that do not have negative experiences at work or in their personal life arguably suffer fewer pressures.

A working life in architecture can be challenging for women and men architects who juggle family or care commitments outside work with work commitments. While flexibility has been increased in the modern life of many architects, working in a neoliberal age has changed the possibilities of what a satisfying career in any field, including architecture, looks like today, as Richard Sennett notes. Economic systems like neoliberalism that operate a model of 'flexible capitalism' (Sennett 1998, pp. 9, 22) have changed the very meaning of what work and a career are from 'long term' to 'No long term.' Sennett (1998, p. 9) reminds us that career "in its English origins meant a road for carriages, and as eventually applied to labor [sic] meant a lifelong channel for one's economic pursuits." However, what 'flexible capitalism' under neoliberalism does is divert employees from 'a straight roadway' in a career (Sennett 1998, p. 9) to work that has returned to an "arcane sense of … job, as people do lumps of labor, [sic] pieces of work, over the course of a lifetime."[2] Under 'flexible capitalism,' the quantifying of work as 'lumps of labour' in architecture seeks maximum return for individual wealth. It similarly creates a system that heightens efficiency enacted by the organisation or individuals who can make savings in time and money. These savings and the need for extreme flexibility can have an effect on the bodies and character of architectural workers both inside and outside the workplace. Groups with different characteristics are affected in differing ways. Here younger workers, the precariat architectural class, are discussed as an example.

By heightening flexibility, neoliberalism diverts workers away from a stable and permanent straight career path – where loyalty and commitment are important – to unstable and impermanent work in which workers – in this case, architectural educators and practitioners – jump around places of work. Increasingly driven by economic imperatives or the fact they have no other options but zero hours-style contracts, workers can have multiple casual contracts to increase their earnings. (Stoyanova and Grugulis 2007, p. 4) As "the curse of oppression from capitalism," (Sennett 1998, pp. 10, 9) flexibility's claim of giving people greater freedom to shape their own life, in fact only diverts work life risks from employer to employee and thereby increases pressure on workers, creating a culture of anxiety because "people do not know what risks will pay off, what paths to pursue." Barry Schwartz (2016) defines 'the paradox of choice' as linked to what economists refer to as 'opportunity costs' where the act of comparing one option to another leads to the feeling of being unsatisfied or unhappy because an opportunity is seen to be have been missed. "… When people make decisions, even if the results of the decisions are good, they feel disappointed about them; they blame themselves." (Schwartz 2005) According to Schwartz (2005), in the myriad of choices that neoliberal life offers us "the secret of happiness [lies]… in low expectations." Unreasonable life expectations can lead to regret, self-blame or harm, depression, or suicide (Schwartz 2005), meaning that greater choice does not assimilate to improved welfare. As is the case with the paradox of choice, Sennett (1998, p. 10) concludes that flexibility can have a significant negative impact on a person's character.

Sennett (1998, p. 10) reminds us that since antiquity, character has meant "the ethical value we place on our own desires and on our relations to others" and that Horace wrote that man's character depends on connections to the world. Unlike the cult of 'personality,' human character encompasses far more. In Sennett's (1998, p. 10) opinion, "character… focuses upon the long-term aspect of our emotional experience. Character is expressed by loyalty and mutual agreement, or through the pursuit of long-term goals, or by the practice of delayed gratification for the sake of a future end… Character concerns the personal traits which we value in ourselves and for which we seek to be valued by others."

Building upon Sennett's (1998, pp. 93–94) argument that 'flexible capitalism' disadvantages some workers over others, Management, Employment, and Organisation expert, Dimitrinka Stoyanova (Russell) and Professor of Work and Skills, Irena Grugulis (2007, p. 4) argue in *Fragmented (Working) Lives* that 'flexible capitalism' "puts special emphasis on youth" who, because they are paid less, are less judgemental, can be more flexible because they are not yet partnered, with family or care commitments, or are not in large debt yet, become easily exploitable labour. This precariat class of architectural workers have less past experience with which to criticise workplace expectations. Brown's (2015, p. 33) 'neoliberal subjects' accept rather than challenge increasing demands on their work productivity. Younger, mostly more energetic workers, increase in commodity value in the market and some workers of older generations can be undervalued. Stoyanova and Grugulis (2007, p. 4) explain, "Past experience does not matter as much as it used to" and respect for experience as a "signifier of greater competence, skills and hence value" and the hierarchies that accompany experience are 'diluted.'

While the youthful worker is a demographic at greater risk of exploitation, what Sennett notes (2006) is that the character of any worker who wants to be successful or survive in competitive workplace conditions requires a particular type of flexibility no matter what age. That type of worker needs "to be able to manage short-term relationships in the context of frequent changes to tasks, jobs and places. They have to be able to update their skills and abilities and be socialised in the new culture which values potential ability and not past performance. And finally, they have to be prepared 'to let go of the past.'" (Stoyanova and Grugulis 2007, p. 4) This ability to 'twist and turn,' as the 2007 version of *The Game of Life* included, becomes an increasing feature of game play in the virtual and real world. However, workers who are not resilient or capable of surviving in this workplace landscape can suffer emotionally and physically because of an ongoing feeling of inadequacy; that there is always more they need to do, regardless of how many trophies they are winning.

Younger critics of Sennett, such as Serge Natarajan (2003) describe the picture Sennett presents – in which new opportunities for fulfilment instead only create "new forms of oppression ultimately disorienting individuals and undermining their emotional and psychological well-being" – as bleak. Natarajan (2003) challenges Sennett's contention that 'flexible capitalism' cannot last and that Sennett's (1998, p. 148) claim that "a regime which provides human beings no deep reasons to care about one other cannot long preserve its legitimacy." Natarajan challenges Sennett's suggestion that character is being eroded alongside rising information technologies and objects to Sennett's suggestion that "With no orientation that guides the individual, he or she is not capable to shape a meaningful narrative of his or her future." (Natarajan 2003, p. 2) Sennett considers that information technologies and optimisation strategies which decentralise and increase audit control dismantle institutions and disorientate workers. For Sennett, because workers are not only told what to do but also how to do it. They are losing the ability to be able to proactively act to control their own lives. Being time-consumed by work, means work dominates the time to think about controlling one's own life narrative. However, not all see that younger generations are disempowered by new technologies. Natarajan (2003, p. 7) explains that "While information technology has reinforced supervision of organisational processes, it also has provided a formidable tool to bypass control and to disseminate information within an organisation," arguing that it is the potential of new media that creates new communities that were previously not able to unite. The relationship between an individual and a community operating in a neoliberal age is an area of important debate.

For Sennett a solution is the revaluing of teamwork as a genuine collaborative mode of working collectively, rather than its tokenistic form as used by modern managers. Teamwork which resists market competition has the potential to counter disorientation and fragmentation that disables a worker from creating a balanced and satisfying work-life.

In *Liquid Times*, Bauman (2007, pp. 55–70) discusses the seismic shift in modern society in the relationship between state, democracy, and the management of fear. Referring to the work of Robert Castel (2003), Bauman (2007, p. 68) contends that "Once competition replaces solidarity, individuals find themselves abandoned to their own … resources." Uncertainty inevitably leads to fear and loss of trust. (Bauman 2007, pp. 94–95) In order to show different approaches to how we participate in an uncertain world, Bauman proposes two types of mentality, that of the gamekeeper and the gardener. The gamekeeper approach to living in the world – which we are all compelled to adopt in 'liquid times' – is the defensive mentality of hunters who kill and "don't care less about the overall 'balance of things'." (Bauman 2007, p. 100) Their duty is to defend territory to ensure order. "Hunting is a full-time task, it consumes a lot of attention and energy, it leaves little or no time for anything else; and postpones … reflection…." (Bauman 2007, p. 107) It becomes addictive and catching prey can be anticlimactic, leading only to the compulsion for the next kill, a point that Sennett agrees with. Satisfaction becomes an unreachable state. Instead, the gardener "assumes that there is no order in the world at all … were it not for attention and effort." (Bauman 2007, p. 99) While the gardener approach is emerging as a more favourable option, "… the prospect of an end to hunting is not tempting but frightening in a society of hunters…." (Bauman 2007, p. 108) Shedding architecture of its neoliberal game-playing individualistic mentality offers potentialities to improve work-life balance in architecture, society, and the environmental world at large.

Collectivism and Empathy for Work-Life Balance in Architecture

This book argues that a balanced life in architecture which enhances wellbeing and happiness needs to go beyond a short-term approach to playing out our lives – what Michel Foucault describes as 'biopolitics,' the political rationality that takes the administration of life and populations as its subject – and devise ways to resist its stronghold. Sennett's (1998, p. 10) questions posited in *The Corrosion of Character* are therefore applied here to a life in architecture: "How do we decide what is of lasting value in ourselves [as architectural workers] in a society which is impatient, which focuses on the immediate moment? How can long term goals [in architecture] be pursued in an economy devoted to the short term? How can mutual loyalties and commitments be sustained in institutions [in architecture from university to private practice] which are constantly breaking apart or continually being redesigned?" And how can we retain architectural workers who are atypical, who don't want to play the game in architecture in the same ways?

If we are to modify the neoliberal system or game in which architects currently operate, the relationship between architects, the architectures they produce, and the communities they operate within needs behavioural modification. This book does not aim to provide a list of solutions or recommend any quick fixes but instead speculates through transdisciplinary reflection on future possibilities to alleviate the causes of pressures that exacerbate worker's stresses, dissatisfaction in, and drop out from architecture. In this concluding section of the book, responses to Sennet's questions are offered only in the two trajectories an architect's life, i.e., working in architectural education or architectural practice. In each case, the neoliberal 'enterprise of self' comes under review. By prioritising what Peter Kelly (2016) describes as 'enterprise of self,' social relationships are sacrificed, which in turn affects quality of life. In *The Self as Enterprise: Foucault and the Spirit of 21st Century Capitalism*, Kelly (2016) sees that our energies must be diverted away from the 'enterprise of [an architect's] self' that neoliberalism and 'flexible capitalism' prioritise and return to value empathic, care-driven teamwork. Understanding the nature of empathic relations is therefore essential, so reference is made to the writings on empathy and the lack thereof for others, by Frans De Waal (2008), Jeremy Rifkin (2009), and Simon Baron-Cohen (2012).

After the global financial crisis of 2008, in *The Age of Empathy: Nature's Lessons for a Kinder Society*, American scientist and Professor of Psychology, Frans de Waal (2009, p. ix) states that greed is on the decline and "empathy is in." At that time, De Waal (2009, p. ix) argued that it seemed as if the world was "waking up from a bad dream about a big casino where the people's money had been gambled away, enriching a happy few without the slightest worry about the rest of us." He claims the nightmare started 25 years earlier, begun by "Reagan-Thatcher trickle-down economics and the soothing reassurance that markets are wonderful at self-regulation." (De Waal 2009, p. ix) While De Waal saw that belief in the system had been lost, society has returned quickly to valuing material over social wealth, suffering a form of amnesia. While De Waal (2009, p. ix) cites that empathy became commodified even by the Barack Obama administration who defined 'our empathy deficit,' empathy is recognised as often deficient in an economically-driven society, although this isn't what was advocated by the father of neoliberal economics, Adam Smith.

De Waal (2009, p. 1) notes that Smith himself understood that "the pursuit of self-interest needs to be tempered by 'fellow feeling'." Smith (Smith and Stewart 1869, quoted in De Waal 2009, pp. 1–2) opens *The Theory of Moral Sentiments* by noting that "How selfish soever man may be supposed, there are evidently some principles in his nature, which interest him in the fortune of others, and render their happiness necessary to him, though he derives nothing from the pleasure of seeing it." (De Waal 2009, pp. 1–2) Smith's coining of the phrase the 'invisible hand' of the free market was meant to care for all of society's woes. De Waal (2009, p. 222) explains that "[Adam] Smith saw society as a huge machine, the wheels of which are polished by virtue, whereas vice causes them to grate. The machine won't run smoothly without a strong community sense in every citizen. Smith frequently mentioned honesty, morality, sympathy, and justice, seeing them as essential companions to the invisible hand of the market." Unlike sympathy, empathy's precursor, which means to have sorrow for someone else's plight, empathy requires one human 'changing places' with another human being to better understand their feelings and emotions, and from that emotional transaction, better understand their history of life experience of cumulative advantage or disadvantage that create the conditions that form identity and shape their life narrative. Empathic consciousness, as first defined by Arthur Schopenhauer (1995) in *On the Basis of Morality*, describes "the empathic process, within which compassion is the action component." (Rifkin 2009, p. 350) Empathy is not only about feeling one's pain but equally "one can empathize with another's joy." (Rifkin 2009, p. 13) Essential on the part of the empathiser is a willingness to exhibit empathic behaviour.

Published in the same year as *The Age of Empathy* was Jeremy Rifkin's (2009, p. 1) more expansive *The Empathic Civilization: The Race to Global Consciousness in a World in Crisis.* This book sets out the history of how empathy – a term that comes from the German word, *Einfühlung*, coined by Robert Vischer in 1872, but which did not enter the human vocabulary until 1909[3] – has evolved in humans, and how it has shaped our development and influenced the fate of the human race as a species. In his history of empathic civilization, Rifkin notes how "The Romantic Movement was a reaction to the Enlightenment fixation on reason" which surged and then declined. (Rifkin 2009, p. 350) Rifkin (2009, p. 343) explains that "the Romantics, like the Enlightenment rationalists, believed in progress, but for them it had nothing to do with accumulation of wealth but, rather, the accumulation of natural wisdom." (Rifkin 2009, p. 343) During the Romantic era, "Marianne" become the image of an ideal citizen who "in her openness, […] expressed the ideal of 'equal care for all.'" (Rifkin 2009, p. 336) The Romantic movement went beyond the notions of solidarity and fraternity that defined the French Revolution and instead sought to put women and men back at the centre, with strong human relationships as a central ambition. (Rifkin 2009, p. 344) The rise of *homo empathicus* or 'Empathic [wo]Man' in the 18th and 19th centuries forced "us to rethink the long-held belief that human beings are, by nature, aggressive, materialistic, utilitarian, and self-interested. The dawning realization that we are a fundamentally empathic species has profound and far-reaching consequences for society."

At the core of the story of the empathic civilization is what Rifkin (2009, p. 2) describes as "the paradoxical relationship between empathy and entropy." [4] He (Rifkin 2009, p. 2) claims that to rethink new models of how we live in society we need to resolve the empathy–entropy paradox. While Rifkin examines empathy in civilization more broadly to argue for societal and environmental perpetuity, in this book the redeployment of empathy in architecture's cultures, academic and professional, is being proposed to sustain a fulfilling life for architects. That someone working in architecture realises they have been 'deeply heard' (Rogers 1958, pp. 15–17 in Rifkin 2009, p. 14) when celebrating their accomplishments or dealing with obstacles is necessary to nurture workplace communities throughout their life. Nowadays, Human Resource auditors with managers in architecture schools and architectural offices (who can afford to have them) mainly deal with struggling or unsatisfied staff. Emotional intelligence is a phrase co-opted in the neoliberal workplace and is increasingly battered around by "educators [who] have picked up the banner of empathic attunement [sic]," but Rifkin (2009, p. 15) does note, as an example, that "Early evaluations of student performance in the few places where the new empathic approach to education has been implemented show a marked improvement in mindfulness, communication skills, and critical thinking as youngsters become more introspective, emotionally attuned, and cognitively adept at comprehending and responding intelligently and compassionately to others." Embedding genuine empathic skills that nurture "non-judgemental orientation and tolerance of other perspectives" (Rifkin 2009, p. 15) would offer a marked improvement in many architectural workplaces. Enactment of empathy that is reciprocated in architecture's workplaces has the potential to alter imbalanced work cultures to impact positively on work-life balance.

Three years after *The Empathic Civilization* was published, the British clinical psychologist, Simon Baron-Cohen (2012, p. xii) in *Zero Degrees of Empathy: A Theory of Human Cruelty and Kindness* endeavours to understand the essence of empathy through a study of emotions, where human empathy is absent. Baron-Cohen's research examines the ways in which empathy is lost, and the link between the erosion of empathy (a feature of character) and its effect on the community, family, and nation, for which there is a vast range of consequences. (Baron-Cohen 2012, p. 130) As a Jew whose parents migrated to the U.K., Baron-Cohen refers to the stories of cruelty his father experienced under the Nazis to show the extreme consequences of the total loss of empathy. In this example, he (Baron-Cohen 2012, pp. 3–4) recognises that there is a marked shift in thinking of humanity as 'subjects' or 'mere objects' rather than as human, and refers to *Ich and Du (I and Thou)* first published in 1937 by Martin Buber (1958) – the German philosopher who resigned his professorship when Adolf Hitler came to power – which discusses the devaluing of humans. "When our empathy is switched off, we are solely in 'I' mode" and in "such a state we relate only to things, or to people as *if they were just things*." (Baron-Cohen 2012, p. 6) Baron-Cohen (2012, p. 4) concludes that:

> Empathy erosion can arise because of corrosive emotions, such as bitter resentment, or desire for revenge, or blind hatred, or desire to protect. [...] [or] as a result of the beliefs we hold (such as the belief that a class of person is unworthy of human rights) or because of the goals we have (such as defining our country), or because of our intentions (for example to make an employee redundant). Empathy erosion can even occur as a result of fear [...] or obedience to authority [...] [or] wanting to conform.

A key conclusion that Baron-Cohen (2012, pp. 6, 11) makes is that when a person is solely focused on "their own interests they have all the potential to be unempathetic" to others. Being empathic allows the person for whom empathy is felt to "feel their thoughts and feelings have been heard, acknowledged and respected." (Baron-Cohen 2012, p. 13) Arguing that empathy is the most valuable but under-utilised resource in the modern world, Baron-Cohen (2012, p. 13) concludes that "erosion of empathy is an important global issue related to the health of our communities, be they small (like families) or big (like nations). [...] With empathy we have a resource to resolve conflict, increase community cohesion, and dissolve another person's pain." (Baron-Cohen 2012, p. 130) He sees that empathy acts as 'a universal solvent' able to dissolve, as well as anticipate, any 'interpersonal problems.' (Baron-Cohen 2012, p. 132) So, how can we break the cycles in architecture using collectivism and empathy to enhance work-life balance in education and industry? How can we revise how to manage?

The rhetoric of control is fundamental to understanding management. (Höpfl 2008) In *Management in Liquid Modern World*, Bauman et al. note that management most often nowadays refers to the managing of formal organisations but it "can also refer to coping or muddling through… Sometimes we manage others, sometimes ourselves; sometimes we manage to change things, sometimes to adjust to what we cannot change." (Hatch in Bauman, Bauman, Kociatkiewicz, and Kostera 2015, p. vii) "To manage can mean not only to handle, but also to cope, and organizations are as much sites of compassion and poetic ambivalence as they are of hierarchical order and symbolic violence." (Kociatkiewicz in Bauman, Bauman, Kociatkiewicz, and Kostera 2015, p. 143–144) Considering how to manage an organization, group, family, or oneself in liquid modern society in a neoliberal age has become a challenge with many arguing that the very essence of what it means to manage is in crisis. More radical solutions explore forms of 'revolutionary management' such as 'management without managers' (Bauman, Bauman, Kociatkiewicz, and Kostera 2015, p. 31) which seeks "ways to manage ourselves out of the current crisis we, as humanity, have found ourselves in […] beyond the managerial elite." Collective challenges to hierarchical organizational structures are a radical option. There are also opportunities to challenge 'organisational class' stereotypes of managers and workers and attitudes to unpaid work.

Architecture educators, students, and 'the managerial elite' will play a seminal role in changing the work culture of how graduates manage and balance their work-life time in the future. Models of unhealthy work enacted in architecture school can become normalised in industry and many offices exploit what Peggy Deamer (2018) defines as an '(un)free work' culture. Deamer refers here not to the free work or unpaid work done by *femina domestica* to support *homo oeconimus* (although this is an invisible part of the profit equation), but rather unpaid architectural work. Her argument is that:

> Architecture cannot produce spaces of freedom – public spaces, healthy spaces, accessible spaces, affordable spaces, sensually liberating spaces – for the society architects presume to serve if they are produced in unfree circumstances such as unpaid labour, gender inequality, generational hegemony, unsustainable work hours, non-existent work–life balance, lack of collegiality or discipline-crippling competition.
>
> *(Deamer 2018, p. 17)*

She contends that the models of work which include "division of labour, lack of creative autonomy of all workers, disappearance of work/life balance" can be resisted and rejected as the norm through the reversal of how the body of architectural workers are used in practice to respect architectural workers of all classes, clients and consultants involved. (Deamer 2018, p. 23) This is a form of collective and united action that returns to a welfare state tradition for immediate change in how long, when, and where architectural labour is enacted.

In *Liberalism, Neoliberalism, Social Democracy*, Mark Olssen (2010, p. 14) claims that neoliberalism's departure from the welfare state tradition has attacked the notion of public interest, which had formerly underpinned western models of bureaucracy and government. The nurturing of competitive marketplace tactics that pit design studios or research clusters against one another are short term and not necessarily constructive. According to Olssen (2010, p. 14) "although it is essential in economic contexts to ensure norms of fair cooperation in order to avoid monopolies and the centralization [sic] of economic power, in many community contexts, including families, and frequently in work places, reciprocal social relations depend upon cooperative behaviour, and facilitation, rather than competition. One of the crucial failings of unbridled neoliberalism from the perspective of educators, [...] is that it seeks to institute competition as the central structuring norm of a society on the grounds that this best promotes efficient institutional and behavioural forms." (Olssen 2010, p. 14)

Activism which challenges the notion of fast and optimal productivity in the university are beginning to emerge, including the slow scholarship movement, but many more resistances are possible. The 11 female authors and members of the Great Lakes Feminist Geography Collective argue that a slow scholarship movement is one way of resisting the university pressures put on academics for high productivity. (Mountz et al. 2015, pp. 1249–1253) Alison Mountz, Anne Bonds, Becky Mansfield, Jenna Loyd, Jennifer Hyndman, Margaret Walton-Roberts, Renu Basu, Risa Whitson, Roberta Hawkins, Trina Hamilton, and Winifred Curran (2015, p. 1249) set out a range of "strategies to resist the compressed temporal regimes of the neoliberal university [so as] to stop, reflect, reject, resist, subvert, and collaborate to cultivate different, more reflexive academic cultures." They are to: 1. Talk about and support slow strategies; 2. Count what others don't; 3. Organize; 4. Take care; 5. Write fewer emails; 6. Turn off email; 7. Make time to think; 8. Make time to write (differently); 9. Say no. Say yes; and 10. Reach for the minimum (number of outputs and amount of grant funding). These are some practical proactive steps to surviving in short-term pressures that have come to define labour within architecture schools. They can help architecture educators challenge the efficiency and the quantitative valuing demanded of *homo oeconomicus* academics.

In response to the unmanageable demands of economic optimisation and productivity that are driving the U.K. H.E. sector, the University Trade Unions, which support architecture educators who are paid members, has been increasingly active in making demands for change to improve work life conditions in the university. While there are independent unions and union style activist writers, (Deamer 2018) here a proposal for managerial resistance by architectural managers is flouted.

Contesting Neoliberalism (Leitner, Peck, and Sheppard eds. 2006) argues that improving worker wellbeing is best facilitated by what is being defined as 'empathic managerialism,' which actively resists the tendency to qualify and count architectural productivity by instead focusing on qualitative and emotional empathy. Rifkin (2009, p. 544) states that, "empathic sensibility lies at the heart of the new management style". The architectural managerial class have the capacity to enact genuine (not token) empathic managerialism and devise strategies with their team/s relating to time management and work allocation (including the rise in administrivia audit culture) to address the problem of time pressures that impact negatively on wellbeing of the bodies and minds of architectural students, educators, and practitioners of differing demographics.

Some universities employ senior manager-interlopers who have no training or understanding of the discipline they are managing or how a university differs from a commercial business. They are often brought in to enact 'slash and burn' type optimisation strategies to enhance productivity and profit. These types of managers often do not understand, or care enough to understand, or feel the repercussions on others of their policy changes. For wellbeing to be supported, a university should not be run as an 'edufactory.' Its history differs to a traditional commercial business and if business-mindedness is to take over the purpose of a university, then academics who know business inside and outside the university would be better placed to contribute to leadership. Empathic management is leadership by academic/managers who understand the machinations of architectural education in the university, and its historical past and present, but who, through their empathy and experience of having worked on the shop floor and felt the detrimental impact of poor management decisions on wellbeing, can empathise with workers. From that interior perspective, a pathway toward empathic managerialism is possible because it can critically and deeply understand, to return to Sadler (in Deamer ed. 2014, p. 125), how to "locat[e] the contradictions in the rules and systems necessary to production." These leaders can challenge and decelerate the audit culture and the expectations of academic production within the university, in order to resist the depletion and exhaustion of its essential and valuable workforce resource. Neoliberal governance has forced many U.K. universities into unreasonable and unhealthy austerity with negligible time to think. As the 'edufactory' is showing an increasing number of breakdowns in its machinations, empathic managerialism is more vital than ever.

There is a growing body of literature that argues that the current demands by organisations on the bodies of their employees and workers needs to change to engage in a more participatory rather than hierarchical, directorial, and surveillance manner. Paul Miller and Paul Skidmore's (2004, p. 14) *Disorganisation: Why Future Organisations Must 'Loosen Up'* recognises the history of organisations being "insensitive, frustrating, unresponsive, painful places... at the mercy of managerial whim." They recognise the benefits of "flattened hierarchies" and of technology that can unleash "new possibilities for organising work in ways that are more aligned with other priorities, from family life to civic duty." Due to their claim that there is an "inherent unsustainability ... emerging in current patterns of organisation," which is increasing stress levels and decreasing levels of employee job satisfaction, but not felt by the organisation itself, Miller and Skidmore (2004, pp. 16–17) argue for disorganisation "to unravel or explode the closed routines and forms of control upon which organisational security and predictability have traditionally relied." This most readily happens by diversifying leaders in organisations to include more women, people of different race and ethnicity, class, and generational age. As one step of many there is a 'genderquake' (Wilkinson 1994) taking place. Essential is the understanding that diversification of architecture offers the profession the capacity through a diverse body of leaders to manage empathically in order to nurture and support 'otherness.' Empathy requires having had prior experience of discrimination because of difference.

The ability to assimilate or 'fit in' that is enabled by powerful social networks and the opportunities they provide is not possible for everyone during their architectural life, unless the profession changes to open demographically, ideologically, and ethically. Still, as has been argued in other publications, regarding gender diversity in architecture, (Troiani 2024; 2019; 2018; 2012) integration into the profession should not be about having to assimilate to the historical masculinist centred mode of a work-only life. (Martin in Berkeley ed. and McQuaid assoc. ed. 1989) This is because a work-only centred architectural life is not the only kind of life that should be endorsed, nor is it a model for sustainable architectural communities in H.E. or professional practice.

In the academy we need to strive for work-life harmony in redefining other forms of 'professional' in architecture. To achieve new definitions of the architect, architectural students and educators must actively resist 'academic capitalism' (Slaughter and Leslie 1997) that sacrifices individualism for standardisation or normalisation and jeopardises mental and physical wellbeing. Architectural education must explore the possibilities of creative labour and thought not for economic imperatives. Women and men architects need to resist the long hours, competitive, and career- and quantitatively-driven culture in architectural universities. By working with or against managers, external accreditation bodies, architectural students, and staff need to employ collaborative, empathetic work environments in the studio and beyond to reduce the increasing stress and inability-to-cope culture emerging in architecture schools. Alternative pedagogical practices initiated by academics with other professional drives beyond generating economic wealth will question the rise of corporatisation in architectural education research and practice.

In professional practice, architecture is complicit in supporting large scale corporations and private development. What Jackson describes as the "dilemma of growth" needs to be reconsidered to create alternative modes of architectural work that are not solely economically driven and support sustainable practice. Young architects need to understand the options available to them beyond the corporate lifestyles of starchitects. Alternative practices and expectations of architects, government, users, and the public at large about economic growth, status, and wealth accumulation are the way forward to offer new practice freedoms. In these ways, improving work-life harmony in all aspects of an architect's is possible.

Notes

1 Guattari (2014, p. 145) argues "that we should use our expanded understanding of the whole range of ecological components to set in place new systems of value. A market system which regulates the distribution of financial and social rewards for human social activities on the basis of profit alone, is becoming less and less legitimate. The time has come to take serious account of other value systems: of 'profitability' in the social and aesthetic sense, of the values of desire, etc."

2 "The word 'job' in English of the fourteenth century meant a lump or piece of something which could be carted around. Flexibility today brings back this arcane sense of the job, as people do lumps of labor, [sic] pieces of work, over the course of a lifetime." (Sennett 1998, p. 9)

3 "The term 'empathy' is derived from the German word *Einfühlung* or 'feeling-in', coined by Robert Vischer in 1872 and used in German aesthetics. *Einfühlung* relates to how observers project their own sensibilities onto an object of adoration or contemplation and is a way of explaining how one comes to appreciate and enjoy the beauty of, for example, a work of art. [...] In 1909, the American psychologist E. B. Titchener translated *Einfühlung* into a new word, 'empathy.' (Mark H. Davis, *Empathy: A Social Psychological Approach,* Boulder, Co.: Westview Press, 1996.)" (Rifkin 2009, pp. 11–12)

4 "Entropy is a scientific concept as well as a measurable physical property that is most commonly associated with a state of disorder, randomness, or uncertainty." https://en.wikipedia.org/wiki/Entropy, Accessed November 06, 2023.

References

Ančić, B. and Domazet, M. 2015 January. Potential for Degrowth: Attitudes and Behaviours Across 18 European Countries, *Teorija in praksa*, 52 (3): 456–475.

Aristotle, Trednnick, H. ed., Barnes, J. (Introduction), and Thomson, J. A. K. (Trans.) 2004. *The Nicomachean Ethics*. London: Penguin Classics.

Baron-Cohen, S. 2012. *Zero Degrees of Empathy: A Theory of Human Cruelty and Kindness*. London: Penguin Books.

Bauman, Z. 2007. *Liquid Times: Living in an Age of Uncertainty*. Cambridge: Polity Press.

Bauman, Z., Bauman, I., Kociatkiewicz, J., and Kostera, M. 2015. *Management in a Liquid Modern World*. Cambridge: Polity Press.

Bonaiuti, M. 2014. *The Great Transition*. London: Routledge.

Bourdieu, P. and Nice, R. (Trans.) 1996. *Distinction: A Social Critique of the Judgement of Taste*. Cambridge, Mass.: Harvard University Press.

Bourdieu, P. 1986. The Forms of Capital. In Richardson, J. G. ed. *Handbook of Theory and Research for the Sociology of Education*. New York; Westport, Conn.; London: Greenwood Press, pp. 241–258.

Brown, W. 2015. *Undoing the Demos: Neoliberalism's Stealth Revolution*. New York: Zone Books.

Buber, M. 1958. *Ich und Du (I and Thou)*. New York: Scribners (2nd Edition). [First published in 1937.]

Castel, R. 2003. *L'Insécurité Sociale. Qu'est-ce qu'être protégé?* (*Social Insecurity: What is it to be Protected?*), published in the collection "The Republic of Ideas," The editions du Seuil.

Castle, H. 2017. Find Your Inner Entrepreneur. *The RIBA Journal*, January 03, 2017, https://www.ribaj.com/intelligence/find-your-inner-entrepreneur Accessed August 03, 2023.

D'Alisa, G., Demaria, F., and Kallis, G. eds. 2015. *Degrowth: A Vocabulary for a New Era*. New York; London: Routledge. [E-book]

Deamer, P. 2018 May. (Un)Free Work: Architecture, Labour and Self-Determination, *Architectural Design*, 88 (3): 16–23.

De Waal, F. 2009. *The Age of Empathy: Nature's Lessons for a Kinder Society*. London: Souvenir Press.

Fleming, P. 2017. *The Death of Homo Economicus: Work, Debt and the Myth of Endless Accumulation*. London: Pluto Press.

Fulcher, M. 2013. The Thatcher Years: Architects Reflect on the Legacy of the Iron Lady, *Architects' Journal*, April 11, 2013. 237 (13): 12–13. https://www.architectsjournal.co.uk/archive/the-thatcher-years-architects-reflect-on-the-legacy-of-the-iron-lady, Accessed November 06, 2023.

Georgescu-Roegen, N. 1971. *The Entropy Law and the Economic Process*. Cambridge Mass.: Harvard University Press.

Guattari, F. 2014. *The Three Ecologies*. London: Bloomsbury Academic.

Guattari, F. 1989 Summer. The Three Ecologies, *new formations*, 8: 131–147.

Harvey, D. 2019. *Spaces of Global Capitalism*. London: Verso.

Harvey, D. 2007. Neoliberalism as Creative Destruction, *The Annals of the American Academy of Political and Social Science*, 610: 33–44.

Harvey, D. 1982. *The Limits of Capital*. Oxford: Blackwell.

Holliss, F. 2015. *Beyond Live/Work: The Architecture of Home-based Work*. London; New York: Routledge.

Höpfl, H. 2008. Sacred Heart: A Comment on the Heart of Management, *Culture and Organization*, 14 (3): 225–240.

Jackson, T. 2009. *Prosperity without Growth: Economics for a Finite Planet*. London; Sterling, VA: Earthscan.

Kaplan, V. 2006. *Structural Inequality: Black Architects in the United States*. Lanham; Boulder; New York; Toronto; Oxford: Rowman & Littlefield Publishers, Inc.

Kelly, P. 2016. *The Self as Enterprise: Foucault and the Spirit of 21st Century Capitalism*. London: Routledge.

Lefebvre, H. 2014. *Critique of Everyday Life*. London: Verso.

Lefebvre, H. 2002. *Everyday Life in the Modern World*. London, England; New York: Continuum.

Lefebvre, H. 1991. *The Production of Space*. Oxford: Blackwell.

Leitner, H., Peck, J. and Sheppard, E. S. eds. 2006. *Contesting Neoliberalism: Urban Frontiers*. New York: Guildford Press.

Lewis, W. A. 2003. *The Theory of Economic Growth*. London; New York: Routledge.

Martin, I. 2015. The City that Privatised itself to Death: 'London is now a set of improbably sex toys poking gormlessly into the air,' *The Guardian*, February 24, 2015. https://www.theguardian.com/politics/2015/feb/24/the-city-that-privatised-itself-to-death-london-is-now-a-set-of-improbable-sex-toys-poking-gormlessly-into-the-air, Accessed November 06, 2023.

Martin, R. 2003. *The Organizational Complex: Architecture, Media and Corporate Space*. Cambridge, Mass.; London: The MIT Press.

Martin, R. 1989. Out of Marginality: Toward a New Kind of Professional. In Berkeley, E. P. ed. and McQuaid, M. Assoc. ed. *Architecture: A Place for Women*. Washington, DC: Smithsonian Institution Press, pp. 229–236.

Meadows, D. H. 1972. *The Limits to Growth: A Report for the Club of Rome's Project on the Predicament of Mankind*. London: Earth Island.

Miller, P. and Skidmore, P. 2004. *Disorganisation: Why Future Organisations Must Loosen Up*. London: Demos.

Mountz, A., Bonds, A., Mansfield, B., Loyd, J., Hyndman, J., Walton-Roberts, M., Basu, R., Whitson, R., Hawkins, R., Hamilton, T., and Curran, W. 2015 December. For Slow Scholarship: A Feminist Politics of Resistance through Collective Action in the Neoliberal University, ACME, *International E-journal for Critical Geographies*, 14 (4): 1235–1259.

Muraca, B. 2013 April. A Project for a Radical Transformation of Society, *Environmental Values*, 22 (2): 147–169

Natarajan, S. 2003 March. Richard Sennett: *The Corrosion of Character: The Personal Consequences of Work in the New Capitalism*. https://www.yumpu.com/en/document/read/12447649/richard-sennett-the-corrosion-of-character-the-personal-, Accessed November 06, 2023.

Newman, J. 2012. *Working the Spaces of Power: Activism, Neoliberalism and Gendered Labour*. London: Bloomsbury Academic.

Oliver, M. L. and Shapiro, T. M. 2006. *Black Wealth/White Wealth: A New Perspective*. New York: Routledge.

Olssen, M. 2010. *Liberalism, Neoliberalism, Social Democracy: Thin Communitarian Perspectives on Political Philosophy and Education*. New York; London: Routledge.

Rank, M. R., Hirschl, T. A., and Foster, K. A. 2014. *Chasing the American Dream: Understanding what Shapes our Fortunes*. Oxford: Oxford University Press.

Rifkin, J. 2009. *The Empathic Civilization: The Race to Global Consciousness in a World in Crisis*. Cambridge, U.K.: Polity.

Rogers, C. R. 1958. Reinhold Niebuhr's The Self and the Dramas of History: A Criticism, *Pastoral Psychology*, 9: 15–17.

Sadler, S. 2013. The Varieties of Capitalist Experience. In Deamer, P. ed. *Architecture and Capitalism: 1845 to the Present.* London: Routledge, pp. 115–131.

Scaria, D., Brandt, M. L., Kim, E., and Lindeman, B. 2020. In Kim, E. and Lindeman, B. eds. 2020. *Wellbeing.* Switzerland: Springer Nature, pp. 3–10.

Schaffner, A. K. 2016. *Exhaustion: A History.* New York: Columbia University Press.

Schneider, T. and Till, J. 2007. *Flexible Housing.* Amsterdam; Boston; London: Elsevier.

Schopenhauer, A., Payne, E. F., and Cartwright, D. E. 1995. *On the Basis of Morality.* Providence; Oxford: Berghahn Books.

Schwartz, B. 2016. *The Paradox of Choice: Why More is Less.* New York: Ecco.

Schwartz, B. 2005. *The Paradox of Choice.* TedGlobal X 2005 talk. July 2005. https://www.ted.com/talks/barry_schwartz_the_paradox_of_choice?language=en, Accessed November 06, 2023.

Sen, A. and Nussbaum, M. 1993. *The Quality of Life.* Oxford: Clarendon Press.

Sennett, R. 2006. *The Culture of New Capitalism.* New Haven: Yale University Press.

Sennett, R. 1998. *The Corrosion of Character: The Personal Consequences of Work in the New Capitalism.* New York; London: Norton.

Sennett, R., and Cobb. J. 1977. *The Hidden Injuries of Class.* Cambridge: Cambridge University Press.

Slaughter, S. and Leslie, L. L. 1997. *Academic Capitalism: Politics, Policies, and the Entrepreneurial University.* Baltimore: The Johns Hopkins University Press.

Smith, A. and Stewart, D. 1869. *The Theory of Moral Sentiments: To Which is Added, A Dissertation on the Origin of Languages.* London: Bell & Daldy. [New ed., with a biographical and critical memoir of the author by Stewart, D.]

Spencer, D. 2016. *The Architecture of Neoliberalism: How Contemporary Architecture Became an Instrument of Control and Compliance.* London: Bloomsbury Academic.

Standing, G. 2016. *The Precariat: The New Dangerous Class.* London: Bloomsbury Academic.

Stiglitz, J. E. 2013. *The Price of Inequality.* London: Penguin Books.

Stiglitz, J. E. 2009 September. Moving Beyond Market Fundamentalism to a More Balanced Economy, *Annals of Public and Cooperative Economics*, 80 (3): 345–497.

Stiglitz, J. E., Fitoussi, J.-P., and Durand, M. 2018. *Beyond GDP: Measuring What Counts for Economic and Social Performance* (Report). Paris: OECD Publishing. https://doi.org/10.1787/9789264307292-en

Stoyanova, D. and Grugulis, I. University of Bradford. School of Management. 2007. *Fragmented (Working) Lives.* Bradford: Bradford University School of Management.

Troiani, I. 2024. Not A One-Size-Fits-All Architectural Education. In Choi, G. and Durham, H. eds. *Inclusion Emergency: Diversity in Architecture.* London: RIBA Publishing.

Troiani, I. 2021 December. The Elephant in the Room: How Neoliberal Architecture Education Undermines Wellbeing, *Charrette*, 7(2) Autumn: 9–33.

Troiani, I. 2019. His House, Our House and Her House: A Filmic Place for Women. In Troiani, I. ed. and author and Campbell, H. ed. *Architecture Filmmaking.* Chicago, Bristol: The University of Chicago Press/Distributed by Intellect Ltd, pp. 225–238.

Troiani, I. 2018. Zaha Hadid's Penthouse: Gender, Creativity and 'Biopolitics' in the Neoliberal Workplace. In Staub, A. ed. *The Routledge Companion to Modernity, Space and Gender in Section: Liberal and Neo-liberal Values.* New York: Routledge, pp. 131–149.

Troiani, I. 2012. Zaha: An Image of 'The Woman Architect,' *Architectural Theory Review*, 17 (2–3): 346–364. Republished as Troiani, I. 2014. Zaha: An Image of 'The Woman Architect.' In Stead, N. ed. *Women, Practice, Architecture: 'Resigned Accommodation' and 'Usurpatory Practice*.' London: Routledge, Chapter 10.

Unknown. 2011. Hawkins Brown, The Hub, Coventry University, 2011. https://www.harkinsbrown.com/news-and-events/press/mix-magazine, Accessed December 21, 2021.

Unknown, 2007. Plastic Surgery, Faddy Diets and Celebrities: 'Game of Life' gets a Modern Makeover, August 15, 2007. https://www.dailymail.co.uk/news/article-475584/Plastic-surgery-faddy-diets-celebrities--Game-Life-gets-modern-makeover.html, Accessed November 06, 2023.

Wilkinson, H. 1994. *Turning Back: Generations and the Genderquake*. London: Demos.

INDEX

Note: *Italic* page numbers refer to figures and page numbers followed by "n" refer to end notes.